Amazing Texas Monuments & Museums

Amazing Texas Monuments & Museums

Ann Ruff

Lone Star Books
A Division of
Gulf Publishing Company
Houston, Texas

Dedication

To John Hamilton and Logan Cravens for great "graving" and to Earl Ruff for great support—and to all those marvelous Texans who gave us these amazing monuments and museums for me to write about.

Front cover photos:

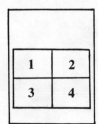

1. The Orange Show, courtesy of Stephan Myers Photography, Houston, Texas.
2. Big Tex, courtesy of the State Fair of Texas, Dallas, Texas.
3. Boom Town, courtesy of East Texas Oil Museum at Kilgore College, Kilgore, Texas.
4. The Cadillac Ranch, courtesy of McSpadden Photography, Amarillo, Texas.

Back cover photo:

Dinosaur State Park, courtesy of Texas Department of Highways and Public Transportation, Travel and Information Division, Austin, Texas.

Amazing Texas Monuments and Museums

Copyright © 1984 by Gulf Publishing Company, Houston, Texas. All rights reserved. Printed in the United States of America. This book, or parts thereof, may not be reproduced in any form without permission of the publisher.

ISBN 0-88415-564-1

Library of Congress Cataloging in Publication Data

Ruff, Ann, 1930–
    Amazing Texas Monuments and Museums.
    Includes index.
    1. Monuments—Texas—Guide-books. 2. Museums—Texas—Guide-books. 3. Texas—Description and travel—1981– —Guide-books. I. Title.
F387.R83 1984   917.64'0463   83-18726
ISBN 0-88415-564-1

Contents

Foreword

When I tell people that I am a museum buff, the unspoken response is that museums are dusty and dull.

When I mention that it is impossible for me to go by a monument—any monument—without stopping to read the entire inscription, my listener shrugs the shrug that says, "This guy is suffering from terminal blahs."

When I make the observation that the best way to learn about a town is to visit the local cemetery, because it changes the least, the look turns from ennui to doubt, my listener usually turns away.

Silly people, do they not know all of this to be true? And, what's more, do they not realize that right here in Texas we have undoubtedly the strangest collection of markers, museums, monuments, and grave sites in captivity?

We do, and now, thanks to Ann Ruff, we have a guidebook. Her collection of collections, *Amazing Texas Monuments & Museums*, is just that. Not the well-known art museums, the Texas Hall of State, the Alamo or the state archives. Everyone knows about them. No, these are the semi-buried Cadillacs of Stanley Marsh 3, the world's largest mosquito, the water museum, and the cemetery on Peckerwood Hill, reserved for convicts (complete with their execution number).

Without leaving Texas you can visit the Globe Theater and watch Shakespeare's plays, check out the biggest beer bottle collection on earth, or take your choice of three telephone museums. You can visit the graves of Machine Gun Kelly, Howard Hughes, and Big Al (the latter was an alligator).

It has been said that the world is divided into two kinds of people, those who divide the world into two kinds of people, and those who do not. I would differ: The world is neatly divided into those with curiosity, energy, and a sense of humor, and those who are not interested in this book. Besides, where else can you find the answer to a question which has been bothering people for years: Where is the *second* best little whorehouse in Texas?

Lynn Ashby
Houston, Texas

Preface

Someday I am going to write a book about writing this book. It was one of the most pleasurable experiences of my life. Every museum, every monument, every grave provided a unique experience. Sometimes it was the location, sometimes it was the people I met, sometimes it was the story involved, but most of the time it was all of those factors that made every entry in this book a great adventure.

I shall never forget going into the Foard County courthouse in Crowell. It was nearly noon, and I was searching for a monument Ed Syers had described in his book *Backroads of Texas* (Lone Star Books, Houston, Texas) as "pointing a silent finger to the sky." Wondering just which finger was doing the pointing, I thought someone in Crowell could tell me about such a strange monument. I went first to the sheriff's office, but nobody was there. Then I went to the county clerk's office, but nobody was there. Even the library was empty, so I went to the bathroom, and nobody was there. I was the only person in the Foard County courthouse.

A check at the two filling stations in Crowell only brought blank looks from the attendants. Not willing to give up my quest so easily, I followed the book's meager directions and drove nine miles west of town. Sure enough as Syers had described, there was a paved road heading south; so I figured somewhere out in these scrubby wastes there just might be a finger pointing to the sky.

After a few miles, the pavement ended and turned into gravel. It always brings me a queasy feeling to be a lone woman on a road to nowhere, totally unsure of what my goal is, but part of the fun of a search is finding your own way. However, I can never get rid of the thought of finding myself standing for hours (even days) waiting for just one helpful soul to come by and rescue me from car trouble.

The gravel kept flying, the miles flew by, and absolutely *nothing* gave me a clue to a funny monument. I resolved to make one final effort and ask at the first house I came to. After what seemed forever, I came upon a lovely modern home by the side of the road. With dogs yapping at my heels, I rang the bell.

When a lady answered the door, I found myself babbling like an idiot and showing her the book where the monument pointed its finger to the sky. The lady said, "Well, there's a monument on our property, but it doesn't point any finger. I'll take you out to see it in my truck." As we walked through the house, pet birds screeched a welcome, and a chaparral perched on the garage's rafters.

After bouncing over a lot of ruts, we came upon the monument, which turned out to be a rather unimpressive pile of stones in the shape of an obelisk. No hands, no fingers, just a pillar of rocks. I decided not to write about it, since Syers already had and, as Texas' monuments go, this wasn't among the more "Amazing."

Then my hostess, Betty McAdams, said, "Perhaps you would like to see my museum?"

I didn't have the heart to tell such a nice person I was not including pioneer museums in my book; but I certainly didn't want to be rude, so I said, "Of course! I'd love to!"

When we got back to the house, people were standing in the garage, so I suggested I come back later, since she had company. Betty said, "Oh, no, we keep a phone outside for the neighbors to use in case we aren't home." I was very impressed with Betty's idea of the good neighbor policy.

As we walked back to the old house that was now the museum, I couldn't believe my eyes—the entire yard was a prairie dog town. The little varmints were everywhere, popping up and down in their burrows, and so cute I wanted to watch just them, not some antiques.

As expected, Betty's old homestead was a real treasure of pioneer memorabilia with every room furnished in authentic antiques of gracious ranch living at the turn of the century.

As we walked past a long showcase filled with old knick-knacks, Betty said, "Well, I guess you want to see Lee Harvey Oswald's can opener?"

Mouth agape, I gasped, "You better believe it!"

Betty opened the case and took out an ordinary can opener used to puncture cans before the days of pull tabs and said, "Here it is."

I don't know what I expected, but as I looked at the common, everyday object, I asked her how she managed to acquire Lee Harvey Oswald's can opener.

"Oh," Betty said, "Lee's mother used to work for me, and while Lee was in Russia, he wrote and asked her to send him some of his things— one was his can opener. Marge told me she had packed Lee's away and could she borrow mine. She would later give me Lee's, which she did."

As I stood there, out in the middle of nowhere, amidst the barking dogs, a chaparral that lived in the garage, people using an outside phone, and prairie dogs popping up all around, discussing Lee Harvey Oswald's can opener, I wouldn't have been surprised if Mr. Spock had beamed me up to the *Starship Enterprise*.

When I asked Betty if she thought Lee was guilty, she said, "Oh, no, you should have read the letters he wrote his mother." I kept wondering if the Warren Commission had ever talked to Betty.

I really hated to leave this new friend, and when Betty asked me to stay for supper, I had to make the true excuse that now sounds so silly, "Golly, I'd love to, but I have to be in Turkey before dark."

As I drove back on the flying gravel, I promised myself I would return to the boonies of Crowell, the prairie dog town, the chaparral in the garage, and Lee Harvey Oswald's can opener. Maybe Mr. Spock will beam me down again someday.

Ann Ruff
Llano, Texas

How to Use This Book

This book is an eclectic collection of museums and monuments and is divided by category rather than region. The attractions are listed under the appropriate city in the index, and a map that precedes each entry shows the general location in Texas.

Since many of these museums are private collections, most are shown by appointment only. Even some with regular hours are in a business office and are not open on weekends. In all instances, it is advisable to call in advance before driving miles to see these unusual collections. The museum owners are all wonderful people, and they thoroughly enjoy sharing their hobbies with visitors. Usually the owners are a source of fascinating information, so when possible, try to arrange your visit when the owners can show off their museums.

The monuments are always available for photographs, but should you want more information about them, your best source is the local chamber of commerce. In nearly every town I found the chamber to be helpful, cooperative, and anxious to promote their particular monument. Another helpful source is the local town or county museum, and often I got interesting facts from historical societies.

The last part of the book is about interesting graves or interesting people who now occupy those graves. Please note that exact locations are vague, for I did not want to make the headstones easy targets for vandals. Dedicated "gravers" will enjoy the search and will figure out how to find the grave they are looking for. I found local mortuaries and cemetery attendants excellent sources; gravestones have a tendency to all look alike, and you could search the rows for hours. (A word of caution about graveyards: Don't think a cemetery is only a resting place for the dead; often it is alive with unseen inhabitants—and they aren't ghosts. When the cemetery chiggers find a real live warm body, they attack with a vengeance.)

So pick a section and learn about telephones or trains, cowboys or cows, saints or sinners, and all about the *Amazing Texas Monuments and Museums*.

Monuments Instead of Money

When it comes to spending money, Texans have a real flare for the unique and sometimes outrageous, and their monuments take strange shapes and forms. Surprisingly enough, even those with modest incomes are often as flamboyant as the filthy rich . . . in their own way.

Garden of Junk

Hallsville

In tiny Hallsville in East Texas, David Romero turns his Garden of Junk into a Christmas wonderland that attracts more than 4,000 visitors each year. It takes this landscape gardener three months to put up his manger scene, miles of tinsel and lights, hundreds and hundreds of ornaments, and outdoor fireplace arrangement. Santa and his helpers make toys in the front room of Mr. Romero's extremely modest hut. A fence made from bed springs is a convenient rack for many of the Christmas decorations.

Every year the spectacular becomes more elaborate. Just the job of storing all that glitter and sparkle is mind boggling. But, from the first of December until the first of January, David Romero's fantasyland is a joy to young and old, and it's just a dedicated man's way of saying "Merry Christmas."

The Milkovisch Collection

222 Malone Street
Houston

One look at this glittering house and you expect Hansel and Gretel to come tripping out to greet you, but instead, you meet Mr. and Mrs. John Milkovisch. Beer can collectors usually put their prizes on a shelf and dust them occasionally, but John Milkovisch's 17-year collection of beer cans is a display to end all displays. The entire home is a tribute to the pleasure of the brewer's art. Every inch of the outside walls of this small bungalow is completely covered with flattened beer cans securely nailed in place. Every brand is well represented with perhaps a few more Jax cans, but as John said, "I just buy anything on special."

But, the walls are not all, by any means. This aluminum version of a fairy tale house is literally dripping in beer cans. John cut the bottoms out of the cans, fastened them together, and they dangle from the eaves of his home.

Shimmering in the sun, the silver disks give the appearance of giant stalagtites hanging from the roof. When the wind blows, the ropes of silver clang together with a noise guaranteed to frighten any bird on Malone Street. Strings of can bottoms dangle from every tree and not just from the limbs John could reach. This enterprising decorator created the world's largest windchime by tying the chains of bottoms to rocks and throwing them to the highest branches.

You can tell John marches to a different drummer (or should it be a different brewer) for his garden is a masterpiece in marbles as well. No, not the marble from quarries, the marbles kids play with. The sidewalks and planters are set in marbles and rocks, and the patio fence has holes drilled in it with embedded multi-colored "toys" and "aggies." Mrs. Milkovisch's sole contribution to the garish setting is a plastic tree hung with plastic lemons that once contained synthetic lemon juice.

The Milkovisch's have lived on Malone Street since 1942 and obviously plan never to leave, for finding the right buyer for their tinsel house might be a bit of a problem. Also, John has another project in mind. He is going to cover his garage with the same siding as used on his house, so he has a lot of drinking ahead.

Cadillac Ranch

I-40 West
Amarillo

Of all the Texas eccentrics, none are in the league with Stanley Marsh 3 of Amarillo. (Marsh insists on the Arabic numeral.) Stories of Stanley's pranks and peccadillos are the stuff legends are made of. A local citizen in describing Marsh said, "If he were poor, he'd be called crazy, but since he's rich, he's just eccentric."

This oil, cattle, and banking mogul even married money, as Mrs. Marsh 3 added a cattle fortune to her husband's wealth. Now Stanley has ventured into real estate and a television station, and both are quite lucrative.

The Marsh 3 mansion is named Toad Hall, and the grounds are stocked with exotic animals usually found in

John Milkovisch's Houston home glitters and glistens with his beer can collection.

Call it "Fins Farewell" or "Millionaire's Madness" but whatever its title, these ten half-buried Cadillacs are Stanley Marsh 3's contribution to the art world.

zoos. However, llamas, rheas, and zebras seem right at home in the Texas Panhandle. Marsh 3's philosophy is, "I use frivolity the way other people use golf, whiskey, sin: to keep from getting bored." One of Stanley's ideas of frivolity is to drop water bombs from the balcony of his thirtieth floor office. At a dinner he had for Japanese students, the only Texans invited were over six feet four inches tall. Marsh 3's 14 by 18 inch stationary is marked "Top Sacred." When the great prankster found a car parked in his spot, he had the offending vehicle welded to a lamppost. At a society wedding, Stanley arrived with a dwarf dressed as Aunt Jemima. Marsh 3 says, "My favorite cause is lost."

As a patron of the arts, the millionaire commissioned a group called The Ant Farm to create a noteworthy masterpiece. The result of this artistic endeavor is a vacant field sprouting ten Cadillacs buried hood down, fins in the air. Beginning with a '49 fastback coupe, the models go to a 1960 Sedan deVille—all the years tailfins were in vogue. You can draw your own conclusions and make up any explanatory title you want from "Fins Farewell" to "Detroit Decadence," or even "Millionaire's Madness."

Stanley once called this Cadillac junkyard a memorial to the day of the auto—a symbol of escape, money, and personal freedom. It was also referred to as a monument to teenage dreams and lost youth. Marsh 3 even tried to get Evel Knievel to jump his motorcycle the length of these ten fins.

The gate to Cadillac Ranch is padlocked, but an easy climb gives you a closer look at the stripped, faded, and rusted old status symbols of American wealth. Graffiti is everywhere on the ruined bodies, and most of it is angry and vulgar.

Most old cars end up in the scrap heap, but at least these ten have achieved an unusual form of immortality—thanks to Stanley Marsh 3 and his Ant Farm.

C. W. Post Statue

Courthouse Square
Post

Indians danced for it, God-fearing souls prayed for it, but C. W. Post blasted for it. Rain! That rare element on the High Plains was the target of tons and tons of dynamite in a revolutionary attempt to squeeze moisture from Texas' unwilling clouds.

C. W. Post was not some wild-eyed fanatic, nor was he a con man out to fleece the farmers with some hokus-pokus scheme. This was a man of the highest moral principles

who sincerely wanted to make West Texas more habitable. After all, Post had built the town bearing his name and had enticed people to move there; he loved this harsh land.

Generations of Americans have grown up on Post Toasties (originally called Elijah's Manna) and Grape-Nut Flakes for breakfast. C. W.'s main contribution to the stomachs of America, however, was a concoction of wheat, bran, and molasses called Postum. This forerunner of Sanka and Brim turned a handsome profit of $1,400,000 in 1908, with Post Toasties and Grape-Nuts racking up about $3,500,000.

Post was not a native Texan, but he had been a real estate developer around Fort Worth before changing the eating habits of the country. When Post devised the concept of creating a perfect community, he came back to Texas. Dreamers of perfect communities have a blind spot when it comes to human nature, but this devoted family man was deeply religious, a teetotaler, and determined to build the ideal town.

Work began on this new Texas town in 1907, and after it was half finished, every building had to be picked up and moved five miles. The original site was ten miles from the center of Garza County, and the law in Texas states that the county seat cannot be more than five miles from the county's center. But, location was not the only problem. As a harbinger of things to come, the first well struck salt water. Also, the high winds and the task of carrying supplies (the 70 miles from Big Spring took 4 days) slowed the town's progress considerably.

Water continued to be a problem. When Post purchased his 225,000 acres, the plains had experienced several years of unusual rainfall, but by 1907, the weather was back to normal—either hot and dry, or cold and dry. There was a suggestion of building a pipeline from the water level under the caprock down to Post, but Amarillo went berserk, claiming it would drain off their water supply. Engineers finally decided the plan was unfeasible, and Amarillo breathed easily again.

Post laid out his farm plots in squares of four with the four homes built in the common corner, and all four households shared one well. Post's theory was that part of the plight of the pioneer farmwife was loneliness, and sharing a common area would give the ladies someone to visit with on a daily basis. Well, chickens kept getting mixed up, dogs and children fought, and the ladies did not get along. Also, C. W. had over-developed his project, and most farmers could not afford his land prices. The land ended up being leased rather than becoming the independent farms Post had envisioned.

By 1911, water was really scarce. The act of rainmaking is as old as man, and at least the runner-up to the world's oldest profession. The turn of the century was the heyday of rainmakers, and the divining rod business boomed. C. W. decided he would blast the rain from the heavens with dynamite. In July, 12 stations were built on the rim of the caprock, and blasts were set off at three-to-five-minute intervals. The first two rain battles were failures, but a few days later, it sprinkled. The August battle resulted in drenching downpours, and also the October onslaught was won with rain soaking the land.

The 1912 offensive began in April with only hail, but in May it rained at nearby O'Donnell. In June the time of day was changed and also the blasts increased to 12,000 pounds of dynamite. The prairie sounded like no man's land, and rain poured everywhere but on Post's farms.

For the 1913 campaign, the general moved the battle-ground, and it rained two days later, and it kept pouring until August. By the end of August, however, the fields were dry again.

The next year Post underwent a successful operation for chronic appendicitis, and yet for some unexplained reason, this great humanitarian seemed to lose the will to live. Post died before the 1914 rain battle, and dynamite no longer shook the High Plains. Post paid for all of the dynamite and expenses himself, and his 23 salvos cost $50,000. Ironically, 1914 and 1915 were splendid years for rain.

C. W. is not remembered much for his efforts at Post. His many civic donations to the town, his awards for the best yards, his Algerita Hotel, and his plans for a brilliant future for his town are mostly forgotten. Post even drilled an oil well when oil was never dreamed of in West Texas, and he missed by 300 feet. But, millions of Americans know Jell-O, Log Cabin Syrup, Maxwell House Coffee, Birdseye Frozen Foods, etc., for the Postum Cereal Company is now the mammoth General Foods Corporation.

Post's biography ends with the statement that the town itself was monument enough for its creator, and no statue was needed. Mrs. Post did not agree. So several years later, Mrs. Post had the patriarch of this unpretentious small town cast in bronze for the courthouse lawn.

The 1914 ammunition for the rain battle was stored until World War I began. Post citizens were so fearful of German sabotage, all of the dynamite was exploded. No, 1917 was not a good year for rain.

Orange Show

2401 Munger
Houston
Open weekends
Admission

Just a few blocks off the hectic Gulf Free-way in Houston is a one-man fantasyland built as a tribute to that nutritious fruit, the orange. In Greek mythology, the eleventh of Hercules' 12 labors was to gather the "Golden Apples of Hesperides," long thought to be merely oranges. After pulling a con job on Atlas to secure the

Wheels whir, gears mesh, and the magic color is orange in this masterpiece of junk.

treasures, Hercules was off for Labor No. 12. The "Golden Apples" would feel right at home in the Orange Show, which is a herculean task in itself. For 26 years Jeff McKissack labored to build a temple to the orange.

A factual description of the Orange Show would take volumes, and even actually looking at it leaves you awe-struck that one man's creative talents were spent in fashioning and building such a strange monument. You enter a door into a world of weird machine parts, colorful tiles, plaster shapes of nothing, and junk of every description. You posi-tively marvel at the assortment of oddities McKissack pre-ferred to money.

A mosaic sign greets you with "We are glad you are here," and other signs proclaim "Go Orange" and "Love Me Orange." Windvanes, metal birds, and statues are intertwined in an amazing confusion.

The outdoor theater is simply called "The Side Show." Purple, pink and yellow tractor seats, placed on different levels provide seating. No one seems to know exactly what kind of performances were planned for this stage—dancing oranges perhaps.

Over in one corner of the collection is a small obelisk simply explained as "Monument to the Orange." Nearby is the door to the Museum to the Orange. As you enter, a mechanical bird chirps a greeting without stopping. You feel you have entered a rather unusual garage sale. A clown's large sign states he found happiness by trying cold fresh orange juice. On one wall manikins enact Longfellow's "Under the Spreading Chestnut Tree," and John Brown "(1890–1975)" said, "I love oranges. They help make me strong and healthy—delicious and refreshing, too." Wooden

Indians, stuffed bears, a teepee—all are here in the museum. Even a happy frog croaks, "I can make it," after falling into a churn. He kicked until a cake of butter formed, and McKissack's moral is "Never give up. Keep kicking."

Jeff McKissack was a retired U. S. Postal Service employee and financed all of this wackiness with his social security check and small pension. All by himself, Jeff built every piece of the Orange Show. Biking around Houston, McKissack looked for discarded objects to put in his ever-growing memorial. Bits and pieces of many demolished buildings found their way to a place of honor on Munger Street. The star attraction of the Orange Show is a large metal pond filled with water and a real steam-operated steamboat. Spectators watch it go around the pond on a track from an amphitheater filled with tractor seats. The steamboat's boiler was put together by McKissack, and he always did his own electrical and plumbing work. The entire Orange Show is totally McKissack, and he even sewed his own drapes for the museum.

A ballot box asked visitors to vote yes or no as to the Orange Show being the most beautiful, unique, and colorful show on earth and whether Jeff D. McKissack was a creative, artistic building genius. He hoped to establish some sort of record for the *Guinness Book of World Records*, but the results of the ballots are unknown.

McKissack also published a booklet entitled "How You Can Live 100 Years and Still Be Spry." There were no monumental secrets to eternal youth. You should merely dine at home or at cafeterias because you can see what you are getting. Meals should be mostly protein with no sugar or starches. Shun preservatives, eat lots of Vitamin C, preferably in oranges, and eat at least three of those a day. Proper exercise and rest are very important, and you should not smoke. About the only slightly daffy rule is to sleep under an electric blanket, because a lot of cover is not healthy. Also, Jeff thought everyone should spend their vacation in Hot Springs, Arkansas, taking the mineral baths and drinking the water. The book is also loaded with little quotes from St. Thomas Aquinas, Benjamin Franklin, Aesop, and other philosophers.

In spite of all of his emphasis on health, Jeff McKissack only made it to 77. But, the Orange Show was not doomed to destruction, for a group of Houstonians purchased it from McKissack's nephew for $10,000 and completely restored it. The Orange Show Foundation is a non-profit, tax-free educational organization.

The Orange Show is really much more than just a silly old man's monument to a citrus fruit. It was a statement of his life. McKissack considered himself lucky to have something to do, a goal in life, a purpose. And, as the builder saw it, his purpose was to construct something uniquely his own. You cannot help but feel that Jeff McKissack was having a wonderful time laughing at life.

Appropriately enough, McKissack was cremated and his ashes scattered in the flower beds of his Orange Show. His neighbor, Ty Eckley, who now sort of oversees the Orange Show, gave the eulogy for McKissack: "Wouldn't it be grand if we could do as well with our tasks as did Jeff McKissack."

The Eye of the World

J. J. Steak House
6685 N. 11th
Beaumont

 It only took God 6 days, but it took John N. Gavrelos 25 years to create the world. Considering he included the entire Bible, the complete pantheon of Greek mythology, the empire of Alexander the Great, the pyramids of Egypt, famous churches of the world, plus numerous well-known moments in history, 25 years doesn't sound too long for just one mortal man's work.

The J.J. Steak House looks like thousands of other Texas eateries, and the menu is typically Texan including basic steaks and chops. However, in an addition to the dining room is a production in miniature that would warm the cockles of Cecil B. DeMille's heart. From 1923 until 1948, this Beaumont restaurateur shaped a vast landscape of all of civilization with bits of wood, cigar boxes, and a small knife.

Behind a huge glass case, pipe cleaner trees shade these exact replicas of the wonders of the world. Glowing with a shellac patina, the edifices, rocks, statues, and artificial plants depict 160 Biblical scenes, including the "Beginning of the World," "Adam and Eve in Hard Labor for Their Sins," the "Tower of Babylon," "The Temple of King Solomon," "The Nativity Scene," and "Golgotha."

Equally impressive is the "Ancient Persian Palace of King Zerxes," not far from a tiny Socrates sipping his bitter brew of hemlock. The rather enigmatic buildings "The Temple of French," and "The Temple of England" are actually Notre Dame and St. Pauls. San Sofia and "The Temple of Alexandria, Louisiana," share honors with "The Temple of the Buddists [sic] in China," and the Parthenon.

American history has not been neglected either. Our forefathers come alive under Gavrelos' knife, signing the Declaration of Independence while Betsy Ross sews her flag and the Statue of Liberty holds her torch high.

Gavrelos worked on his microcosm of history in his spare time, using fruit crates instead of masonry and steel. This Greek immigrant had no more than a third grade education, but he probably knew more about the Bible, literature, and history than a college graduate. Using pictures from books as his models, Gavrelos' monuments and scenes are remarkably authentic.

The dedicated artist was never married and died at age 88 in 1979. With a hobby this demanding, it is doubtful if John had time between smashing fruit crates for romance. Pictures are exceedingly difficult to take of this masterpiece in kindling, for the case has been sealed, and the glass doors will not slide open. Fortunately, the new J.J. owners do not mind if you stand in the "museum" as long as you like as you try to absorb all the infinite details and imagine all the patience that John Gavrelos had to have had to create his gift to posterity.

Nowhere Else But Texas

You can travel the entire United States and probably the world and never find a museum to chili. Only in Texas is this noble dish so revered. And out in San Angelo, Miss Hattie's stands as a tribute to the world's oldest profession, and where else but Texas could there be a museum to one of the most colorful mounted police forces in history—the Texas Rangers. Odessa honors our presidents, and the only taurine museum in the United States is in El Paso, glorifying bull fights. The one thing these diverse subjects have in common is that they are only found in Texas.

Museum of the Chili Culture

Frank X. Tolbert's Chili Parlor
4544 McKinney
Dallas

 Every good Texan knows his state dish is chili, but you might not know there are as many different versions of the fiery fare as there are chili cook-offs. Lyndon Johnson had to have a bowl of Lady Bird's Pedernales (that's purr-DIN-alice) River Chili with milk and saltine crackers three times a week. The late president took his chili as seriously as he did the black box capable of triggering doomsday, and went into a rage over the slightest bit of grease floating in his Texas version of ambrosia.

This food for the gods has been around for a long time. Columbus sailed back to Spain without any gold, but with a gift of chili peppers for Isabella and Ferdinand. The royal chef probably stirred up the first bowl of chili in history. By the end of the nineteenth century, San Antonio's chili queens were staging nightly cook-offs on Military Plaza for such judges as writer O. Henry and orator William Jennings Bryan. For a dime, each queen's bowl of red was served with bread and a glass of water to quench the fire ignited by her particular brew. Unfortunately, this noble tradition was squelched by the health department in 1943.

By that time, William Gebhardt had invented chili powder, and Lyman Davis had put Wolf Brand chili in cans. Davis named his product for his pet wolf, Kaiser Bill, and Will Rogers dined on Wolf Brand for his "bowl of blessedness" when he could not get the real thing hot from the fire.

In 1967, a desolate ghost town in the Big Bend country achieved national fame when Terlingua was the site of the first World's Championship Chili Cook-Off setting a tradition that promises to endure as long as people eat chili. Devoted chili fans descend on this wilderness the first Satur-

day in November for the big contest. The whole crazy show began as a joke when Frank X. Tolbert, a Dallas newsman and author, was researching the history of this popular dish. For the momentous occasion there were only two contestants: Wick Fowler of Four-Alarm Chili fame and the memorable H. Allen Smith. Astoundingly, 500 spectators braved the desert sands to torture their palates. Since that day, Texas has gone chili cook-off mad, and so many contestants vie for the Terlingua sweepstakes, they have to win other preliminary cook-offs to qualify. (See *Traveling Texas Borders*, Lone Star Books, Houston, Texas, for a description of this lively annual event.)

Tolbert, "The Grand Sage of the Pod," has since cooked chili everywhere in the world, including reindeer chili up in the Arctic Circle at Honnengsvag, Norway. For years, Tolbert's Native Texas Foods and Museum of the Chili Culture was in a dumpy chili parlor at 802 Main in Dallas. Walls were strung with Terlingua clippings, posters, and photos as well as bad paintings of chili pods and related subjects. Armadillos abounded, in company with a dragon breathing fire from a recent chili cook-off. A marvelous letter to Henry Ford dated April 10, 1924, waxes eloquent over Ford's invention:

> While I still have breath in my lungs I will tell you what a dandy car you make. I have drove Fords exclusively when I could get away with one. For sustained speed and freedom from trouble the Ford has got ever other car skinned and even if my business hasn't been strickly legal it don't hurt enything to tell you what a fine car you got in the V8.
>
> Yours truly,
>
> *Clyde Champion Barrow*

But the best exhibit was the one set down on your table—a $3 bowl of Tolbert's red. The recipe for this famous dish goes on for four detailed pages in the great chef's book, *A Bowl of Red*, and naturally the main ingredients are the peppers. Ask for sun-dried *anchos*, and for a very "elevated" flavor, use four pepper pods for each pound of lean beef. Other recipes in the book include Lady Bird's Pedernales River Chili.

The museum cleaned up its act when it moved to its new location on McKinney. All the tacky armadillos are gone, but a lot of the memorabilia from Tolbert's chili exploits is still stuck around. And, most importantly, the bowl of red is superb. As you get ready to smack your lips over the state dish of Texas, dwell a moment on Matthew (Bones) Hooks' chili prayer:

> "Chili eaters is some of your chosen people. We don't know why you so doggone good to us. But, Lord, God, don't ever think we ain't grateful for this chili we about to eat. Amen."

Miss Hattie's

"The Second-Best Little Whorehouse in Texas"
San Angelo

Working conditions at Miss Hattie's were excellent for her girls, but there were on-the-job hazards.

The Chicken Ranch and Miss Mona have achieved national notoriety from the musical *The Best Little Whorehouse in Texas*, but way out in the West Texas town of San Angelo is the "Second-Best Little Whorehouse in Texas." Miss Hattie's closed before the media could secure her claim to fame, but from 1896 to 1946, this lady ran a Texas institution that did not need television or movies to publicize its charms.

Nowadays, San Angelo touts all sorts of wholesome entertainment for its visitors. Even the name of the town is synonymous with purity. In 1867, the same year Fort Concho was built, Bart DeWitt founded his trading post. His wife named her new home Santa Angela for her sister, a Mexican nun, and somehow the feminine Santa Angela evolved into the masculine San Angelo.

Fort Concho occupied a central position in a chain of defense against Indian marauders, so more troops were stationed here than at any of the other frontier posts. Fort Concho was abandoned by 1889, but the railroad had arrived by then and San Angelo was firmly entrenched as the center of ranching activity for the surrounding counties.

As the town grew out of mud huts and adobe shacks, so grew its wild and wooly ways. East Concho Street, bordering the Concho River, became renowned in the annals of Texas' infamous dens of corruption. You can't even buy a bottle of whiskey in the city limits of San Angelo today, but at the turn of the century, East Concho Street alone had 13 bars. Nestled in among them was Miss Hattie's.

Miss Hattie ran a genteel establishment in spite of the neighborhood. At some point in her life, Miss Hattie had married the keeper of the saloon on the first floor of the building. When they divorced in 1902, Miss Hattie's settlement was the upstairs bordello while her ex-husband continued in the saloon business downstairs. Usually, ten or so girls made up the work force, and some were such loyal employees they stayed on for years. If they gave gold watches for length of service in bawdyhouses, Miss Blue, Rosie, and Goldie would have qualified for the award. Goldie was the star attraction in the trade and charged the exorbitant sum of $2 for her favors. She obviously derived a great deal of job satisfaction from her position at Miss Hattie's.

A brothel was not always some sleazy run-down old dump with pityful-looking creatures inhabiting it. In fact, these houses were such an integral part of frontier life that many had the most elegant and tasteful decor in town. Miss Hattie's was no exception. Even now, the pressed tin ceilings are absolutely magnificent. Gilded in gold, these ornate designs are as gorgeous as they were when first installed. Miss Hattie's even had the first bathroom in San Angelo, and Miss Blue rated her own cold water tap to her room.

Life at Miss Hattie's had many fringe benefits. None of the ladies did a lick of housework. Even though the tiny kitchen was available, the girls preferred to have their meals catered. Neither did their hands touch dirty soapy water nor did their backs bend over steaming washtubs, for all laundry was sent out and delivered daily. Maids came to clean, mop, and dust all the rooms and parlors, so plenty of time was left to ride around town in Miss Hattie's Model T sedan. With the top back, the madam, three of her employees, and two white dogs cruised the streets waving gaily to acquaintances—sort of a subtle advertising pitch. Don't you know there were some hard-working pioneer wives that gritted their teeth with envy and venom as Miss Hattie and her girls drove past.

Naturally, some marvelous stories originated about Miss Hattie's. The bank was next door to this thriving enterprise, and some clever soul dug a tunnel from this staid firm to the house of pleasure adjoining it. Clients would enter the bank to ostensibly conduct their business affairs, go through the tunnel to visit their favorite girls, and return the same way. There was certainly nothing unusual about conferring with one's banker, even if the conferences did go on for hours sometimes.

Of course there were raids. What would a bawdyhouse be without raids! Warning lights and bells would sound the alarm at both the front and back stairs. The girls and their customers would flee the premises by way of catwalks to nearby "boarding houses." During one such melee, Miss Blue fell through the skylight, but the doctor who treated her is still living, and said she wasn't hurt too badly. It was business as usual in a few days.

There were a few other hazards in the girls' line of work, and it wasn't unusual for babies to arrive. The camaraderie among the girls was wonderful, however, and those without customers would provide a bawdyhouse version of a daycare center while the mothers were "working."

When two airbases were built near San Angelo, they created a bonanza for Miss Hattie's, and business boomed.

Goldie just loved soldiers, and they must have loved her, too, for they presented her with all sorts of presents and mementos—medals, insignias, and printed satin pillows dripping with fringe. With the end of the war came the demand for purity and righteousness, and such blatant sinning could no longer be overlooked. Miss Hattie's had to go.

When the Texas Rangers closed down this West Texas way of life in 1946, the bawdyhouse was locked away, but not forgotten. Evelyn Hill, who has lived in San Angelo all of her life, remembers a day when she was about five years old. When her mother took her to a store on Concho Street, Mother threatened Evelyn with, "Keep your eyes straight ahead and don't look around." The admonition came too late, and Evelyn shocked her mother with, "What are all those girls doing hanging out of their windows in their nightgowns in the daytime?"

Years later, Evelyn bought the old saloon and brothel and opened an antique store downstairs. Having Miss Hattie's overhead, locked and rotting away, was just too much. Evelyn said, "I couldn't stand it. I just had to restore it." So, after two years of cleaning, searching, unpacking, and just plain digging out (plus two cases of dust pneumonia), Evelyn Hill has restored Miss Hattie's into a museum dedicated to the world's oldest profession.

When you tour Miss Hattie's, the only things missing are its madam and her girls. The gentleman's parlor, where the men waited for the lady of their choice to be free, is just terrific. Velvet drapes, lace curtains, a pink silk sofa with crocheted doilies, pictures of soldiers, and even a wall board of Goldie's collection of military souvenirs complete the furnishings. Miss Hattie's private parlor and room look as though she might enter at any moment from a ride with her girls and dogs.

Even though Miss Hattie had her own suite, the other girls had mighty fine working conditions. Ornate iron, brass, and oak beds (double, of course) were covered with velvet and satin spreads. Even the original feather matresses are still on the beds. The lace panels on the windows, oriental rugs, and upholstered chairs and sofas created a really elegant atmosphere. Boots are still lined up at the foot of Miss Blue's bed. Evelyn said that when a pair is stolen by some souvenir hunter, word gets around, and one of the ranchers will come by with another pair. They still consider it a very special honor to have their boots under Miss Blue's bed. One room has the wicker baby basket which held the girls' mistakes.

If those rooms could talk, it boggles the imagination at the stories they could tell. Several of the girls still live in San Angelo and are now in their seventies. Evelyn said they came to visit one day and stayed for hours upstairs laughing and reliving their working days. However, they are still true professionals and would tell none of their secrets. Even Miss Hattie came by with her granddaughters and loved the way her house looked after so many years.

After their enforced retirement, Miss Hattie and her girls were left numerous ranches and property by grateful clients, so none were destitute by any means. Miss Hattie died in the spring of 1982 at age 104 and rich as Croesus. So much for the wages of sin.

Texas Ranger Hall of Fame and Museum

Fort Fischer Park
P.O. Box 1370
Waco 76703
817-754-1433
Hours: 9–5
Admission

"You Rangers don't fight like palefaces."

Quanah Parker, 1870

 In the saga of western heroes, no stars shine as brightly as the stars of the Texas Rangers. Volumes have been written lauding the exploits of this dedicated group of men who set the standard throughout the world for mounted police forces. Their stories are the stuff of Hollywood's most exciting westerns, but are better than fiction, for the Texas Rangers actually lived out their harrowing tales.

From the moment of their inception, the Rangers were unique. The first Rangers were a private army of ten men employed by Stephen F. Austin in 1823 to protect his early colonists from Indian attacks. After Texas became a republic, Rangers were needed on the frontier, but funds for their support and pay were practically nonexistent. When the Texas Army was disbanded in 1841, the Rangers still assumed the responsibilities of a military force. During the Mexican

They didn't ride white horses, wear masks, or shoot silver bullets, but the Texas Rangers were the stuff of legends.

War, the Texas Rangers became a necessary cavalry unit for Zachary Taylor.

After the Civil War, the famous fighting force was disbanded by Reconstruction politicians, and the frontier and Mexican borders became hotbeds of bandits, gunslingers, rustlers, marauding Indians, and every other unsavory type opposed to law and order. This miserable condition existed until 1874 when the Texas Legislature passed a bill creating six companies of Rangers to be known as the Frontier Battalion to serve primarily in West Texas. At the same time, a special force of one company was authorized to rid South Texas of the numerous cattle thieves and outlaws.

By World War I, the Ranger forces were increased to about 1,000 men whose duty it was to protect the Rio Grande. Later, the impossible task of enforcing Prohibition became the Rangers' responsibility. With the discovery of oil, Texas towns boomed with money, but they also boomed with sin and corruption. In Borger, a notice appeared in the newspaper offering odds against Captain Frank Hammer's living 30 days. Only a fool took the bet, and when Hammer arrived, Borger was tamed forever. During the Kilgore boom, "Lone Wolf" Gonzaullas appeared with two pearl-handled revolvers and riding a black stallion and proceeded to arrest 30 lawbreakers in one day.

What kind of man was this Texas symbol of justice? Historian T. R. Fehrenbach describes Ranger captains as "extremely young, volunteers, not merely brave—but with an utter absence of fear—superb psychologists, and their units comprised one of the most colorful, efficient, and deadly band of irregular partisans on the side of law and order the world has ever seen." Two circumstances have been true throughout their entire existence, the Texas Rangers were always outnumbered by their foes, and the battle plan was consistent: attack, dominate, subdue.

As a tribute to these legendary men and their exploits, a museum was built in their honor in Waco. The first 20 men selected for the Texas Ranger Hall of Fame were all Rangers of great bravery who served above and beyond the call of duty. Also depicted in the museum is the most famous Ranger of them all—the Lone Ranger. The Masked Rider of the Plains and his faithful Tonto led a crusade against injustice that has never been equaled in the West. The Masked Man fired silver bullets as a symbol of "the high cost of human life," and as he rode away into the sunset with his famous farewell of "Hi-yo, Silver! Awaaaaay!" you knew he would soon be back if needed.

Down-to-earth Rangers did not shoot silver bullets, but Captain Jack Hays was the first man to use the Colt six-shooter on Plains Indians. How the famous pistols arrived in Texas is not known, but in 1840 Hays and 14 men were attacked by 70 Comanches. Hays lost several Rangers, but killed 30 Indians with the new Colt revolvers. A demoralized but brave Comanche chief declared, "I will never again fight Jack Hays, who has a shot for every finger on the hand."

A fleet horse and a trusty six-shooter that "run together like molasses" became one of the most effective weapons systems known until the arrival of the "accurate" breech-loading rifles in the 1870s. After Hays' success with the

six-shooter, Captain Samuel H. Walker went East, looked up Samuel Colt, suggested some improvements, and out of this visit came the world's first martial revolver—the Walker Colt. It would kill more men than any handgun ever made. Rangers and their six-guns went on to enduring fame in the long Mexican border wars.

The standard set by Captain Jack Hays was so superb, every Texas Ranger wanted to be "like Jack Hays." Many achieved that desire, such as the heroic Ben McCulloch, Sam Walker, L. H. McNelly, John B. Jones, and even Big Foot Wallace. Also in the Hall of Fame is John S. (Rip) Ford of Civil War fame; L. S. Ross who rescued Cynthia Ann Parker; Ira Aten; George W. Baylor; and Frank Hammer. Ranger John Armstrong made the brilliant arrest of John Wesley Hardin who with more than 40 notches in his gun was Texas' most wanted killer. And in 1878, Ranger Dick Ware ended the outlaw career of Sam Bass in Round Rock. (See "Saints and Sinners.")

One of the Hall of Fame's original honorees was W. L. Wright. His son, E. A. (Dogie) Wright, has a collection out in Sierra Blanca of memorabilia of his father's as well as his own exploits. Dogie is past 80, but his memories and stories about West Texas and his days as sheriff, Texas Ranger, and Border Patrolman are priceless.

When Ranger Bill McDonald was sent to put down a riot in Columbus, the town was aghast that only one Ranger had been sent for such a perilous situation. McDonald's taciturn reply was "Well, you ain't got but one mob, have you?" This went on to become the Ranger motto "One riot, one Ranger." Up in Quanah in a shootout against four rustlers, McDonald took a bullet through his coat, one in his left side, one in his arm, and a fourth in his right side. The undaunted Ranger caught the hammer with his teeth, killed his opponents, and a few weeks later was saddled again ready for another assignment.

With such true stories as that to build upon, the Texas Ranger Museum and Hall of Fame fascinates every generation. Thanks to the overwhelming efforts of Captain Clint Peoples, these Texas heroes are honored and remembered in one of the finest museums in the nation.

A diorama of Jack Hays on Enchanted Rock tells the story of how this Ranger held off 100 Indians for over an hour with a single-shot rifle and two five-shot pistols. A collection of Bowie knives, including an original made and designed by Jim (or his brother Rezin) is on display. This was the "ultimate weapon" of the West until the arrival of the six-shooter, and was standard equipment for a Ranger. In addition to his Bowie knife and Walker Colt .44, a Ranger's artillery included a single-shot rifle or double barrel shotgun, and a hatchet.

The gun collection is spectacular. Billy the Kid's Whitney shotgun, Tom Horn's Colt that captured Geronimo, Tom Mix's .38 Colt, and a Colt found at Little Big Horn are just a few of the museum's pieces of weaponry. Bat Masterson's cane and gun, along with the most beautifully engraved revolvers ever made tell stirring tales of the Old West.

An exciting multi-media presentation, "Tradition of Courage," and the Moody Texas Ranger Memorial Library further enliven the history of the Rangers, tracing this purely Texas organization from its formation to the present, through 150 years of glory.

Among the many photographs of old Rangers are the priceless treasures of their guns, spurs, badges, and honors. Climaxing the museum is the bronze statue of one of these typical "bigger than life" men. Engraved on the base are Captain Bill McDonald's immortal words "No man in the wrong can stand up against a fellow that's in the right and keeps on a-comin.'"

Presidential Museum

622 N. Lee
Odessa 79761
915-332-7123
Hours: 10–12, 1–5 Mon.–Fri.
Admission free

 After the assassination of John F. Kennedy in Dallas, a group of concerned Texans worried about their state's image and planned a monument to the office of the presidency. A museum was organized and opened to the public in 1964 as one small room in the basement of the county library. Over the years, the museum has evolved into an institution that attempts to deal with the process of becoming president and how the presidency operates.

The collection relates not only to presidents, vice-presidents, and first ladies; also-ran candidates are remembered as well as Presidents Jones, Houston, Lamar, and Burnet of the Republic of Texas. Even Jeff Davis is honored here.

Stamps from all over the world picturing American presidents, postcards of their birthplaces, plates, signatures, campaign memorabilia, and even political cartoons depict the highest office in the land. Particularly delightful is the doll collection of First Ladies. Mr. and Mrs. Gayle Dishong did extensive research and painstakingly arrayed each doll in authentic gowns and hair styles. Nearby, Lyndon Johnson's favorite rocking chair sits as though waiting for its famous owner to relax from a busy schedule.

An extensive noncirculating research library is available for scholars.

Bullfight Museum

Del Camino Motel and Restaurant
5001 Alameda (US Highway 80 East)
El Paso

 The history of bullfighting is as old as the history of man. Paleolithic man scratched the bull's image on his cave walls at Altamira, Spain, in a primitive attempt to capture the animal's great spirit. From man's earliest beginning, bulls were considered the supreme symbol of strength and fertility.

Mythology abounds with bulls. Theseus became the world's first bullfighter when he slayed the Minotaur, and ancient Minoan youths engaged in the sport of "bull-dancing." An agile girl or boy would face the beast, grasp the horns, and somersault over the bull's back. By the time Rome ruled the world, the grandfather of bullring empresarios, Julius Caesar, instigated bullfights as part of his big spectaculars at the Coliseum.

Bullfighting moved to Spain with the Moors, and even with the Christian reconquest, the Church accepted the sport. The opening of the season was Easter, and fights were held to commemorate canonization of saints. But, the bullfight as we know it today began in the eighteenth century in the slaughterhouses of Spain. At first, the most important moment was the kill, not the *arte de torear*, or playing with the bull. Now fans anticipate the artistic cape work of the matador prior to the bull's "moment of truth."

The star of the show is always the matador. This maestro must possess a deep passion and desire to fight bulls more than anything else in the world, regardless of reward. Controlling his fear in order to control the bull gives a man deep satisfaction for having such self-mastery.

Every piece of the star's *traje de luces*, or "suit of lights" is steeped in ancient tradition. The pants (talequilla) are always skin tight with no protection for the genitals. That is considered totally dishonorable. The white shirt must be ruffled and the black tie and sash of a specific length. The flat shoes (zapatillas) are black with ribbon laces, and the pigtail (coleta) is usually made from a sweetheart's or mother's hair. This tradition originated with Roman gladiators, who wore pigtails as caste marks. When a matador retires from the ring, he publicly cuts his coleta. His ornate jacket (chaquelita) is heavily encrusted with gold or silver embroidery. Jacket, vest, and pants must always match, but can be of any color. Most matadors are extremely superstitious and consider red the greatest danger in spite of the fact bulls are color blind. Completing the 14-pound costume is the *montera*, or hat, which itself weighs a pound and is very expensive.

The most costly item in the bullfighting profession is the cape, the tool of the matador's art. El Toro has never seen a cape before this moment, and the artistic part of the show is when the matador performs his cape work.

At "The Moment of Truth" the sword must be placed correctly on the bull's back for a clean kill. Novice bullfighters often create a bloody lingering death for their antagonist. If the matador has performed well, the crowd awards him the bull's ear. If it has been an outstanding show, he is awarded two ears. For a really spectacular show (very rare) the matador earns two ears and the tail. As for the bull, if he was brave, he is dragged around the ring *twice*. Bullfight *aficionados* find this very thrilling for an animal that has lived 4 years preparing for a 20-minute death scene.

Sometimes the crowd is so emotional over a particular matador's artwork, they not only throw flowers, they hurl fighting cocks, lambs, artificial limbs, underwear, and even human babies have been tossed at his feet. Now, that is enthusiasm. But, there is a definite element of risk in seeking such adoration. Luis Freg experienced 90 *cornados*, or horn wounds. Out of those 90, 72 were severe, and he received extreme unction five times. Obviously, he loved his work.

At the Del Camino Motel, Bill Adams has filled his restaurant with bullfight trophies. "El Finito's" head presides over the collection. He was the only bull in history to be pardoned in the State of Chihuahua. The great Manolete's life and death is presented with his suits, pictures, and paintings. Also, the unique "El Cordobes," who made $4 million in 5 years, is described in photographs and memorabilia. "El Cordobes" was unique for his style and also for the fact that he quit while he was rich and famous—not dead.

A replica of a bullfighters chapel is here in the museum of tauromachy as well as a model of the Plaza de Toros in Madrid. Many, many photographs of other matadors are in the collection, including those of Patricia McCormick, the first American lady bullfighter. Signed capes and shirts of other great matadors adorn the walls as well.

If this taurine paraphernalia doesn't interest you, you can still enjoy a good meal at a reasonable price—and that's no bull.

One of a Kind in Texas

Texas may not have the nation's only space, biblical, circus, wax, or energy museums, but the one of each the state does have is outstanding.

Lyndon B. Johnson Space Center

Nasa Road 1 Exit off I-45
Clear Lake
713-483-4433
Hours: 9–4
Admission free

 The role of most museums is to imbue you with a sense of the past, but at the LBJ Space Center, you are overwhelmed with what the future has in store. At the visitor center you can choose between a self-guided tour, guided tour, and a driving tour. Why not take all three?

The magnificent mural "Opening the Space Frontier—The Next Giant Step" by Robert T. McCall portrays the past and future of manned space flight. On the opposite wall are the space suits worn by astronauts on various flights. You can try on a space helmet like the one Alan Shepard wore when he became the first man in space. The lunar module and the moon rover that took the Apollo 17 astronauts to the moon are back here on Mother Earth at the space center. You can even see a piece of the moon brought back by Dave Scott and Jim Irwin in July 1971. These hunks of basalt are about 3,320,000,000 years old.

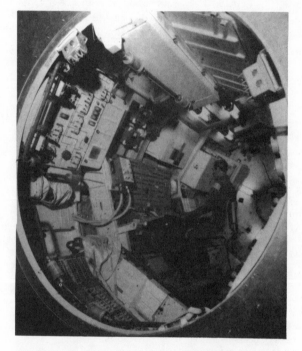

The LBJ Space Center is a display of man's most ingenious technology, and it is open year round.

Six moon landings brought back 842 pounds of the moon's surface, and most of it is still at the JSC for future research.

A beautiful theater runs continual shows on flight preparations, actual flights, and problems encountered and solutions. In the Exhibit Hall is a full-scale mockup of the space shuttle orbiter, with a description of how man can survive in a world without gravity. Upstairs is a display on the history of Mercury and Gemini. The Mercury flight was to discover if man could survive in orbit, while the Gemini tested man's efficiency in space for extended periods of time.

When you tear yourself away from the visitor center, Building 5 houses the Skylab trainers and the simulators currently used by astronauts to train for the shuttle mission. Building 9A has the full-scale Space Shuttle trainers for the manned missions of the 1980s. There is no end to the projects on the planning boards for the successful Space Shuttle: a complete scientific laboratory, a solar power station, and perhaps even communities of workers.

Obtain a pass at the visitor center and follow the red signs to the incredible Mission Control Center. The most historic words of the twentieth century were first heard here when Neil Armstrong reported, "Houston, the Eagle has landed." You can sit in the Control Center's viewing room and receive a presentation on the history and future of the exploration and exploitation of space.

Over 4,000 people a day come to the Johnson Space Center, and you can hear every language in the world. Even if you don't understand one word, you can tell from the tone of their voices, they are impressed!

Exploration of space opens up a limitless frontier with never-ending adventures, and it is this boundless universe with its countless mysteries that appeals to all Americans. You know the planets are in your near future, and then . . . the stars.

The Hertzberg Circus Collection

210 W. Market (Main Library Annex)
San Antonio
512-299-7810
Hours: 9–5:30, closed Sunday
Admission free

 One famous All-American boy, Huckleberry Finn, thought the circus "was the splendidest sight that ever was." But, the circus is far from being an All-American phenonmenon. This truly international art form began about the fourth century B.C. with the Romans. Even the word "circus" is Latin for a roofless, oval enclosure surrounded by tiers of seats used for public spectacles.

During the Middle Ages wandering jugglers and animal trainers brightened the dreary life of serfdom, and in 1768 Philip Astley became the "Father of the Circus" with an exhibition of trick riding in London. John Bill Ricketts brought the circus to America with the same type of show, and it was an immediate success—even George and Martha Washington applauded.

Hackaliah Bailey of New York made so much money exhibiting an elephant, that exotic animal shows became lucrative businesses. Somehow the animals and acts evolved together to form the opulent show America loves so well. Small Town, U.S.A., lived for the great day the circus came to town. The lavish parade announcing its arrival was almost as exciting as the show. Lengthy pageants of splendor featured gilded chariots, rare animals, the performers, and at the end a great steam-powered organ or calliope

(pronounced cally-ope by circus people) enticed thousands of people into the big top.

Harry Hertzberg, a San Antonio lawyer, civic leader, and state senator was an avid circus fan and a prolific collector. Thanks to Hertzberg's love of the circus, his collection is nationally recognized as one of the significant circus memorabilia collections in the United States.

The largest item in the museum is an ornate parade wagon built in 1902. Talk about versatile! The wagon was pulled by a team of ponies in the morning parade, became a ticket office in the afternoon, and carried gear at night to the next town. This particular wagon belonged to the Gentry Bros., a circus typical of the small dog-and-pony shows that appeared in rural communities.

Today when you hear the name P. T. Barnum, you immediately think of the circus, but in the nineteenth century, the showman operated a big museum of curiosities in New York City. Barnum's prize exhibit was the midget, General Tom Thumb. Tom Thumb certainly was not the smallest man who ever lived (he was 40 inches tall), but he was certainly the most famous midget.

One of the tiny general's earliest coaches is part of the Hertzberg collection along with his miniature violin, a tiny muzzle-loading rifle, a vest and cane, a cast of his foot, and even a piece of the General's and Mrs. Tom Thumb's 1863 wedding cake. The little people were actually a part of the circus on very few occasions.

Clyde Beatty, the greatest animal trainer of all time, has donated his safari costume from his movie *Ring of Fear* and also here are two claws from Beatty's lion, Simba.

One room in the museum contains a marvelous miniature circus, lacking only miniature people to sit in the bleachers. This masterpiece was the 13-year undertaking of ringmaster Harry Leska Thomas, and illustrates a tented railroad circus popular in the 1920s and 1930s.

The Hertzberg Collection features many examples of pioneer outdoor poster advertising. Among Hertzberg's nearly 1,000 posters are some advertising Clyde Beatty, the wire-walking Wallendas, and cowboy Tom Mix. These wonderful posters are a vivid history of American entertainment during the nineteenth and twentieth centuries.

So much is here in this delightful museum. Broadsides (handbills) boast of a circus "unequaled in extent, unparalled in attractiveness, matchless in the mighty majesty of magnificence." Little booklets that contained descriptions of the animals, songs and jokes of the clowns, and accounts of the lives of the freaks and novelty acts in the side shows were sold. The Hertzberg's collection of these booklets tell much about the tastes of American audiences.

So many journals, route books, programs, photographs, prints, music sheets, paintings, manuscripts, and scrapbooks have been amassed, the library is widely used for circus research. Materials may only be used on the premises, but a fulltime librarian is prepared to aid researchers.

Kids don't run away from home to join the circus anymore, nor can they sneak under the flap of the big top, but they can still thrill to the amazing feats of skill by talented performers. The circus will continue to survive as long as there are "little kids," no matter what their age. It is hoped somewhere another circus fan is following in the late Harry

Hertzberg's footsteps and preserving circus memorabilia. Then, he will receive a tribute such as this:

"Dear Harry Hertzberg,

We love you as you love a circus. Can more be said?
The Alfredo Codona Tent, 1938."

Biblical Arts Center

7500 Park Lane at Boedeker
Dallas 75225
214-691-4661
Hours: 10–5 Tues.–Sat., 1–5 Sun.
Admission

One of the most fateful days in the history of Christianity was the Day of Pentecost, for it marked the beginning of the Church. Christ's chosen Apostles received the power of the Holy Spirit as recorded in Acts 2 of the New Testament.

Few artists have attempted to portray this momentous event that affected mankind so profoundly, but Dallas artist Torger Thompson was committed to this masterpiece. Thompson devoted all of his spare time to his "Miracle" project. He placed his Day of Pentecost in the Upper Room as is traditionally accepted. However, after hundreds of sketches, his intensive research into the original Hebrew text of the Bible and consultations with leading theologians convinced the artist the event took place on Solomon's Porch of Herod's Temple in Jerusalem. Years of work had to be revised, but Thompson was committed to accuracy.

Finally, when all preliminary sketches were completed, the artwork had outgrown his home. The next logical step was to begin the mural and find a patron who believed in the project. In a way, another miracle occurred, for Torg met Mattie Caruth Byrd who commissioned Torg and his associate, Alvin Barns, to begin the "Miracle at Pentecost."

The Garden Tomb of Christ at Calvary is duplicated at the Biblical Arts Center in Dallas. (Photograph courtesy of Biblical Arts Center.)

The two artists spent a year just composing the pilot painting 24 feet wide by 4 feet high which now hangs in the Biblical Arts Center. Overshadowing the pilot art, however, is the massive mural itself, 125 feet wide by 20 feet high. Painted on the finest imported linen canvas with countless tubes of paint, the painting was completed in 1969 after more than two and one-half years of constant labor. It took another two years to build the perfect home for the 200 witnesses to the miracle on that eventful day on Solomon's Porch.

The presentation of the "Miracle" is awesome. You enter a theater, and the room darkens. A melodious voice begins the story with, "In ancient Jerusalem about 2,000 years ago, it was a time of waiting. When the Apostles heard the news that Jesus Christ had risen from the dead, they were to wait in Jerusalem, but for what, they did not know. Day after day the devoted followers waited. All they knew; 'You shall receive power when the Holy Spirit comes upon you.'"

Throughout the narration of the "Miracle of Pentecost," spots of light hit the main characters in the story. At the end, the curtain parts, and the entire painting is on view. It takes several moments to adjust to its magnitude. The familiar strains of "He walks with me, and He talks with me, and He tells me I am His own . . ." are heard throughout the auditorium. The Biblical Arts Center is proud that "The Lord did not call a renowned muralist, nor a celebrated gallery exhibitor, but Torg who headed his own commission. The wisdom of God's choice is shown in the painting."

Even the architecture of the Center is reminiscent of structures built in the early Christian Era. The limestone entrance with heavy, carved wooden doors is modeled after Paul's Gate at Damascus (Acts 9:25). Massive stone columns and vaulted ceilings add to the Romanesque features of the building.

In the atrium is a donation by an anonymous patron of a replica of the Garden Tomb of Christ at Calvary, a site in Jerusalem believed to be the actual burial place of Jesus. Plants indigenous to the Holy Land are added to this beautiful setting.

No matter what faith you profess, you are welcome at the Biblical Arts Center, for viewing the expertise of superb craftsmen is almost a religious experience in itself.

Insights

El Paso Science Center, Inc.
303 North Oregon (Mills Bldg.)
El Paso
915-542-2990
Admission free

Crammed into a basement room of the El Paso Electric Company building are magical displays explaining the wonders of modern science that delight and excite curiosity in school children. Randall Hays, the director, says a bigger location is planned for the more than 80 exhibits now cramped for space. You can learn about seeing, touching, smelling, hearing, motion, light, illusion, electricity, solar power, space science, energy, and the human body in a classroom unlike any other.

You can test your peripheral vision, watch floating rings, draw with sand, get lost in an optical cube, and watch solar energy as it continues to function even after 9,500,000,000 years of service. A mirror talks to you, gravity is defied, and computers whiz out answers in seconds.

If you remember the childhood poem "I have a little shadow that goes in and out with me," you can now step into a phosphorescent box and leave your shadow behind. This "magic trick" is a museum favorite.

Special programs are held, guest teachers give talks, and Insights publishes a book about El Paso's history and environment. Its newspaper *Boing!* entertains school-age children with stories and projects. This unusual museum is one of the most popular classrooms in El Paso.

Evern Wall, president and chairman of the board of El Paso Electric Company says, "We can't do anything about the price of electricity, but we can give good service." Part of the Electric Company's many services to their customers is it science museum, Insights.

Southwestern Historical Wax Museum

601 E. Safari Parkway
Grand Prairie 75050
214-263-2391
Hours: 10–6
Admission

 Alexander the Great not only conquered the known world of his day, he took time off from raping and pillaging to appoint Lysistratus of Sycion as his wax modeler-in-chief. Lysistratus was so grateful for his job, he developed the art of wax molding as we know it. His method of taking plaster molds of inanimate and living subjects and casting the formed impressions in wax has stood the test of time and remains basically the process used today.

Romans liked their exalted statesmen cast in wax; Anglo-Saxons gathered to stare at wax effigies of dead monarchs; and during the Middle Ages the Church used wax figures to explain the Bible. You might say these tableaux were the first wax museums.

Of course the Queen of Wax was Madam Tussaud. Surviving the Reign of Terror by casting death masks of the guillotine's famous victims, this remarkable woman escaped to London to open the world's most renowned wax works. The Chamber of Horrors at Madam Tussaud's set a trend for all wax museums, but none have achieved the perfection of her tortured souls writhing in horrendous agony.

In the Wax Museum at Grand Prairie, the emphasis is on characters that rose to glory in the days of the Wild West. Dick Dowling defeats the Union Navy as they attempt to invade Texas at Sabine Pass during the Civil War. Judge Roy Bean dispenses his unique brand of justice at the Jersey Lilly Saloon in Langtry, while a Longhorn steer stares

Gunslinger Bill Longley is as handsome in wax as he was in the wild west days of Texas.

balefully through the brush, waiting to be herded up the Chisholm Trail. Over in the East Texas section, Pop Joiner brings in the Daisy Bradford #1 in the Great East Texas Oil Field.

Outlaws and lawmen meet once again to talk over the number of men they killed in their assorted careers. The bigoted Bill Longley, handsome John Wesley Hardin, arrogant King Fisher, and elusive Sam Bass rub shoulders with Rangers Jack Hays and Big Foot Wallace. Pat Garrett stands ready to apprehend Billy the Kid, while Billy blasts away from the Lincoln County jail. (See *Traveling Texas Borders*, Lone Star Books, Houston, Texas.)

Several attempts at gore are part of the museum's dioramas, but nothing like the authenticity of Madam Tussaud's Chamber of Horrors in London. A headless corpse of Black Jack Ketchum lies at the foot of the gallows. Before Black Jack fell to his doom, the robber's last word were "Let 'er rip!" The hangman took him at his word, and Black Jack's head was ripped from his body. At the wax museum, a pipe sticks out of the wax body spurting "blood."

Also on view is the car used in the movie *Bonnie and Clyde*. (See "Saints and Sinners.") After 13 killings, 9 kidnappings, and about 100 stolen cars, the notorious couple went on to more fame in Hollywood's version of their career. One of Clyde's automatic shotguns is included in the exhibit.

No wax museum would be complete without its movie stars, and glamorous personalities fill a Hollywood setting. The great John Wayne is larger than life, and Elvis is belting out "Blue Suede Shoes." Biblical scenes are always popular subjects for wax museums, and here at Grand Prairie is the Last Supper in three-dimensional wax.

In 1900, hundreds of wax museums flourished in the world. Now, only a handful do a brisk business. Until the coming of illustrated newspapers and magazines, wax museums served a useful purpose in providing the almost sole means of familiarizing people with the famous and the infamous. Now, wax museums offer the opportunity for the public to mingle with the legendary and the mighty. And, this way, you can say anything you want to about them without hurting their feelings.

Fabulous Flora and Fauna

Naturally if it grows in Texas, it's going to be the biggest, the best, the most productive, or the rarest. Whether it be animal or vegetable, Texas will have the ideal conditions for it to be larger than life and twice as legendary.

World's Largest Strawberry

Poteet Chamber of Commerce
FM 476
Poteet 78065

That luscious red delicacy that goes so well with shortcake and cream is a perennial herb of the genus *Fragaria* in the rose family and is not a true berry, but a fruit receptacle. Strawberries were introduced into the United States early in the nineteenth century from France. Today, 30 varieties of this super source of vitamin C are grown, but the James Wilson strain developed in 1851 was the first to really make strawberries a productive crop.

Strawberries grow best in sandy soil, and around Poteet is just the right combination of sand and temperate climate to make this tiny community of about 3,000 the Strawberry Capital of Texas. Poteet was named for the operator of a blacksmith shop here after the Texas Revolution. Francis Poteet had to make trips to San Antonio for supplies, and he began picking up his neighbors' mail. The post office held the letters in between trips and marked them "Poteet."

Strawberries got to be such a big source of income for Poteet, in 1948 the town launched a Strawberry Festival. The idea was a brainchild of Charles Mullins, Sr. and Mallory C. Franklin. (Franklin never grew a strawberry in his life.) Well, you don't have to know a lot about strawberries to initiate a festival, because by 1981, an estimated 185,000 guests showed up to munch the town's favorite fare. The Grand Championship strawberry crate brought $2,400. Fortunately for the consumers' pocketbooks, it never reached the grocery shelves, but it is interesting to speculate how much a carton of championship berries would cost.

The monument to this bumper crop was built in 1965 as a gift from the Central Power & Light Company and its vice-president, C. C. Wines. Designed by Alfred Hesse of Corpus Christi, the big berry weighs 1,500 pounds and is 7 feet tall. But if you think this monument is "the berries," Poteet has one even bigger and taller. The town's water tower stands 134 feet tall with a 34-foot tank shaped and painted to resemble a strawberry.

Poteet, Texas, so fascinated cartoonist Milton Caniff, he named his new female lead in his Steve Canyon comic strip

for the town. When Caniff was asked why he decided on Poteet, he said that while in Houston at a banquet, one of his dinner partners was a newspaper man who had just done a story on Poteet's Strawberry Festival. The cartoonist became intrigued with Poteet and its festival, so Steve Canyon's precocious blond ward was christened with her Texas name.

Now, right next to the big berry by the chamber of commerce is the Poteet Canyon Monument built in 1967 of tile blocks and patterned on an original drawing presented to the Poteet Chamber of Commerce by Caniff. On Poteet Canyon Day, Caniff arrived in the strawberry city for a big parade and reception.

If you want to head down to Poteet for all the big festivities, the gala is held in April. Contact Sammi Franklin at 512-742-3873. She is the festival's director and can give you the details. They are instigating a new strawberry wine which should be interesting, and perhaps you can even get a taste of a $2,000 crate of berries.

World's Largest Pecan

Courthouse Square
Seguin

If you hear the words Sioux, Wichita, Cheyenne, Chickasaw, Choctaw, and Comanche around Seguin, it doesn't mean Indians are on the warpath. These are some of Texas' favorite varieties of pecans. In fact, Texas is so nuts about its pecan trees, in June of 1919 the pecan became the official state tree. *Carya illinoensis* is a native of Texas from the Piney Woods west throughout central Texas, reaching its peak of development in the watershed of the Colorado River.

The intrepid shipwreck victim, Cabeza de Vaca, was the first European to ever sample this tasty nut. He probably dined on the pecan extensively during the freezing winter of 1532. Held captive for nine years on the "River of Nuts" (the Guadalupe), de Vaca had plenty of time to observe the growing habits of his sustenance. George Washington even

Seguin's oversized fruit of the state tree of Texas is metal and plaster, and not very tasty.

planted the curiosities and developed such a passion for them, much of the time he had his pockets filled with what he called "Mississippi nuts."

Pecan trees prefer deep, fertile, well-watered soil, and if all the conditions are met, this excellent shade tree will reach 100 feet. One monster reached 120 feet and produced 1,600 pounds of nuts in a single harvest. You can see this monarch on the Llano River near Junction, Texas, on the farm of Lewis Jetton.

When the early settlers arrived in Texas, they saw so many pecan trees, it never occurred to them the trees could be exhausted. Many were cut down for firewood, to clear fields, or just to make it easy to pick the nuts. Fortunately, Governor Hogg instigated making the pecan the state tree, and today Texas leads the country in pecan production. In 1981, confectioners used 62 million pounds of Texas pecans in candy.

If you like to keep a bowl of pecans around the house, unshelled nuts store temporarily at room temperature, but should be kept refrigerated for long periods. Shelled pecans must be frozen, as they spoil very quickly. Stored properly, these Texas delights will keep fresh and tasty for about a year.

On the courthouse square in Seguin, next to a monument to all the Spanish explorers who trekked this way (and probably liked pecans, too) is the World's Largest Pecan. Monroe J. Engbrock, a plastering contractor, built this five by two and one-half foot boulder of metal lath and plaster. Set in solid cement, it weighs approximately 1,000 pounds.

A fitting tribute to this beautiful tree came from Governor Hogg, who said:

I want no monument of stone or marble, but plant at my head a pecan tree and at my feet an old fashioned walnut. And when these trees shall bear, let the pecans and the walnuts be given out among the Plain people of Texas so they may plant them and make *Texas a land of trees.*

If you are among the "Plain" people, take Governor Hogg's good advice and get your share of the more than $42 million worth of nuts these trees produce each year.

World's Largest Peanut

FM 140 West
Pearsall

Courthouse Square
Floresville

Even though the lowly peanut is associated with few bucks and lack of status, Texas produces 533 million pounds annually—and that ain't peanuts.

The traditional food of baseball games is not a nut at all. It is a legume or pea that develops underground from flower stalks drooping on the soil. Actually a native of South America, the peanut was later introduced into Africa, Europe, and then Asia. During seventeenth century trade with Africa, nature's best food arrived in the American colonies. The word "goober" was derived from the African word *nguba*, and it was very popular with the chef on slaving ships for his cargo. You could say this was the beginning of "peanut fares." After all, one and one-half cups of shelled goobers is enough daily protein for an adult male.

One of America's favorite uses for peanuts is in plain old peanut butter. In 1890, while looking for a perfect food for his elderly patients, a St. Louis physician came up with the perfect food for everybody—peanut butter. It has evolved from a jar of tasty spread covered with a thick layer of peanut oil to a perfectly homogenized treat that is eaten with everything from mayonnaise to tomatoes. Now one of the most fattening foods on the market is available as "diet peanut butter." It's somewhat bland, but better than no peanut butter at all.

Toasted, raw, salted, dry—even sugar coated, the peanut is an important staple in American diets. The Texas Department of Agriculture has a booklet on all the exotic dishes you can concoct with peanuts, even (gasp!) peanut chili.

Dr. George Washington Carver discovered 300 uses for peanuts. Not only can you eat them, cows and hogs like the leaves. Peanut oil goes into shaving cream, machine oil, face powder, shampoo, nitroglycerine, and sweeping compounds.

In a patch of weeds under a broken sign in Pearsall, the World's Largest Peanut looks ready to be plowed under. In Floresville, their six-foot money-making legume rates a site on the courthouse lawn and looks somewhat like a modernistic sculpture rather than a lowly goober. Even with two of the World's Largest Peanuts, Texas only ranks third in national production. Up in Durant, Oklahoma, the Okies built another World's Largest Peanut out of fine granite with a time capsule. (See *Traveling Texas Borders*, Lone Star Books, Houston, Texas.) But, according to Guinness, the real World's Largest Peanut was grown by Ed Weeks of Tarboro, North Carolina, and it was only three and one-half inches long.

Texas Forestry Museum

1905 Atkinson Drive (Highway 103 East)
Lufkin 75901
409-634-75901
Hours: 1–4
Admission free

Somewhere around 2,000 years ago, a Chinese scholar named Ts'ai Lun got tired of writing on silk and bamboo and decided to invent the oriental version of the Big Chief tablet. Ts'ai Lun pounded the inner bark of the mulberry tree into a pulpy mass, added a dash of water, and cooked up the first paper—unlined, no doubt.

The different types of paper used throughout the world today are countless. Paper runs the gamut from the highly valued paper currency to the lowly, but essential, toilet tissue. The United States alone uses 1.1 million tons of paper a week or about 565 pounds per person per year. Sweden is second and Canada third in consumption, but in

China, where Ts'ai Lun began the whole thing, every person uses no more than 12 pounds per year.

To supply this enormous appetite for an indigestible product, you start with a pine seedling and in 17 to 20 years you will have 500 pounds of wood or 120 pounds of paper. With 6 seedlings, you would have enough wood to make 18,000 copies of a 16-page section of a newspaper.

As for lumber, a 1-inch thickness of wood gives the same insulation as 6 inches of brick or 12 inches of concrete. Unfortunately, wood burns, and too often before it ever gets to the sawmill. All but one percent of the forest fires are caused by man. Those sort of figures bring a lump to your throat.

> You can take a tip from Smokey
> that there's nothing like a tree,
> Cause they're good for kids to climb in,
> and they're beautiful to see.
> You just have to look around you,
> and you'll find it's not a joke
> To see what you'd be missin'
> if they all went up in smoke.
>
> "Smokey the Bear" song
> by Steve Nelson and Jack Rollins

In East Texas, Smokey is a very important character, for this part of the state is called the "Piney Woods" with good reason. Out of 225 species of trees growing in Texas, these southern yellow pines account for 64 percent of the timber volume in commercial forests.

Even before Texas won its independence, the forestry industry was providing the impetus for Texas growth. Towns like Houston, Beaumont, and Lufkin once based their economy on lumber. That fact has not changed much around Lufkin, and to preserve the history of the forestry profession, a beautifully designed museum has been built in a grove of Texas pines.

Huge glass windows bring the trees right into the museum. The "high-wheeled cart" in the center of the exhibits is the forerunner of the modern-day skidder. Drawn by mules or oxen, these 8-foot wheels pulled several logs at a time to the loading site. All the tools the blacksmith used to keep the mill's equipment in top condition are on display as well as an old, old automatic nailer that could pound out 25 million board feet of that southern yellow pine annually.

Many more exhibits portray the importance of the forest to man and depict the creatures who live in its shelter. One of the more humorous and popular displays is an old moonshiner's still. Who knows how many of these illegal little factories are still brewing up various blends of "white lightnin'" out in those piney woods.

Obsolete antiques rest on the grounds. Old Locomotive #3 built a logging town named Manning. Manning has disappeared, but Old #3 endures. The fire lookout tower is just about a relic as well. Helicopters and small aircraft have proved more efficient in locating those ominous spirals of smoke.

For years, one of the shortest railroads in the country was from Camden to Moscow. If you were lucky enough to

"All Aboard" before it stopped chugging its short tracks, you got a good view of about eight miles of dense forests from an old railroad car with hard seats and a pot-bellied stove. At least the Camden Depot has been restored on the museum grounds.

A short forest trail meanders through the surrounding woods. This minitrail typifies the 15 longer trails throughout the state where you can enjoy the peace and solitude of the forest. For information and locations of these beautiful pathways, write The Texas Forestry Association, P. O. Box 1488, Lufkin, Texas, 75901.

Trees are a crop and are tended and harvested like any other farm product, yet many people believe that a forest which is "harvested" is being "destroyed." If properly managed, a tree farm will result in one-third more wood products from the same area. If you are interested in becoming a "farmer," contact the Texas Forestry Association at the museum address.

And, always take that tip from Smokey: "There's nothing like a tree," if you own just a few, or an entire forest.

Monument to the Mule

Muleshoe

The critter looks so real you expect it to open its mouth, curl back its lips, bare those big yellow teeth, and bray a piercing "Heeeeeeeeeeeee-Haw" that can be heard all over the Texas Panhandle. This life-size statue of a mule is not to be confused with your run-of-the-mill reproductions of bulls in front of steak houses or horses advertising western wear—this Texas mule is special indeed!

Standing nobly by the side of Highway 84 in this West Texas town with the unglamorous name of Muleshoe, the monument honors all mules. Without these unsung heroes, the settlement of the vast plains would have been delayed for years. Fierce Comanches, often called the "Centaurs of the Plains," were such snobs about their horseflesh, the braves would not bother to steal mules. After all, it is rather difficult to picture a mighty warrior all decked out in his

This monument to one of Texas' unsung heroes is appropriately in Muleshoe.

warpaint with scalps hanging from his leggings, riding a *mule*.

The Indians did not even consider mule meat worth eating—too tough and stringy when compared to juicy buffalo hump. Well, this tough and stringy animal proved far superior to horses for hauling guns, ammunition, and supplies to the frontier forts. So, ultimately in his own way, the lowly mule defeated the arrogant Comanches who ignored his enduring traits.

The model for this monument was Pete, the 1,100 pound 18-year old offspring of a jackass and a female horse. A mule's ears measure about 33-inches horizontally from tip to tip, and he is better adapted to hot weather than a horse, less likely to overeat or overdrink, and freer from digestive ailments. Therefore, a mule can be fed cheaper, coarse food.

Bret Harte recounts a favorite mule story about a dauntless beast named Rowdy, who during a blizzard ate the ropes off a wagon and the hair off the tails of some accompanying horses. When Rowdy was hungry, he et.

The mule made the Bible 21 times, and Queen Elizabeth I drove around London in a carriage drawn by 6 white mules. Even the Father of our Country recognized the value of this versatile beast and bred a superior ass for mule breeding.

Muleshoe is named for a ranch established from a part of the XIT. The story goes that E. K. Warren, the new owner of the 180 square miles was inspecting his property and discovered an old rusty muleshoe lost by Coronado's expedition. The ranch and brand were adopted by Warren, and the new town named for the ranch. Will Rogers was a frequent visitor and liked to mail his publications with the Muleshoe postmark.

When the town decided to erect a $5,000 monument to the mule, they received more than 500 donations, including 21 cents from a mule driver in Samarkand, Russia. The story doesn't tell how a Russian mule driver heard about Muleshoe, Texas. On July 5, 1965, Waggoner Carr dedicated the statue.

This dependable, untiring, healthy animal is a symbol of courage, hard work, and endurance. Mule owners say their famed stubborness is largely legendary. The same quality in people is described as, "knowing their own minds." So, if someone says you are mulish, think about it. It's not a disgrace to have the good sound qualities of a mule.

Moo-La

Courthouse Square
Stephenville

Cattle ranchers may brag about their Hereford, Charolais, and Santa Gertrudis herds, but dairy farmers compare the values of Jerseys, Guernseys, and Holsteins. Up in the north central part of Texas, the big black and white dappled Holstein is the favorite, and Stephenville and Windhorst are so proud of their bossies they have put a replica of the greatest milk producer among dairy cattle on a pedestal. Folks in this part of Texas realize how much "moola" there is in moo cows—about $25 million annually—so the big gals deserve a statue.

American Angora Goat Breeders Association Museum

Austin Street
Rock Springs
Hours: 9–12, 1:30–4:30 Mon., Wed., Fri.

When Jason and the Argonauts sailed to Colchis in search of the Golden Fleece, that shimmering wooly pelt had to be an angora goat hide nailed to the tree. Jason may be a figment of Greek mythical imagination, but the Kingdom of Colchis was in the direction of Turkey where angora goats were originally bred. The Turks jealously guarded their precious goats and would not export them. Finally, in 1849 James B. Davis was given seven does and two bucks for his aid to the Turkish people with his expertise on cotton cultivation.

Angora goats came to Texas in 1884 when William Leslie Black purchased 8 sires and 4 does for the magnificent sum of $750. Black's return on his investment was staggering, and in 8 years 8,000 nannies, billies, and kids were roaming his ranch in the San Saba River Country. The beautiful limestone hills and deep, rich valleys of the Edwards Plateau were so much like Turkey, the goats thrived. By the 1930s Texas was producing 97 percent of the world's mohair.

If someone invites you over for a chevron dinner, your main course will be angora goat meat. Black tried to sell canned goat meat and gave his goods the unappetizing name of "Range Canning Co. Boiled Mutton." Somehow, that name never appealed to American taste buds, so Black changed the label to "W. G. Tobin's Chili Con Carne." That bit of false advertising netted Black a tidy sum.

Angora goats are actually raised for their luxurious wool of uniform length and quality. Ancients called the wool "select choice," and in Arabic it was *muxayyar* which evolved into mohair. The durable mohair fiber has been fashionable since Biblical times, and Jacob's coat was probably woven from it as mohair has a great affinity for dyes. It takes on brilliant colors and a sheen with a halo-like quality. In addition to all those good qualities, mohair is practically nonflammable. The woolybacks are shorn twice a year in early spring and later summer.

The goat industry got a major boost in the early 1900s thanks to Teddy Roosevelt. On a trip to Mississippi, the president was invited to a bear hunt. Bears were scarce in those parts, and all the host could find was a small cub on a rope. Teddy refused to shoot the bear, and Clifford K. Berryman drew a cartoon of the "hunt."

The drawing inspired a Russian immigrant, Morris Michtom, to create a toy bear and send one to Teddy requesting permission to name it for the president. Roosevelt no doubt exclaimed his famous "Bully!" and the Teddy Bear was born. Michtom's little toy is now a treasure in the Smithsonian.

The Teddy Bear captured the toy market instantly. By 1908 the German toy firm, Steiff Company, had made a million children happy with their cuddly mohair bears. Even now, it is a rare child that doesn't have his Teddy Bear.

Mohair is shipped to England where the luxurious garments are woven and then exported back to the United States. Prior to the plastic age, mohair was used as upholstry for cars, trains, buses, etc.

In tiny Rock Springs is the only goat museum in the United States. Here at the American Angora Goat Breeders Association founded in 1927 by public subscription is a tribute to the shaggy beast with one of the finest coats in the world. It is the only registry office for these animals in the world as well. There is not much to see but a few stuffed goats and some angora products, but some recognition is in order when you consider that about 13 million pounds of fleece leave the Edwards Plateau annually.

White Deer Monument

White Deer

If Texas doesn't have the largest animals in the world, it does have some of the rarest. According to Indian legends, a rare herd of white deer once used this part of the Panhandle as their feeding grounds. Finally too much association with the local Bambi-types wiped out the color line. The only one left is on top of a pedestal in the town bearing its name.

World's Largest Mosquito

Great Texas Mosquito Festival
P.O. Box 523
Clute 77531
409-265-2541

In quest of the World's Largest Mosquito, you could not pick better hunting grounds than the brackish marshes of the Gulf Coast around Clute and Brazosport. During the days when DDT was legal, the fogging machines blasted tons of the chemical over every street. Life would be almost bearable, then a shift in the Gulf breeze would come, and every mosquito in the salt grasses would be swirled into town. You could not get from a building to your car without being covered with the blood-thirsty little beasts. That may sound like a tall Texas tale, but it is very true.

Whoever wrote that the female is the deadliest of the species must have had the mosquito in mind. Those big red itching bites are not inflicted by the docile male; it is the female that causes all the misery. Not only does she spread encephalitis, malaria, and yellow fever in man, but she causes heart worms in dogs. When you get right down to it, there just doesn't seem to be a good reason to have the mosquito around. Frogs and bats like them, but as for humans, the mosquitoes are one pair that Noah should have left behind.

Well, the little demons won't buzz off, so Clute has decided to make the best of them and stage a Mosquito Festival each year. Clute citizens have formed their own

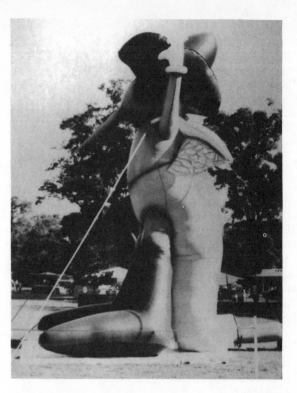

Willy Manchew highlights Clute's Great Texas Mosquito Festival.

version of a SWAT team, and its mascot is a 25-foot parody of the town's most numerous inhabitants. Dreamed up by Linda Hill, this gigantic insect was unveiled during the 1982 festival. A contest was held for the big skeeter's name, and the winning name was Willy Manchew. Wearing a 50-gallon cowboy hat and smiling happily at his guests, the $8,500 Willy Manchew will be a permanent festival fixture.

Held in mid-August when mosquitoes are really rampant, the festival offers entertainment for mosquito lovers of all ages. You can buy a cowboy hat growing mosquito legs and eyes, enter a songwriters' contest with an original ditty about mosquitoes or Clute, or partake in the mosquito calling contest. How do you call a mosquito? Most people don't.

Clute is literally buzzing with mosquito-related activities during its festival, and all visitors are welcome.

World's Largest Rattlesnake

Chamber of Commerce
Highway 59
Freer

Trying very hard to look ferocious and deadly, Freer's concrete diamondback rattler only succeeds in looking pleased with himself. Coiled on the steps of the chamber of commerce and as big as the building (one story), the big snake seems to know he symbolizes the harshness of the land of Southwest Texas. You can make all the snide remarks you wish because snakes are deaf to sound carried by air and have to sense vibrations from the ground.

The Indians worshiped snakes as gods or messengers of gods. During the Hopi Snake Dance, braves carried snakes in their mouths and then released them to the four winds. Snakes were to tell the gods of the need for rain. In April in Freer, the old rattlesnake has his day once again during the Rattlesnake Round-Up sponsored by the Junior Chamber of Commerce.

The objective of the Round-Up is to "bring 'em back alive," and the weather is very important. If it is too cold or too hot, snakes will not crawl, as the cold-blooded reptiles are the same temperature as their surroundings. They spend their winters deep in the ground, so by April they should be out and vulnerable. A special forked stick with a leather loop attached is used to pin down the snake's head. The loop slips over his head and he is thrown into a thick bag along with other writhing bodies.

After all entries have been tossed into a big pen, prizes are awarded for the biggest, the longest, and the one with the biggest rattlers. The rattlers are the most distinguishing feature of the legless reptile. They are composed of keratin, the same substance that forms human hair and nails, bird feathers, and cattle horns. The hissing sound that strikes terror in an intended victim is caused by the clashing of the rattle segments.

Usually 600 to 1,000 snakes end up in the pen. Men from Texas Snake Handlers carry these slithering bodies on their heads and arms, and walk over them barefooted. It is sort of reminiscent of the Hopi Snake Dance, but in Freer the snakes aren't cast to the four winds, just to the charcoal grills.

Yes, some of the great snake hunters do get bitten. Rattlesnakes can bite without coiling, and they do not always rattle before striking. Also, the snakes can bite without ejecting venom. The venom acts like a meat tenderizer, and the rattlesnake is literally preparing the flesh for digestion. Rattlesnake bites are seldom fatal, but the venom causes ghastly scars. One year a doctor from Alice let a snake bite him on purpose to show that if you don't get excited, the bite won't hurt you.

On the frontier a favorite snakebite remedy was whiskey and ammonia. Texas Rangers scarified the bite with deep incisions and packed them with salt. The story is often told of a cowboy bitten on the tip of his finger immediately drawing his six-shooter and blowing off his finger.

Many of the captive snakes are milked for their venom. If you want to try your hand at the sport, hook the snake about the middle, and as you lift it out of the pen, grab it with the other hand right behind its head. The snake will then wind his body around your arm (ugh!), but he is helpless. Have a partner place a small rimmed dish to the snake's mouth. That old snake is fighting mad, and when he opens his mouth, shove the dish inside so that the rim is behind the two fangs. The venom sacs are in the snake's cheeks, so as you press his cheeks, the deadly venom squirts through the fangs into the dish. Now, doesn't that sound more exciting than milking Bossy!

If all that snake activity is not for you, there are other events including an arts and crafts show and a parade.

El Campo Museum

Chamber of Commerce
201 E. Jackson Street
El Campo 77437
Hours: 9–5 weekdays
Admission free

In El Campo you can visit the far reaches of the Arctic, roam an East African veldt, penetrate the dense jungle of India, climb the North American mountains, or explore the depths of the Amazon Basin, and never leave the museum. This startling trip around the world is by means of a big game trophy exhibit.

Greeting you as you enter is a full-grown polar bear magnificently erect on his hind legs. The setting of snow and ice gives the scene an aura of reality. With the big bear is the Arctic fox, a bull walrus, and a sleepy-eyed musk ox. Though far from their natural habitat, they seem right at home in El Campo.

A tiger from the heart of India, with eyes gleaming and fangs ready to strike, stalks out of his lair. You can almost hear his angry roar. This particular marauder had killed two people and a cow, but only after the demise of the cow was there a hue and cry in the Indian village to rid the area of the big cat.

Mountain goats cavort among rocky crags, inspecting the more earth-bound creatures from their perilous playground. Horned heads are everywhere, and every species from the tiny dik-dik, smallest of the antelopes, to the massive placid eland are displayed.

This African display is so complete you almost feel you are on the grasslands of the Serengeti. Against a mural so realistic that the donor of these trophies remarked, "I should have brought my gun," are the "Big Four"—a lion leaping for his kill, an elephant with tremendous tusks weighing over 70 pounds each, a Cape Buffalo glaring with mean little eyes from an almost impenetrable skull, and the rarest of the "Big Four", one of the very few full mounts of the

The African veldt comes alive in the El Campo Museum.

white rhinoceros. Pig-eyed and hideous, the rhino is not actually white, just lighter and larger than the ordinary dull gray beast.

Many of the exhibits here are world class trophies, and all are taxidermy works of art. The stuffed animals are a gift of Dr. and Mrs. E. A. Weinheimer. When the benefactors deeded the building and the trophies to the City of El Campo in 1978, Harlan Hobbs organized a museum committee that encompassed the efforts of all El Campo citizens, both young and old.

Local artists painted the murals, and with a few tears, a lot of laughs, and even more glue, the children created the tons of paper maché used in the displays. Some of the volunteers learned how to use fiberglass to create the rocks, and shifts were kept working morning and night. Clouds were constructed from "every ingredient but quicksand." When the museum was all finished, the city held a grand parade to bring the props and displays from the workshop to the museum. Costumes and paraphernalia from the numerous ethnic groups in and around the city are also exhibited along with the animals.

At Christmas the museum becomes a fantasyland completely unlike any other treat in Texas. The entire community once again becomes involved with a different Christmas show every year. Santa acquires lots of helpers, and the stuffed trophies inhabit a toyland that could only happen in Texas. More than 10,000 lights twinkle and glow as the antelopes are transformed into Rudolphs, the polar bear hands out gifts in a Santa hat, and icycles and snow castles enhance the scene of animals decked out in Christmas finery. No wonder so many visitors come to share this original Christmas panorama.

But, don't wait until Christmas to visit El Campo. The museum is open all year with its animal land and other creative displays.

World's Largest Jackrabbit

Fourth and Sam Houston Streets
Odessa

Out in the Permian Basin where there are far more jackrabbits than people, the citizens of Odessa cherish their Texas "haritage." They feel so strongly about their fuzzy friends, they have erected a monument to these prolific inhabitants.

The big bunny is reportedly the brainstorm of former Texas Highway Department Travel and Information Division Director, Tom Taylor. In a speech during the early sixties in Odessa, the director suggested Odessa honor the jackrabbit because there were so many of them. Under the leadership of John Ben Shepperd, the Odessa Chamber of Commerce adopted the harebrained scheme, and in 1962 this six-foot rabbit became as beloved as his forerunner, Harvey. However, the Odessa mascot is a lot more visible than Elmer P. Dowd's imaginary friend.

Odessa's $2,300 fiberglass statue was often referred to as John Jackrabbit, Ben Jackrabbit, and John Ben's Folly, but a

name for the idiotic looking beast has never really stuck. However, this West Texas version of Hollywood's "Bugs" has performed his intended function as a tourist attraction even without a permanent name. School children loved John Ben's Folly so much, they attempted to secure a mate for him. (Heaven forbid! Odessa's streets might have had a six-foot jackrabbit on every corner!) The creature gained national fame in a way when the Jim Bean Distilling Company made a jackrabbit collector's bottle.

In 1970, the maligned statue came under a great deal of "harassment." Chamber President Dan Hemphill called upon his directors to "correct" calling the statue a jackrabbit. It really isn't a rabbit at all, but a hare. The animal's sobriquet comes from his huge "jackass" ears. Hares are larger than rabbits, they don't dig burrows, and they are born with a full coat of fur.

The hare's strong legs can sprint from 0 to 40 mph in 3 seconds. Most of the time the bunnies bounce about on just three legs and save the fourth for that extra spurt of speed. As for Hemphill's charge, Shepperd retorted, "Hemphill is just splitting hares." Well, hare today, rabbit tomorrow.

So, the World's Largest Jackrabbit still stands alone. If you ever want to nibble on a West Texas dish, here's the recipe for cooking the critter, but you won't find him on many menus:

"First, catch your rabbit. Dress rabbit, salt and soak in brine, then boil till tender. Add pepper to taste, fill pot with dumplings. Cook till dough is done."

Cooked or dashing through the brush on three legs or four, this charming beastie is pure Odessa and 100 percent Texan.

Paisano Pete

Dickinson and Main
Interstate 10
Fort Stockton

> The Road-Runner runs in the road,
> His coat is speckled, a la mode.
> His wings are short, his tail is long,
> He jerks as he runs along.
> His bill is sharp, his eyes are keen,
> He has a brain tucked in his bean.
> But in his gizzard—if you please—
> Are lizards, rats, and bumble bees;
> Also horned toads—on them he feeds—
> And rattlesnakes! and centipedes!

Eve Garson, *Desert Mavericks*

With his gleeful smile, Paisano Pete welcomes travelers to Fort Stockton. This "Symbol of the Great Southwest" is a 12-foot high fiberglass chaparral measuring 20 feet from his beak to his tail. More often known as a roadrunner, he has been permanently endeared to millions of kids through the Warner Brothers cartoons. Wouldn't

This delightful member of the cuckoo family is a fitting symbol of the Great Southwest.

old Wily Coyote's eyes bulge out if he could see Paisano Pete!

Paisano is loosely translated as "fellow countryman," and is probably derived from the word *faisan* (pheasant) that was changed in Mexican Spanish to *faisano*. His Latin name is *Geococcyx californianius*, but the folks in Fort Stockton just call him Paisano Pete. And, paisanos are indeed fellow countrymen of the inhabitants of West Texas. It is a rare trip in this part of Texas that you don't see a smaller version of Paisano Pete racing across the road.

The *Encyclopaedia Britannica* says these birds got the name roadrunner because they liked to chase carriages during the horse-and-buggy days. This member of the cuckoo family can run 10 to 20 miles an hour, and its feet are definitely a little cuckoo, as two of its toes point forward and two point backward. The roadrunner can fly, but it seems to prefer running.

Paisanos are not native just to Texas; they also run in Arizona and New Mexico. They are found in most of Mexico and even as far north as Kansas and Colorado. Paisano Pete was born way up north in Sparta, Wisconsin, at Creative Display at the instigation of The Tourist and Development Board of Fort Stockton. At a cost of $6,200, Pete was sculptured from plastic foam and covered with fiberglass. The big bird arrived at his new nest on December 6, 1979, and seems right at home in spite of all the cars he is unable to chase whizzing by.

There are many legends about the roadrunner, attributing supernatural powers to the bird. Some Indians believed if they ate these birds they would take on the roadrunner's swiftness. Indians also used roadrunner feathers as a leg ornamentation that gave them more speed. J. Frank Dobie tells a tall tale about a paisano building a wall of cholla cactus around a sleeping rattlesnake and then harrassing the snake until he impaled himself on the cactus. Welllllll . . . paisanos do kill snakes by leaping out of range of their deadly fangs until the snakes are exhausted and stabbing them with their razor-sharp beaks.

One fact is certain, the roadrunner is one of the West's favorite birds, and is a true West Texas symbol for this harsh, arid land. *Beep! Beep!*

Buckhorn Hall of Horns

Lone Star Brewery
600 Lone Star Blvd.
San Antonio
Hours: 9:30–5
512-226-8301
Admission

If it grew horns, the Buckhorn Hall of Horns has it—all except the fabled unicorn. Not only are the walls jammed with heads and horns of every description, but chairs and chandeliers are also made from horns. If you are hooked on horns, the Buckhorn is the place for you.

Back in 1881, Albert Friedrich opened a small saloon on Dolorosa Street when all that was in West Texas was distance, dust, and grass. Trappers, traders, cowboys, and cattlemen brought their thirst to the Buckhorn Saloon and often traded horns for a tall cool one. Albert's father was in the business of making furniture from cattle horns, and horn chairs were part of the Buckhorn's decor. Also in the 1880s antelope and buffalo were still plentiful on the plains, and many heads, horns, and hides were brought to the saloon. The collection kept growing and growing, and in 1922 was moved to the corner of Houston and South Flores streets. Lone Star Brewery bought the saloon and collection, and made it one of the major tourist attractions in San Antonio. The collection of horns, animals, and oddities has grown so extensive, it has been divided into five special halls.

The residents of the Asiatic Hall have exotic names like gaur, nilgai, javan russa, and babirusa. In the African Hall, a five-foot four-inch stuffed gorilla looms out of a jungle. Though smaller than King Kong, his chest still measures four-feet six-inches across. Every type of antelope from the huge 1,200 pound eland to the tiny rabbit-sized dik-dik grazes on the Buckhorn's version of the African veldt. Lions, wildebeests, and monkeys as well as many other African trophies complete the scene.

In the European Hall, reindeer share their territory with horns of the rare Irish elk which has been extinct for more than 2,000 years. In the North American Hall a giant polar bear and the fearsome Kodiak from the Arctic regions stand with claws ready to rip their enemies to shreds. A scruffy javelina and a bighorn sheep peer stolidly back at their admirers. A world record rattlesnake killed in the area displays his 29 rattles.

In a plains springtime setting in the Texas Room, "Old Tex" stands with his 105-inch longhorns looking like the weight of the world is on his . . . head. A chandelier of more than 4,000 deer horns lights the hall over a catalow—an experimental combination of a longhorn and a buffalo. (The results were less than hoped for.) Also, in this room are the world-record 78-point and 64-point antlers from whitetail deer.

The Buckhorn's walls abound in animal oddities: two-headed calves, a doe deer with horns, Siamese calves, Siamese lambs, and even dressed fleas. That means fleas with clothes on. (How do you dress a flea? No one knows because their Mexican couturiers have stopped sending the

If it grows horns, it's represented in the Buckhorn Hall of Horns.

curiosities to the Buckhorn. Yes, you view their fashions through a magnifying glass.) The Hall of Fins sports the fish you would love to catch, and the Hall of Feathers displays one of the few remaining pair of passenger pigeons in museums.

The interesting Toepperwein Gallery is a sharpshooter's idea of heaven. Ad Toepperwein's guns and bullet "drawings" shot by the great marksman are on display as well as some "drawings" executed by his famous wife "Plinky." Plinky had never held a gun in her life until she married Ad, but she was definitely a fast learner. She set a record never beaten yet by breaking 1,952 out of 2,000 clay targets in 3 hours and 15 minutes. Ad and his Texas Annie Oakley were frequent visitors at the Buckhorn and brought many famous guests.

A chair made especially for Rough Rider Teddy Roosevelt from 62 sets of buffalo horns and decorated with bluebonnets is on display along with a deer Mrs. Friedrich fashioned from 637 rattlesnakes rattlers. Mrs. Friedrich had a passion for rattlers, and several of her unique designs are here at the Buckhorn.

William Sidney Porter made the Buckhorn his favorite watering hole, and the house he lived in was moved to the museum grounds in 1960. It is open for visitors if they wish to see where one of America's favorite short story writers, O. Henry, lived.

The marble and cherrywood backbar in the saloon are from the old Buckhorn, and the new front bar is an exact reproduction of the original. The brass rail is the same one that felt the many peon sandals and high-heeled cowboy boots of original Buckhorn customers. Around the Viennese beer tables some of the largest cattle deals in the Southwest were made and the Mexican Revolution of 1910 was planned. The spectacular mirror was carved of Lebanese cedar for the Russian Royal Family in 1790, and it is one of the Buckhorn's prized possessions.

When Albert Friedrich was still collecting his massive array of horns, a "free lunch" of sausages, cheeses, hard boiled eggs, and relishes was served. But, in those days beef was a measely 3 cents a pound, chickens 25 cents each, and beer a nickel a mug. At the Buckhorn today, at least one price has dropped—the beer is free—Lone Star, of course.

Albino Buffalo

Courthouse Square
Snyder

If you had a home where the buffalo roamed in Scurry County during the last century, you might have seen one of the seven known albino buffalos on the North American continent. Before the white man came, the best estimates are that 60 to 75 million head of the regular, brown shaggy beasts grazed peacefully on the Great Plains. As late as 1830, after the hunters had begun their slaughter, there were still 40 million bison, but by 1883 less than 1,000 of this truly American animal were left alive.

The durable old buffalo weighed from 2,000 to 2,800 pounds and lived as long as 20 years. He may have looked clumsy, but he could swim and climb slopes with ease. Their herd instinct protected the vulnerable animals from the ferocious cats, and when attacked, the bulls formed a protective circle with the cows and calves in the center.

The buffalo were the Indians' one real industry, and the U.S. Government decided that the Indians could best be "civilized" by exterminating the beasts. Thousands of hunters destroyed the herds without mercy, and it looked like there would not even be one left to pose for the nickel. Fortunately, in 1905 the American Bison Society saved the buffalo from extinction.

One of the believers in the elimination of the buffalo was J. Wright Mooar. For business and adventure, he claimed 22,000 kills. Brother John Mooar marketed the hides (that was all that was wanted), while J. Wright prowled the prairies.

On October 7, 1876, the Mooar outfit was camped on Deer Creek about ten miles northwest of Snyder. At almost sunset, Mooar saw it! Against the glowing horizon was a shiney white creature contentedly munching dinner. Having killed an albino buffalo in Kansas, Mooar immediately knew this to be another.

The hunter rushed to camp and called a skinner to bring his knives. When they got within shooting range, the prize trophy fell with Mooar's first shot. The firing stampeded the herd, and the bison thundered toward the two men, almost in revenge. Quickly, with a cool hand, Wright shot three more buffalo, and the herd turned in the nick of time.

The hide that Mooar took that day was tanned and shown to visitors as long as he lived. It was exhibited at the Chicago World's Fair in 1893, and Mooar's granddaughter, Julia May McDonnell Hays, still has the rare albino skin. Encased in glass, it is kept at a constant temperature to preserve her grandfather's trophy shot near her ranch home.

In 1967 Snyder erected a replica of the albino buffalo on the courthouse square. To finance the fiberglass statue, membership was sold in the "Order of the White Buffalo." Response was so enthusiastic that funds were quickly raised for the town's trademark. The first statue was the victim of modern-day buffalo hunters, and vandals destroyed it. However, a second more durable white shaggy old bull has endured as the town's trademark.

The Flying Red Horse

Main at Akard
Dallas

Dallas, with the largest Pegasus in the world, is more than a one-horse town. The massive 30-foot by 40-foot sign of the flying horse was designed with two horses so the bracing and rotating mechanism would be concealed.

Unlike the Pegasus of Greek Mythology who sprang full-grown from the blood of Medusa, Dallas' winged steed sprang from the head of J. B. McMath of the Texlite Sign Company. In September of 1934 an advertising man for Magnolia Oil Company wanted a neon-lit Flying Red Horse revolving on top of its building. The deadline for the tubes to blaze red was November 8 to impress the annual convention of the National Petroleum Institute.

Pegasus was originally used as the trademark for the Vacuum Oil Company of South Africa in 1911, but that Pegasus was a white winged horse on a red background. When Vacuum merged with the gigantic Standard Oil of New York in 1931 to become Socony-Vacuum, the trademark became the Flying Red Horse. Certainly people everywhere would sense that the Flying Red Horse represented speed and power of surpassing order. Moreover, Pegasus was beautiful, graceful, and in action.

Even the Greek myth of Pegasus is a heroic tale. Athena, the goddess of wisdom, was so incensed over a mortal's beauty that equalled her own, she changed her rival into a monster so ugly that if anyone dared to look at her, he would instantly be turned to stone. The Medusa also was cursed with unmanageable hair—writhing serpents. However, when the brave Perseus used his shield for a mirror and slew the dreadful creature, Pegasus sprang from her blood.

When King Iobate charged Bellerophon with the unpleasant task of slaying the fire-breathing Chimera, Bellerophon begged Athena for the use of Pegasus. Not only did he kill the Chimera, but the youth performed so many amazing feats with Pegasus' aid, King Iobate gave Bellerophon his daughter and kingdom to boot.

Bellerophon didn't handle success too well and decided to fly up to Mount Olympus and join the gods. Zeus decided the upstart wasn't good enough for the Mount Olympus Country Club set, and Bellerophon fell to his death. Pegasus, however, was placed in celestial orbit to fly throughout eternity.

To make certain Dallas' Pegasus flies through eternity, the Flying Red Horse has been placed on the National Register for Historic Places. J. B. McMath's monument was a miracle of engineering and construction considering the incredibly short time factor.

Once the materials were assembled, only six weeks remained before November 8. Smaller pieces were taken to the top floor in the elevator, passed out a window, and then hauled to the roof. Just when victory was in sight, on November 3, a fire swept through the Texlite plant destroying the 1,162 feet of red neon tubing that had been saved until the last minute to prevent breakage. The fire also destroyed the important design plans for the remarkable sign.

A dedicated crew set up an improvised neon tube construction operation, and many human Bellerophons "flew" on Pegasus to make a pattern out of beaverboard. The harried endeavor was worth the effort, for on November 7, Pegasus was ready to become the famous Dallas landmark.

Several nights after the impressive sign was turned on, Mr. Mac received a frantic call—The Flying Red Horse had broken loose, and it looked as though Pegasus would join the original captured in the stars. It had become a flying red blob of neon. Corrections were made, and Pegasus remains a marvelous tribute to the genius of a man who never graduated from high school. When the 29-story Magnolia Building was erected in 1922, it was the tallest building in the southwest. After Magnolia merged into Socony-Vacuum and the whole corporate structure evolved into Mobil Oil, the building was too small. Mobil gave it to the City of Dallas, and it was sold to investors to renovate into offices. Dallas is still responsible for the care and feeding of Pegasus.

Before the advance of the new skyscrapers, the 6,000-pound Pegasus welcomed travelers from every approach into Dallas. If the Flying Red Horse stopped turning, Mobil's switchboard was jammed with concerned callers. Pilots claimed they could see the region's key landmark from as far as Waco.

Dallas boasts another Pegasus other than The Flying Red Horse. This sculpture by Carl Mille is in front of the Dallas City Hall. Here a marble Bellerophon and Pegasus reach for Mount Olympus, or perhaps the dynamic duo just yearn for a rematch with the modern version of the deadly Chimera—Dallas' city traffic.

Now on the National Register, Dallas' Pegasus flies forever.

Git Along,
Little Dogies

"My heroes have always been cowboys."
Willie Nelson

No other symbol of the past has fired the imagination as much as the American cowboy. Even before the distortions of real life on the lone prairie by the silver screen and television, Ned Buntline's dime novels had created a myth that has never been dispelled. Later writers added to the legend with staunch heroes who shot true, spoke sparingly, honored the law, and whose most important women were their mothers or sisters. In Zane Grey's classic *Riders of the Purple Sage*, noble Lassiter spent years penned in a box canyon with his sweetheart, Jane Withersteen, and never laid an amorous hand on her.

The popular Louis L'Amour's heroes are a bit more worldly and even utter some rather poignant oaths, whereas Zane Grey's protagonists never exclaimed anything stronger than "Oh, Buffalo chips!" But, through the decades, western novel plots have not changed a great deal.

With the western movie and television, the cowboy image has spread to just about every country in the world. The Cartwrights endured for 13 seasons on *Bonanza*, and no other star has challenged John Wayne as the greatest cowboy of them all. Another beloved cowboy was Oklahoma's Will Rogers, and a life-size bronze of the immortal humorist "Riding into the Sunset" stands in Fort Worth near the fairgrounds.

Many writers and historians have pointed out that the cowboy actually led a pretty miserable existence, but the pattern is set, and the romance of this brief era far outweighs reality.

When the great cattle drives began, "Point 'em north" could be heard all over Texas. Rangy stubborn Longhorns made their way to Kansas driven by lean, sinewy men with faces sunburned the color of the dark hides of the cattle they punched up the trail. Their dress was destined to become a permanent part of the American West. A colorful bandana worn loosely around the neck, a flannel shirt, tough denim trousers, a broad Stetson hat, clinking spurs, soft, worn leather chaps, and the high-heeled boots constructed to hook behind the stirrups was the uniform of the cowpunchers. This romantic figure rode a mustang pony so much his legs were nearly always bowed, and he was an expert with a lariat and his single-shot .45 Colt (the peacemaker of the frontier). In his plain garb, uneducated, and barely eeking out a living, this uncomplicated man will probably endure in the imagination of Americans even when space explorers move into the galaxy and discover other "Indians" on a new frontier.

Birthplace of the Cowboy

Highway 281, in the center of town
Pleasanton 78064

Where did the cowboy folk hero come from? Ben Parker of the Lazy 2 Ranch claims this different breed of men was born around Atascosa County. In the little town of Pleasanton, huddled under 2,000 oak trees, Parker has built a monument to "the only common laborer to become a symbol of heroism." Here in the *brasada* (brush country) of South Texas the demanding job of tending ornery cattle and enduring the tortures of trail driving year after year began. The hard working puncher never dreamed there might be something else he could do.

The eight-foot two-inch high tribute to this "common laborer" is a typical cowboy cast in bronze and standing on a pedestal of concrete surrounded by century plants. Sculpted by John Tatschl of Austria, the statue carries a plaque that reads:

"In this part of Texas men first used the techniques of handling cattle on horseback. This statue, dedicated to 'The' cowboy was given to the city of Pleasanton, Texas, by Mona and Ben Parker and placed here to mark this area as The Birthplace of the Cowboy."

Pleasanton is the perfect spot for the statue according to Parker's history of the cowboy.

After Cortez conquered Mexico, Gregorio de Villalobos brought six heifers and a bull to Mexico from stock that had come from the plains of Andalusia. Later, the "first trail driver" came to Texas with 500 head of beef to feed his

The "common laborer" of the cattle ranches has been immortalized in Pleasanton. (Photograph courtesy of Ben L. Parker.)

army as he searched for the Seven Cities of Gold. Coronado never found his gold, but he left behind a fortune for Texas. His cattle mixed with cattle brought into the missions in East Texas, and the new breed thrived in the milder grassy plains of the southern part of the state. Back in those long-ago days, there was no market for beef, and the missions raised the animals for their horns, hides, and tallow.

When gold was discovered in California, several Texas ranchers made drives to the west coast, and W. H. Snyder managed to trail 1,500 Longhorns through Colorado, Oregon, and Nevada to San Francisco. It took him two years, but he still made a profit. When the California market crashed, it seemed the beef industry was dead. Then, the prolific entrepreneur, Gail Borden, tried to sell the army on a beef biscuit for the soldiers. Somehow Borden's 120 pounds of beef boiled down to 10 pounds and mixed with flour was not successful. The army never did buy this forerunner to Spam and chipped beef.

After the Civil War about 5 million Longhorns roamed over Texas, but they were practically worthless. The only way to make money and get them to the beef-hungry Yankees was to walk them. A shrewd businessman named Joseph G. McCoy convinced the railroad to come to Abilene, Kansas, and the Texas cattle industry was born. The Chisholm Trail was originally just a short stretch in Kansas, but all trails leading to it soon became the Chisholm Trail as well. The Texas part of the trail basically followed what is now Highway 281 to the Red River.

Thousands and thousands of Longhorns crossed the mighty Red to end up in stockcars heading east from Kansas. Lasting less than ten years, the days of the great trails were killed by barbed wire, railroads, windmills, and law and order. Yet, in this brief span of history, America gained a treasured legend of life on the vast unsettled plains of the West. And it all began in Texas around Pleasanton.

Parker said, "I used to be in the broadcast business. This was my town, and I was successful. I thought I would do something for the city." This civic-minded rancher has done more than just dedicate a statue for his town, Parker has also contributed the Longhorn Museum and spends a great deal of time there telling visitors the story of his book, *The Origin of the Cowboy*. As a friend of Willie Nelson's, the museum also exhibits some of Willie's mementos. Perhaps Willie has Ben Parker in mind when he sings, "My heroes have always been cowboys."

Charles H. Noyes Monument

Courthouse Square
Ballinger

On the courthouse lawn of Ballinger, shaded by ancient oak trees, a bronze young cowboy prepares to mount his horse. Bearing the simple inscription, "Chas. H. Noyes," this striking monument not only perpetuates the memory of a beloved son, but also honors every Texas cowboy.

Charles Noyes was not a heroic figure and certainly not the type that would ever achieve immortality on the pages of a book. This modest, dependable, and well-loved youth was born in 1896, but his brief life came to a tragic end in 1917. Charley, as he was called by his father, had never been farther from home than a brief stint in business college in Abilene after high school. He was a rancher's son and loved his life and planned no other career. On February 17, 1917, Charley started out on a routine day's work on the ranch to separate the weaning calves from the cows. A few calves broke away, and Charley reined his horse after them. As Charles was turning the little animals, his horse ran into a calf, throwing both horse and rider. The horse struggled slowly to its feet, but the boy's body lay inert; his neck was broken.

Gus Noyes was disconsolate over his son's death and decided to erect a statue of the boy at the site of the accident. Only the finest sculptor would do, so Noyes sent for Pompeo Coppini, the Michelangelo of Texas.

This magnificent Italian artist's statues adorn graves, buildings, and memorials all over Texas. Coppini literally gloried in Texas and its heroes. UT students can see his sculpture with the Littlefield Fountain, and Coppini's Governor Sul Ross is traditionally cleaned of mud by Texas A&M freshmen. Sam Houston's grave is another Coppini masterpiece, as is the cenotaph honoring the heroes of the Alamo.

Ballinger is the home of a Coppini masterpiece honoring all Texas cowboys. (Photograph courtesy of Ballinger Chamber of Commerce.)

When Coppini came to Texas from Chicago to talk to Gus Noyes about his son's memorial, the artist's finances were not at their best. Coppini hoped for a substantial commission from Noyes, and was dismayed when he arrived at the Noyes' Ranch. The scanty furnishings and the clothes the Noyeses were wearing gave Coppini the impression that they were poor people. But, the sculptor wanted very much to fashion the statue, so he set the price as low as possible to get the commission. Coppini had originally thought of $25,000, but desire overcame financial necessity, and he answered "$18,000 complete and erected under my supervision." Noyes replied, "It's a deal. I thought it would cost me double that amount."

Coppini worked from the few snapshots of Charley, which were small and of poor quality. The youth's hat, boots, spurs, saddle, and bridle were shipped to Coppini's Chicago studio, and the artist began an intensive study of horses. The model of the horse was done in clay, but it froze during a severe blizzard and "crumbled like flour" when the studio was warmed. Coppini had to start all over.

Finally, in 1918, the memorial was complete. Amazingly, only a few minor changes had to be made in Charley's features to satisfy Gus that it was his son. The statue was then cast in bronze and shipped to Texas. Meanwhile, Gus Noyes was unable to endure his ranch any longer and moved to Florida. The piece was erected on the courthouse lawn as a tribute to all cowboys rather than on the accident site. Coppini was there for the unveiling, but it was too painful for Gus. The Noyeses never returned to Ballinger.

Empty Saddle Monument

Intersection of US 87 and US 385
Chamber of Commerce (806-249-5646)
Dalhart

 A royal or military funeral procession is often led by a riderless horse with the deceased's boots turned backwards in the stirrups. The saddle will never be mounted or the boots worn forward again. This symbolic tribute emphasizes the sad finality of death.

The Empty Saddle Monument in Dalhart is also the result of a death; not of royalty, but of a hard-working cowboy. In the early 1940s, the annual XIT Reunion was getting set for the biggest celebration of its kind in the west. Eagerly looking forward to the famous roundup were John Marsh, who had been a cowpoke on the 3-million-acre spread, and his wife, Flossie, of Miles City, Montana. Almost on the eve of their departure, John was stricken ill and died. His bereaved widow wrote a short explanatory note to the five-man General XIT Committee and asked if a horse bearing an empty saddle could lead the parade in memory of her husband. The request was speedily granted, and every year since then the horse and empty saddle with a beautiful floral wreath on its horn form a touching tableau and tribute to John Marsh, and according to the offi-

cial XIT program, "all other pioneers who now ride starlit trails on illimitable expanses belonging to the Range Boss of Heaven."

Out of this pageantry grew the idea of the Empty Saddle Monument, and the General XIT Committee commissioned Bobby Dycke, a native of Czechoslovakia, to design and build this permanent memorial. After completion, the saddle was kept covered until the next XIT Reunion when Mrs. Marsh unveiled this cowboy tribute.

The Reunion and parade is held the first weekend in August, and it is a Texas spectacular truly unique among Texas' many festivals. The XIT Ranch came into existence in 1881 when Texas had more land than money and bargained with Charles and John Farwell of a Chicago syndicate to build a new state capitol. The Farwell brothers sold $5 million in bonds in England and agreed to erect a $3 million capitol for 3 million acres of Texas. Strange as it seems, Texas got the best of the deal, for millions of other acres, perhaps even better land, could have been bought at that time for less than a third of the price.

When the cattle bawled their way onto the XIT in 1885, they had to be branded. Many have thought that XIT signified "Ten in Texas," as those 3 million acres sprawled over 10 counties. But, the creator of the brand had no such notion, for some of those 10 counties had not been organized yet. The new ranch manager had asked a cowboy who had come in with that first herd, Ab Blocker, to suggest a brand. Blocker dragged his boot heel in the dust to read XIT, a design which cannot be burned over. From that inauspicious beginning, that brand has symbolized a saga of the west that will never be forgotten.

In the 1880s the XIT was the largest ranch in the world under barbed wire. There remain a few strands of the original Brinkerhoff ribbon wire on fences as a reminder of this fabulous rangeland. The XIT is gone now, but folks at Dalhart bring back the good old days at the XIT Rodeo and Reunion every year. The attendance of original ranch hands at the Reunion itself has dropped drastically, for those still alive are in their nineties. A good showing one year was when seven old cowpokes arrived for the annual luncheon.

After the opening parade led by the riderless horse, visitors are treated to hospitality as only Texas can provide. There is a free feed of jillions of ears of sweet corn soaked in butter followed by the juicy red fruit of entire patches of watermelons. A free barbeque with beef, beans, and trimmings for 25,000 guests is also prepared. Slabs of beef are wrapped in wet burlap, and put over hot coals in pits that have to be dug with earth-moving equipment, then covered with tin and dirt. About 13,000 pounds of savory meat are cooked for 24 hours to feed the ravenous guests.

A dance each night features different top country-western stars, and rodeo events lead up to the championship rodeo awards on the last night of the Reunion. Though all the eager contestants are amateurs, there is nothing amateur about the broncs, bulls, and steers. This XIT event is renowned as one of the roughest rodeos ever held, and the 800 rodeoers earn their prize money the hard way. This is one of the biggest and most exciting shindigs held in Texas—where else?

National Cowgirl Hall of Fame and Western Heritage Center

P.O. Box 1742
515 Ave. B
Hereford 79045
806-364-5252
Hours: 8–5 Mon.–Fri.

When Charles Goodnight introduced Herefords into the Texas Panhandle in 1883, the breed became so popular with ranchers, it soon replaced the tough stringy Longhorn. It was only natural that the county seat would be named for this white-faced descendent of Herefordshire, England. Hereford achieved a national reputation as "The Town Without a Toothache" because of the fluorine and iodides in the soil, but now it is famous for the National Cowgirl Hall of Fame and Western Heritage Center.

Cows have to have cowboys, and cowboys have to have cowgirls. Oklahoma City may boast of its Cowboy Hall of Fame, but the ladies have done more than their share in promoting the western tradition of the rodeo. To honor these women for their hard work, the cowgirl honorees in the Hall of Fame are inducted each year at rodeo time in August. These dedicated women do not compete against men, but most of their events are the same as the men's.

In the bareback bronc riding, bull, and steer riding, the contestant must stay on a thoroughly irate animal for six seconds. The rigging can be held with either or both hands, but the contestant must indicate which she will use before the ride.

The most popular event for the gals is the barrel race. The goal of both horse and rider is to turn around three barrels in a cloverleaf pattern without tipping over the obstacles. If a barrel is knocked over, there is a 5-second penalty.

The fastest lady is the winner.

Contestants even perform team roping and attempt to tie up a steer in eight seconds. Another popular event is calf roping, where the girls try to tie down a little dogie in 12 seconds. When they undecorate a steer, it means that the contestants must remove a ribbon taped to the middle of a running steer's back. All the events require a great deal of skill, practice, and courage.

More than 2,000 women between the ages of 14 and 50 belong to the Women's Professional Rodeo Association and compete for the $9 million awarded in cowgirl rodeos annually. While most contestants are students, telephone operators, waitresses, secretaries, housewives, and teachers also compete. These accomplished athletes have tremendous grit and courage for their rough and tough avocation.

Some of the past cowgirls have sported some astounding costumes. Prairie Rose wore elaborate bloomers and a massive sombrero in 1919. A few years later, Mildred Douglas'
costume was a symphony of fringe, and in 1924 Vera McGinnis looked like the female counterpart of Zorro. Today, there is a strict dress code that must be adhered to at all times. The uniform is dress pants, a long sleeved shirt, and western hat. June Ivory, with her dangling rhinestone earrings so popular in the fifties, would not fit in with these modern lasses.

One outstanding cowgirl honoree is Mamie Francis Hafley. From 1908 to 1914, in 628 performances Mamie rode her Arabian horse, Lurline, up an incline to a platform, urged the mount forward, and leapt in the air down to a sunken tank holding only 10 feet of water. Both horse and rider emerged together since Mamie could not swim. Of the feat, Mamie said, "Oh, the glory of it all!"

The first cowgirl to ride under her horse's belly was Bonnie Gray. Known as "The King Tut Cowgirl," Bonnie rode her palomino, King Tut, to broadjump and highjump over a four-door touring car filled with brave passengers. Bonnie went on to Hollywood, but not as an actress. She was the stunt rider for Hoot Gibson, Tim McCoy, Helen Twelvetrees, Tom Mix, and Ken Maynard. When she wasn't hanging under Tut's belly, Ms. Gray socialized with Enrico Caruso, General John Pershing, and the Duke of Windsor.

During the 1930s Baby Lorraine Graham thrilled thousands as she stood on her head in the saddle, slipped back on her horse's haunches, and hanging to the saddle, jumped between the horse's hooves, while the horse raced around the arena. At the ripe old age of four, Baby Lorraine left the crowds gasping.

So many famous women are part of the Cowgirl Hall of Fame, and each has truly earned her niche. But, there is much more, for this museum honors the strength, spirit, stamina, and courage of all western women. Not all rode the rodeo circuit, but their pioneer determination is invaluable. Henrietta King, the matriarch of the largest ranch in the world, is here as is Louise Massey, the composer of "My Adobe Hacienda." Pamela Harr is recognized for her flawless bronzes, and Margaret Harper for creating the stirring pageant *Texas!*

The Cowgirl Hall of Fame was begun by the Deaf Smith County Chamber of Commerce in 1976 and was housed in the library. In 1981, Debbie and Marsh Pitman donated the Hall's permanent home, a house with 6,000 square feet and 16 acres.

Three sections to the museum are planned. The part for the rodeo queens will be centered around a cine robot of a cowgirl in full parade costume, riding her pony, and carrying Old Glory. She will introduce visitors to the displays of photographs, trophies, costumes, and other rodeo memorabilia.

For the women in the Western Heritage section, photographs and biographies of their lives will be presented along with articles from their personal collections. Entries are accepted from all parts of the western United States, and the main requirement is that the ladies proudly convey a certain passion for the western way of life.

The third part of the museum is the art gallery of works based on western themes by western artists, many of whom are male. Appearing on the 1982 cover of the Association's magazine *Sidesaddle* is Utah's Butch Krieger's portrait of

Fern Sawyer. Krieger saw in Fern the epitome of the American Cowgirl, rugged in character but completely feminine in style.

The success of this museum can be credited to Hereford's citizens and its volunteers, particularly the director, Margaret Formby. In its short history, much has been accomplished to honor "the women who won the west."

Big Tex

Texas State Fair
Fair Park
P.O. Box 26010
Dallas, Texas 75226
214/565-9931

In perfect accord with Texas' idea of the biggest, greatest and most spectacular, nothing is more appropriate for Texas' contribution to American folklore than a cowboy larger than life. And what better place to display this gigantic monument than at the State Fair in Dallas.

Just in case you don't know, the State Fair has always been held in Dallas, and the first recorded fair was way back in 1859. Although the Civil War did not stop the festivities, two years of World War I and four years of World War II interrupted the frivolities. The State Fair was also suspended in 1935 when Texas celebrated its centennial. It still adds up to an impressive fair record.

Today, the finest livestock in the state are still judged along with prize-winning jellies, jams, and other delicious goodies, but a lot of added attractions bring in the crowds.

Football fans are riveted to the annual University of Texas and University of Oklahoma contest, while others go for the nation's top rodeo competition. If that's not enough, a free circus, parades, contests, shows of every description, and even a Broadway musical vie for your attention. Also more than 200 restaurants vie for your appetite. For seventeen marvelous days in October, the Texas State Fair is the show of shows and outshines any other fair in the nation.

For this Texas-size extravaganza, a Texas-size welcome awaits you—Big Tex booms out "Howdy folks, this is Big Tex," and then tells you what wondrous events are in store as you enter the gates of Fair Park. Since 1952, Big Tex has been on hand as the official greeter for the fair, and he has performed magnificently.

Big Tex did not begin his illustrious career as the official greeter of the State Fair. He actually started off in show biz as Santa Claus for Kerens, Texas, in 1949. This oversized Saint Nick was so popular he caught the attention of R. L. Thornton, State Fair president. For a bargain $750, Thornton moved Big Tex into the bigtime in 1951.

Big Tex is mighty big indeed! Fifty-two feet of cowboy is tall by anybody's standards. To outfit Big Tex in suitable attire, the H. D. Lee Company tucked a 100-yard shirt (University of Texas orange, of course) into size 276 Lee jeans with a 23-foot waist size. Big Tex's hat will hold 75 gallons of Lone Star beer, and his size 70 boots are 7 feet 7 inches high. It takes a 25-foot hydraulic crane using 100 feet of boom to lower this Texas Paul Bunyan into his footwear. How's that for a boot jack?

Of all the monuments to the Texas mystique, Big Tex has probably been seen more than any of the others throughout the state. After all, a 52-foot cowboy does grab your attention.

Disasters

Texas is always proud of being the largest, the best, the most flamboyant, the richest, and other superlatives, but one phrase Texans do not like is "the worst," particularly when it involves loss of life. However, Texas was the site of some of the worst disasters in the history of the United States. Some were manmade, and others were caused naturally, such as the horrendous hurricane of 1900 that practically wiped Galveston off the Texas Coast. Two of the country's worst manmade holocausts occurred in Texas, as well, one at the rural community of New London and the other at the massive chemical complex in Texas City. Both shook the world, one as far away as Nazi Germany.

New London Cenotaph

New London

In the archives of the West Rusk High School in New London lies a faded telegram of condolences signed "Adolf Hitler." The year was 1937, and Texas was reeling from one of the saddest tragedies in history. No matter how horrible a disaster is, it is always so much worse when it happens to children. In the New London School Disaster, an entire generation was lost. Telegrams and aid poured in from all parts of the world, even from a man who would cause the death of millions. The following essay by Kevin C. Evans, the grandson of two of the survivors, is an account of that day of horror as recalled by his grandfather.

The New London Cenotaph
By Kevin C. Evans

The Cenotaph in front of West Rusk High School has been a fixture in my life just as the event it symbolizes is a fixture in the memories of the generations before me.

At the top of the thirty-two foot structure is a twenty ton block of Texas granite that is seven feet high and four feet thick. Life-sized figures representing ten children bringing gifts and homework to two teachers are carved around the sides of this block. The block is supported by two huge granite columns with fluted sides. These columns are twenty feet tall and are supported by a granite platform. The sides of the platform are enclosed by a short wall of granite. Inside this wall are the names and grades of the 280 students and fourteen teachers that lost their lives in the New London School Explosion in 1937.

This monolithic structure is placed in the center of a grassy island that divides the highway serving our school.

The whole structure costing $20,000.00 was paid for by donations from citizens of the community. Many nickels and dimes were donated by school children.

I find it hard to think of the disaster as being an actual happening. I tend to place it with such fanciful stories as the Legends of King Arthur and the Greek myths. Each time I speak to one of those enigmatic people called "the survivors," however, I see a sheer horror in their eyes that must only mirror the horror of the actual tragedy. Each time I speak to one of these survivors, I know without a doubt that the disaster was real. I can only thank God I was not born then.

My grandfather, whose name was Carroll Evans but was affectionately called Boxhead, was a teacher at the time of the tragedy. He came to New London in August of the year

The New London Cenotaph is a reminder that an entire generation was lost in the tragic school explosion of 1937.

1933 with his wife Mildred. This was the time of the East Texas Oil Boom. New London along with the rest of East Texas had grown by leaps and bounds. The school here had grown in enrollment just as the town had grown in population. A brand new school building had just been erected and new teachers had been hired. My grandfather was to be New London's new football coach and my grandmother was a first grade teacher. Granddad paid sixty-five dollars for the recently vacated house of the then superintendent Mr. W. C. Shaw. He then moved it to the school teacherage behind the main buildings.

My grandfather lived next door to the shop teacher Lemmy Butler and his wife. For the four years that he knew him they came to be friends.

On March 18, 1937, my grandfather was coming from the science room, heading home. He had just spoken to the science teacher about a visual aid he had used in another class. He had explained how to use a basketball, painted half white, to show the phases of the moon.

He stopped to wait for the elementary classes to enter the gymnasium to see a P.T.A. presentation. The meeting was originally planned to be held in the school auditorium but was moved to the gym because of a schedule conflict. That conflict may have saved their lives. My grandmother was one of the teachers attending.

He then went to his house perhaps passing my three-year old father who was leaning against the homemaking building watching the tennis practice. He entered his home thinking of what would need to be done before he left on out-of-town business. He opened the door of the refrigerator to get a drink of ice water when he heard a nerve shattering explosion that shook the building. There had been other explosions in the oil fields but nothing like this. He ran outside but the settling concrete dust impaired his vision so badly that he couldn't see his hand in front of his face.

He immediately began to worry about his family and ran to find my father. My father was frightened by the blast and ran toward the house. He tripped over a lawnmower however and began to cry. My grandfather heard this sound and followed it through the dust to find him.

My grandmother was sitting in the gymnasium stands with her class at the time of the blast. Bricks and dust flew through the windows on the opposite side of the building. Worrying about the safety of my father and grandfather she left her class and ran to find them. She too heard my father's crying and reached him about the same time as my grandfather did.

My grandmother then took her son inside and left my grandfather to see what was going on. It was then that he surveyed the ruined remains of the high school building. There wasn't much left of the building to see.

A small leak in the natural gas lines beneath the school had occurred. This happened because of a change from commercial to raw natural gas. Six thousand five hundred and sixty cubic feet of gas was estimated to have been under the building at the time of the explosion. It could have taken days to accumulate. The gas occupied the pocket of air between the building's floor and the ground. The gas had seeped from there into the air spaces in the very walls of the building. This gas was theoretically ignited by a spark from electrical equipment in the shop. The resulting explosion literally blew the building apart. The roof was reported to have been blown up in the air and then fell back down to crush what little was left standing.

The first thing my grandfather said he did was remove his jacket and hang it on a fence post. He found it days later trampled and torn.

The second was to dig a little girl out of the remains of the science room. She died later, he once calmly added.

Then he went to see the remains of the shop. There he found a boy who was pinned, from the waist down, under a slab of concrete. He couldn't do anything for the boy so he rested his head on a piece of board and told him to rest quietly until help came. Grandfather found him that evening in a Henderson mortuary while identifying bodies.

It was after this that my grandfather came across the body of his next door neighbor Lemmy Butler. He found him slumped over his desk. Mrs. Butler did not know of Mr. Butler's death. My grandfather knew this and removed Mr. Butler's pocket watch to give to his wife. Mrs. Butler spent all that afternoon driving injured students to Henderson for treatment. She did not come home till late and Grandfather could not wait. He left Lemmy's watch on his desk inside the Butler's home. When Mrs. Butler came home the sight of that one grimy watch was enough to tell her of Lemmy's death.

I have heard many stories about the disaster. Stories of the roughnecks who worked day and night with their employers' permission to clean away the rubble. A story of a pre-school boy who had come with his mother to pick up his brother and sister. The boy ran ahead of his mother into the building, and the mother survived all three children. Stories about the Texas Rangers who were called in to keep order, and the Salvation Army that fed the workers. Stories of make shift mortuarys [sic] on the campus and exhausted mortitions [sic] that slept in rooms full of bodies, in cots they had just removed corpses from. The stories go on and on.

A new building now replaces the old one, and the school has a new name. All of the faces have changed though some of the names are the same. Nothing is left of the old building now, but the dark memories of those who were there, and a granite Cenotaph for those who were lucky enough not to be.

Grandcamp's Anchor

Texas City Pier
Texas City

One of the most famous cities in Texas is not known for its size, its beauty, or as the title of a popular television show. This city is known for one of the most disastrous fires in the history of the United States.

Wednesday, April 16, 1947, dawned clear and cool, a beautiful day with a late norther clearing the skies. The

This anchor from the freighter Grandcamp *was found one and one-half miles away from the explosion site in Texas City.*

French freighter *Grandcamp* lay along the wharf with its hold loaded with tons of ammonium nitrate fertilizer. A thin ribbon of smoke began to drift upward along the inshore side of the ship behind the sweatboards. An alarm rang out! A soda-acid extinguisher was emptied! Fire pails were lowered, but the blaze grew! A hoseline was called for, but not used for fear water would damage the cargo. Later inquiries would reveal this was perhaps the fatal decision.

At 8:33 A.M., a fire alarm brought fire fighters to the scene of the threatened port facilities. Crowds began to gather to watch the spectacle. A warning passed among the longshoremen that ammunition was on the ship, and it might blow. At a hearing later, an expert testified that small arms ammunition is not a dangerous cargo, but "ammunition" was terrifying, and the fear probably saved many lives when some of the curious spectators left.

The captain of the *Grandcamp* ordered the crew to abandon ship, but many stood on the wharf to watch the fire or drink coffee at a nearby restaurant. Burning fragments of paper bags began to float across to two nearby ships. The *High Flyer* and *Wilson B. Keene* battened down the hatches, and hoselines were laid with streams of water to extinguish any sparks.

At 8:37 A.M., an officer on the *High Flyer* walked along the wharf snapping pictures of the firemen fighting a losing battle with the *Grandcamp*, then returned to his ship. All of Texas City's firefighting equipment arrived, and Monsanto Chemical and Republic Oil Refining Companies sent truckloads of foamite and men to the wharf.

By 9:00 A.M., smoke and flames belched from the hatchway of the *Grandcamp* as though the gates of Hell had burst from their hinges. The steel deck of the blazing ship was so intensely hot that water poured on it vaporized instantly into steam. In 12 minutes, the gates of Hell did burst. The *Grandcamp* blew apart at the seams in an explosion so violent it was heard as far away as Houston and Galveston. The Monsanto plant went next. The sky rained flaming metal on homes, businesses, and citizens, causing death and destruction wherever the massive chunks fell. So potent was the blast, two airplanes were knocked from the sky, killing all passengers.

At 1:10 A.M., April 17, *High Flyer's* 900 tons of ammonium nitrate defied all efforts of firemen from four towns, and nothing remained of the vessel as it was blasted into eternity.

The horror of the Texas City Disaster has been captured in many, many photographs, but pictures cannot portray the hopeless searching among mangled and mutilated bodies for loved ones. Volunteers came from everywhere to help, and some were wounded and killed trying to save others. The ghouls arrived also, to rob bodies of valuables that might have identified them.

The death toll mounted to an incredible 576 with only 398 identifiable bodies. More than 5,000 were injured, and $67 million in property was destroyed including 200 businesses and 3,382 homes. Only seven of the *Grandcamp's* crew survived; its captain was lost forever.

How did it start? No one knows. Perhaps a careless cigarette, perhaps sabotage, or perhaps the weight of the sacks of fertilizer may have started spontaneous combustion.

On June 22, 1947, 63 bodies whose identities are known only to God were buried in Texas City's Disaster Cemetery. All that remains is the *Grandcamp's* anchor, a 10,640-pound hunk of steel that was blown through the air 1.62 miles and buried 10 feet in the ground.

Colossal Collections

Everyone collects something. It may be gimcracks such as matchbooks, hats, t-shirts, salt and pepper shakers, or thimbles. Some lucky collectors spend fortunes stockpiling antique cars, art, precious gems, etc. Some just store away money, and others only collect memories. The possibilities are endless.

Renaissance man collected cabinets of rarities that evolved into museums, and modern man has followed in his footsteps. While all curios today may not make fine art museum showcases, collections are always interesting. It may be the sheer number of a particular curio that is impressive, or it may be the way the little treasures are displayed that is appealing. Regardless, some unique Texans have amassed some unusual collections deserving of their own museums.

The Stamp Window

U.S. Post Office
Eastland

 It is a rare U.S. Post Office that can boast of an art treasure. About the only decorations you ever see on those sterile walls are advertisements for a new stamp issue, the check-cashing policy, and a sign saying "This window closed." However, in Eastland, you can feast your eyes on a beautifully designed and colorful window. No, it is not a stained glass masterpiece; its panes are a galaxy of stamps. What is unusual is how they came to be on this window.

Philatelists abound throughout the world, and there is certainly nothing unusual about collecting stamps. In fact, it is the most pursued of all hobbies. The traditional method of collecting is to paste those little pictures in albums, or if especially rare, tuck them neatly in plastic covers. But, one very special philatelist has created an amazingly lovely showpiece with her collection, and what more appropriate place to mount it than a post office.

Marene Johnson Johnson was postmaster from 1957 until 1968, but she ran her office a little differently than most. Not only did she remove the ancient spittoons from the lobby, she painted her office purple and blue. (Perhaps it was U.S.-Government-stamp-dye purple and blue.) When Marene requested permission to contribute the stamp window, she was denied many times. Marene finally had to go to the Postmaster General before she could embark on her project.

For 7 years this inspired lady collected her 500,000 "paints," but her canvas only used 11,217. As her theme had been carefully planned, the finished composition was assembled in four months and dedicated on Flag Day, 1963.

Ben Franklin beams benevolently down from the top center pane, and this huge five-cent stamp took 4,700 of the rust-red issues of his portrait. Beneath Ben is the Great Seal of the United States, and below that complicated design is a map of Texas "painted" with nine-cent Alamo stamps, three-cent whooping cranes, and four-cent Sam Rayburns. The Lone Star flag waves from the center with the American and Confederate flags to the sides. Lincoln is portrayed with the stamps bearing his famous profile, and George is there in his two-cent image with Martha in her one-cent likeness. A lush rose pattern of three-cent Statue of Liberty stamps with three-cent horticulture stamps for leaves borders the entire collage.

The most prized acquisitions are the numerous autographed stamps. United Nations stamps are signed by various delegates, and the living presidents and vice-presidents of the United States in 1963 (Hoover, Garner, Eisenhower, Johnson, Nixon, Kennedy, and Truman) donated their signatures. The Betsy Ross stamp was signed by her great-great-granddaughter.

Marene soaked the stamps to remove the glue and dried them between newspapers and glass to make certain they would lie flat. The six-foot by ten-foot Stamp Window has a face value of $820.00, but the actual cost for Marene Johnson Johnson was $15,000. Every cent came from her own personal funds with absolutely no expense to the U.S. postal system.

Marene is dead now, but she left Texas and America a gift that will be treasured and loved by everyone, not just her fellow philatelists.

A 1765 Queen Anne doll is one of the fairest beauties of the Franks Doll Museum.

Franks Doll Museum

211 West Grand Ave.
Marshall 75670
214-935-3065/3070
Hours: Appointment only
Admission

If you have always wanted to meet Shirley Temple, Snow White, the Campbell Kids, and other unusual ladies and gentlemen, they are all here at the Franks Doll Museum. Some of these little folks have been around a long, long time, their original names lost in antiquity. You cannot help but wonder what personalities their owners endowed them with, for so often a doll is an extension of a child's ego, becoming almost a real person.

Today, so many grownups love dolls that only stamps and coins are collected more. The Frankses have sought out their 1,600 of the world's oldest, rarest, and prettiest dolls for more than 30 years. Mrs. Franks said that when they began their collection, "We used to find real bargains, but not anymore. Once we found a Dresden doll for ten dollars which was worth one thousand dollars."

Most of the dolls in the Franks Museum were found in New England or the Midwest, and a very rare black slave doll was discovered in Pennsylvania. Other dolls were obtained through a friend in France and the National Federation of Doll Collectors. Several years ago the Frankses purchased a trunk full of old material and trimmings, and Mrs. Franks prides herself in making sure each doll is dressed as accurately as possible.

A large number of the dolls are French and German bisque, a pottery that has been fired once, but not glazed. Mrs. Franks noted, "The French dolls are probably the best

made dolls in the world, however it is not uncommon to find a doll with a French head and a German body.

The oldest doll in the museum is a 1765 Queen Anne doll, sort of tattered and worn for her years, but still a lovely lady. In one case are the Bru dolls with their distinctive wide eyes so real they seem to see you admiring their beauty. Other famous dollmakers, such as Jumeau, Steiner, and Joel Ellis, are represented, and there is an outstanding exhibit of the French fashion dolls once used to display women's elegant costumes.

Mechanical dolls today can perform all sorts of human activities, but that concept is not original by any means. The Frankses' dolls can pour tea, dance around a pedestal, make human sounds, and they are much more endearing. Chatty Cathy, Ken, and Barbie just lack the class that comes only with age.

While the Frankses do not have to provide the continental menus most of their little people would eat if they could, the temperature must be maintained for their wax guests, and all have to be checked periodically for any deterioration.

A visit to this doll house is a delightful experience. Ladies will find their memories reaching back to the doll they loved so dearly as little girls. It probably wasn't as expensive as a Bru or as gorgeous as a French fashion model, but it is very hard not to be overcome with nostalgia for an age when your best friend was your doll.

Beer Bottle World

Dittlinger Feed Mill—Wurstfest Grounds
New Braunfels 78130
512-629-1913

If you can spare thirteen 8-hour days plus another 7 hours, you will have time to read all of the labels in Jerome Nowotny's collection of more than 15,000 beer bottles. The biggest beer bottle collection in the world was housed at Nowotny's Bavarian Village Restaurant for years. You could have your choice of 93 brands of beer to drink along with the specialty—a foot-long egg. When the master collector sold the restaurant, he donated his beer bottles to the Wurstfest Association for a permanent display at a restored feed mill. The display is scheduled to open at Wurstfest 1984.

Some of the categories for the museum will be beers named after automobiles, cigarettes, animals, cities, Indians, and beer joints. There is even a "Yuk" category for concoctions such as beer and cola or beer and lemonade. The oldest bottle dates back to 1760, which Nowotny found in Modesto, California. This old pottery bottle required a deposit, and with it came the warning, "Anyone keeping this will be prosecuted." It was 1840 before the delectable brew was sold in glass bottles.

The highest price Nowotny ever paid for a bottle (not counting travel expenses) was $75 for a Christian Moehrlein from Cincinnati. It took this avid collector quite a while to decide to pay that much for a new addition, but the temptation was too great. As Nowotny said, "I had to have it."

Beer must be the universal drink, for here at Beer Bottle World is a bottle from every country in the world that operates a brewery. The United States alone supplied 9,000 of the collection. Back in 1870, there were 3,000 breweries in America; now only 31 keep beer drinkers supplied. Texas alone had more than 100 different beers, but now only 7 breweries operate in the Lone Star State.

All of Jerome Nowotny's life has revolved around beer. As a lad in New Braunfels during Prohibition, he made his money showing topers where to buy bootleg beer. It was a profitable era for this young entrepreneur, and at 14 he loaned his father $7,000. This brash 18-year-old Texas youth was in New York when Prohibition ended, and he bought a Trommer's beer. "You cannot imagine the ecstasy of buying a legal beer," Nowotny remembers. In one week he had bought every brand of the precious brew he could find in New York.

By 1936 this independent businessman had been in every town in the country that was shown on a state map. Jerome earned his way by selling tiny monkeys whittled out of peach seeds for 25 cents each. (One wonders if some forgotten whatnot shelves have a Nowotny peach pit monkey.)

The dedicated collector had amassed 6,000 bottles by the time he married Hattie, but Nowotny says, "She took a dim view of me spending fifteen cents for a bottle of beer just to get the bottle when the restaurants were selling three bottles for a quarter." For more than 49 years, Nowotny's

collection has grown, and its originator still adds to his rows of dead soldiers. Beer dealers help Nowotny find bottles, and country stores are a good supply source. One of his latest acquisitions is the Ceremonial Ale bottled in 1981 for the royal wedding of Prince Charles and Diana.

Traveling and collecting became an avid avocation with Nowotny, but part of his benefits was his getting to drink all but 25 of his entire collection. He could not say how many eight-hour days that took, nor will he commit himself on which brew is his favorite.

In between all these duties with his beer bottles, Nowotny designs and makes coats-of-arms. His designs include every flag in the world, hundreds of cities, and numerous hex signs. Using the College of Arms in England as his reference source, Nowotny can turn out 900,000 different heraldic bearings. So, if you have always wanted a family crest, just drop Jerome Nowotny a line.

New Braunfels is the ideal location for Beer Bottle World, as it is nationally known for its annual Wurstfest. The first Wurst festival was in 1961 for one day with only 2,000 sausage-and-beer lovers quaffing suds and nibbling the succulent wurst. Now attendance exceeds 150,000, and the feasting and festivities rock New Braunfels for 10 days. It takes that long for visitors to consume the 22,000 shish-ka-bobs, 19,000 ears of corn, 10,000 turkey legs, 42,000 Kartoffel Puffers (potato pancakes) and 42 *tons* of sausage. Proceeds from all this superb food and beer go to the beautification of this old German town and to other non-profit organizations. For dates and details, just write the Wurstfest Association, P.O. Box 180, New Braunfels, 78130.

Clock Museum

929 East Preston St.
Pharr 78577
Hours: 10–12 2–6
512-787-1923
Admission: Donations to Boy Scouts

One of the wonderful delights of owning your own museum is that you get to show off your treasures continually, and James Shawn is a master at telling tales about his gorgeous collection of rare antique timepieces. Shawn was originally a machinist, but his hobby of acquiring and repairing clocks soon mushroomed into a full-time occupation. Since 1968, this clock museum has been ticking out a welcome to visitors from all parts of the world.

This expert clock repairman hand makes clock parts and is often called to all parts of Texas to cure an ailing ticker. The museum showcases are stocked with old timepieces waiting for his healing hands. Shawn estimates that over 70 percent of his 1,650 clocks are in good working order, and most he repaired himself. Amazingly, this dedicated clock lover never had any official training. He "just picked it up."

To describe each of the numerous and varied clocks in this wonderful museum would take a thick catalog. When Shawn started collecting the Nicholas Muller castings, he could buy them for $40 or $50. Muller was not a clock

James Shawn's clock repair hobby has led to a jewel of a museum in Pharr.

maker; he built cases. He had to make a wooden pattern before casting the clock forms in lead base metal. Muller, a German foundryman, lived in New York and put out a catalog of his castings. Clock makers would look at his designs and order the ones they wanted for their particular clock.

Shawn has 200 of these Muller castings now, including case 3 and 1102. (The case number is also the pattern number.) Through Shawn's interest in Muller's castings, people have realized the amount of work that went into them, and now the cases sell for $500. Shawn has reproduced some of the Muller cases from cast iron and aluminum, and they are for sale.

A calendar clock in the museum dates back to 1865, and the Steeple and Beehive Clock made from 1840 to 1910 was the common clock for pioneer households. Even an old 1900 timeclock is on display where a worker's badge number was punched on a wheel. A telephone clock used by the long distance operator to time calls is part of the collection as well as "Blinking Eye" clocks, French skeleton clocks, lyre clocks, and even a metronome keeping time for visitors.

The oldest clock in the collection was made about 1700 by the father of W. M. Claggett who came to this country in 1713. However, Shawn is perhaps proudest of his pre-Civil War clock which was shipped from Indianola to Boston Harbor, and from there brought by oxcart to San Antonio. For 180 years the clock passed time in the city's oldest jewelry store before Shawn acquired it for $850. In mint condition, its 48-pound mercury pendulum keeps the antique accurate within five seconds each month.

Among these marvelous clocks are also music boxes, playing as they did long ago, and old printing presses and scales. Shawn has also collected what he calls "mystery clocks," odds and ends he uses to build some new and unusual methods of telling time. There is much to see and enjoy here at the Clock Museum, and perhaps the most enjoyable of all is its owner. If you arrive at Preston Street and the museum is closed, just go next door and ring the bell. Mr. Shawn always has a Texas welcome for his visitors.

Music Box Museum

City Library
214 Houston Street
Sulphur Springs 75482
214-885-4179
Hours: 10–6 Mon, Wed., Fri. 4–5, Tues., Thurs. 10–12 Sat.

In an upstairs corner room of the Sulphur Springs Library is one of the most delightful museums in Texas, thanks to one of the state's most charming citizens. Leo St. Clair has donated his fabulous music box collection for the world to enjoy, and if you are lucky, St. Clair himself will tell you about his treasures.

Just meeting St. Clair is a treat, and his story sounds like it should begin with, "Once upon a time. . . ." In 1919, Leo St. Clair was a Storekeeper First Class aboard the *U.S.S. George Washington*, and it was his duty to handle the mountain of luggage for the ship's royal passengers, the King and Queen of Belgium, as they made their first visit to the United States. To the young Navy man's horror, one of the valises was accidentally dropped, and the fall activated a music box packed in the luggage.

At the end of the voyage, Queen Elizabeth presented the miniature gilt and silver music box with her portrait on the back to St. Clair as a memento of their trip. It is shaped like a chair, and its tune is from the opera *Faust*. The picture of the queen was made on her eighteenth birthday. Naturally, this tiny chair is the star of St. Clair's musical extravaganza, for his life was tremendously enriched as he searched the world for more music boxes for his collection.

Every music box is in perfect working condition, and all sorts of creatures and characters come to life when their keys are turned. A little Helen Hayes dressed in a costume the famous actress herself made for St. Clair, is portrayed in a scene from the play *Victoria Regina*. The furniture, along with a picture of the music room, was sent to the music man so he could make the background authentic. The tune played is, of course, "God Save the Queen."

The world is encapsuled in music at Sulphur Springs. A tiny singing bird smaller than one inch in an 1885 Black Forest setting trills "Ach De Liber Augustine," while an oil derrick pumps to "Deep in the Heart of Texas." Seated at a piano, a gorgeous French lady plinks a tune, as Madame Pompadour powders her face and turns to gaze in her hand mirror. From India comes a hand-etched silver and brass replica of the Taj Mahal that plays "Farewell, My Love." Meanwhile, a musical stein from Heidelberg plays three German beer drinking songs.

The oldest and most romantic piece in the collection is the Silver Cross. This crucifix was worn by a Spanish sailor from the Spanish Armada in 1588. When his ship was sunk, the sailor escaped to England, and the crucifix remained in his family until the early 1900s. While on a visit to California, the family's last descendent, Mrs. J. Rutherford saw a program by St. Clair on occupational therapy with hospitalized servicemen making musical articles. She presented St. Clair with this rare gift set in a silver triptych and playing "Holy God We Praise Thy Name." In 1950, this beautiful music box was blessed by His Holiness, Pope Pius.

St. Clair still has some of the musical devices made by servicemen as part of their therapy including a toy white shotgun that plays "The Wedding March."

If you try to pick a favorite from these 175 treasures, the choice would be difficult. Perhaps it would be the jug that plays "Little Brown Jug," or the animated six dogs and a teacher that delight you with "School Days." A real favorite is a rabbit that rises out of a cabbage head. This funny little character was a gift from the actor, Lionel Barrymore, who used the music box as a prop in his movie, *You Can't Take It With You.*

There is still a great deal of sentimental attachment to these old-fashioned melodic devices, and music boxes remain extremely popular as gifts. Elvis plays "Love Me Tender" and a whimsical frog with a crown plaintively measures out, "Someday My Prince Will Come." These wholesale editions may be far removed from museum quality, but their simple little tunes continue to strike responsive cords in human emotions.

R. L. More, Sr., Bird Egg Collection

1905 W. Wilbarger St.
Vernon
Appointment only—Easter to Thanksgiving

In a dusty room over a tire store in Vernon is the R. L. More, Sr., Bird Egg Collection. Locked in glass cases are 10,000 bird eggs from all over the world. From the gigantic ostrich eggs to the minute hummingbird eggs, W. T. More, Sr., assembled an ornithologist's delight. Nothing has been added or changed since 1941 when Robert Lee More, Sr., went to that great aviary in the sky.

All of the eggs have been meticulously drained of their contents by inserting a needle in one end. The tiny numbers on each egg correspond with the files and records of the collection, as all have been scientifically marked. Most of the eggs are in clutches, which means the number of eggs produced by a bird at one time.

More began collecting the eggs in 1888 and continued his hobby for 53 years. He wrote a book about the birds of Wise County, and his collection is considered the finest west of the Mississippi and one of the outstanding private collections of the world. Interestingly, More had only five years of formal education.

The bird egg room is just a part of this small museum. In real life, More was the partner-manager of W. T. Waggoner's Three D Ranch. Vernon was on the old Western Trail into Oklahoma, and thousands and thousands of Longhorns crossed the Big Red just north of Vernon at Doan's Store. The Waggoner Ranch was established during this era, and

oil was discovered in 1911, making the Waggoner fortune one of the largest in the Southwest.

R. L. More, Sr., dealt with the rich and famous of those times. Teddy Roosevelt was here to have his picture made, as was Will Rogers and J. Frank Dobie. The old office door with its sign "Waggoner Estate" still stands, and over it is written, "Through this door passed the oil and cattlemen of the 1920's, 1930's." W. T. Waggoner's motto is among the displays of Waggoner Ranch memorabilia, "Never do anything you can't swear to afterward. When you start lying, you hobble yourself in the short grass."

R. L. More, Sr.'s, grandson Patrick takes care of this small museum, but he requests appointments be made to see the collection. While "spectacular" is hardly appropriate to describe the exhibits, there are not many people who have seen 10,000 bird eggs at one time. For a devotee of museums or a collector of the unusual, the R. L. More, Sr., collection is definitely a "must."

Koliha Pencil Collection

Czech Heritage Museum
SPJST
520 N. Main
Temple
817-773-1575
Hours: 8–5 Mon.–Fri.
Admission free

Temple's citizens all know about the SPJST, but it takes special people to know how to pronounce *Slovanska Podporujici Jednota Statu Texasu.* The Slavonic Benevolent Order of the State of Texas was organized in La Grange on December 28, 1896, and the Lodge has developed into a progressive, meaningful organization. Its life insurance company offices are housed in a modern new building, but down in the basement is a museum dedicated to preserving the Czech heritage in Texas.

Czechoslovakians have made a momentous contribution to Texas and the United States. A Czech played "Come to the Bower" as Sam Houston marched to San Jacinto. Michael Strank raised the flag on Iwo Jima during World War II and was later killed in action. Another famous Czech family, the Gil Baca group, and their polka music have survived generations. These and many, many more Slavic people are honored at the SPJST with relics of their pioneer days in Texas and their colorful Old World costumes.

Among all of these memories of the Czech past is the lifetime collection of pens and pencils of Joseph Koliha that goes back more than fifty years. Mr. Koliha was treasurer of the SPJST and also ran a grocery store. His pens and pencils were all advertising gifts such as firms still give away today. A display case is filled with Koliha's pencils, and Otto Hanus, the curator, has formed a giant pencil from the pencil collection. Mrs. Bartosh, the assistant to the curator, said there are 80,000 of the giveaways. It would be interesting to know how many of the businesses that gave out their pens and pencils are still surviving. Joseph Koliha may truly have a one-of-a-kind, collection.

When Dinosaurs Roamed the Land

About 135 million years ago, give or take a few million, Texas was a vast swampy place lush with reedy plants, strange palms, ferns, conifers, and ginko trees. The landscape may have been unfamiliar, but a few unpleasant inhabitants, such as flies, beetles, termites and the eternal cockroach, would have been easily recognizable, even back in prehistoric times. Strange as it seems, there was no grass, but the majority of the population could not have cared less. They either ate those exotic plants or each other, for during the Mesozoic Age, hoards and hoards of dinosaurs roamed the land.

Dinosaurs (*deinos* for terrible, *sauros* for reptile) and fossils have fascinated people for ages. The ancients thought fossils were writings of underground spirits, and if they had ever unearthed a complete dinosaur, all of those big bones would have confirmed their belief in dragons and other mythical beasts. The entire earth's crust is a huge graveyard of everything that once had life. The remains of two thousand million years (that's a lot of zeroes) are entombed in the earth's sedimentary rocks.

The "time of great dying" for dinosaurs came at the end of the Cretaceous Period, and it was a tremendous crisis in the history of life. Land masses shifted, the climate changed, and regardless of size or strength, the reptilian civilization could not adapt. Mammals would dominate the earth henceforth, but who can predict what will roam the land in another two thousand million years when we, the living, are fossils.

Dinosaur State Park

Glen Rose

 We know for certain that dinosaurs roamed the Paluxy River banks, or whatever boggy swamp the land was, because they left behind birdbath-sized footprints big enough for an ostrich. The thick plastic mud was ideal for fossil-making, even when covered by water.

Ernest T. Adams of Glen Rose was a lawyer that should have been a paleontologist, because Ernest spent most of his career tracking dinosaurs rather than legal cases. In the lean years of the late thirties, Ernest must have had a lot of spare time, for he quarried 26 tracks of a creature 33 feet long 13 feet tall with a 7-foot stride. No matter how you add up all those figures, the "terror of the conifers" was *big*.

In 1930 a smart advertising man came up with the clever idea of using dinosaurs to publicize Sinclair Oil Corporation's petroleum products. Even if fossil fuel came from fossils 100 million years before the advent of dinosaurs, the green

"Terrible lizards" still roam the land at Glen Rose.

brontosaurus, Dinny, helped sell a lot of gasoline. The campaign was extremely successful. Even until the late fifties, inflatable "Dinnys" hung from Sinclair's green and white signs and floated in many swimming pools. After Sinclair's merger with ARCO, Dinny once again became extinct.

In 1964 Sinclair really impressed the crowds at the New York World's Fair with wildlife sculptor Louis Paul Jonas' fiberglass tyrannosaurus rex and a big version of Dinny. The tyrannosaurus rex is always a movie monster favorite because the big bugger walked semi-upright and had a head and teeth that make "Jaws" look like a goldfish. The expression on his face would curdle milk, and he was as mean as he looked.

The brontosaurus was named "thunder lizard" because the earth shook when the 40,000 pound "Dinny" stomped through his feeding grounds. If you had removed the brontosaurus' brain, he would have weighed only 39,999 pounds. With beady eyes and round clawless front feet, the brontosaurus was actually a mild-mannered vegetarian. He hung out in swamps a lot, but it has been disproved that old Thunder Lizard needed water to support his three-story frame. He could walk on land as well as his fellow lizards.

After the Sinclair merger, both fiberglass dinosaurs were given to the Dinosaur State Park. The brontosaurus arrived in 84 pieces, but this replica is 30,000 pounds lighter than the extinct original.

You can still see the tracks of these massive beasts at the park, but the hot dry months when the Paluxy is low are the best times for viewing. The park rangers give excellent guided tours as you walk back 135 million years in time. Actually, these prints were made by a sauropod smaller than the brontosaurus.

So many of the tracks have been quarried, that the best viewing is in different museums around the country. In Austin, a special glass case outside the Texas Memorial Museum displays in fossilized footprints a Paluxy River sauropod's race for life from a pursuing carnivorous theropod. The sauropod's 10-inch stride is interrupted by the fleet theropod's 9-inch stride. A 15-ton slab of tracks are set behind a brontosaurus skeleton at the American Museum of Natural History in New York, and Baylor, SMU, Brooklyn College, and the Smithsonian all have Texas dinosaur tracks. At Dinosaur Park you can experience the same feeling of loss as countries with ancient cultures who find most of their treasures displayed elsewhere in the world.

Dinosaur Gardens

Highway 59 North
Moscow
Hours: 9–sundown

Dinosaurs have held such a fascination for Don and Yvonne Bean that they commissioned Burt Holister of Clarksville to build them some of their own. To find the perfect home for their new pets, the Beans had to do some searching, since you don't just walk out and casually install dinosaurs on your front lawn. Now, 11 horned, scaley, gigantic prehistoric beasts roam the land in East Texas.

To greet visitors to their new menagerie, the Beans have placed a 15-foot allosaurus at the entrance to the museum. Ally is a predecessor of the mammoth tyronnosaurus rex and only 35 feet long, but just as mean.

Before you meet the rest of the unique group at Dinosaur Gardens, Don and Yvonne are usually on hand to tell you how their extinct friends found a new home in Texas' piney woods. Don was a "dinosaur freak" from the moment he visited a similar park on an Oregon vacation, although Yvonne's interest in "terrible reptiles" took a few years to develop.

In July of 1980, the search started for the right dinosaurs to begin their collection with. Yvonne said, "I almost lived in the Texas City library for almost a year researching the various types of animal life which existed on earth between 70 and 300 million years ago."

Another problem was finding an artist to build their fearsome friends. Hurricane Allen turned out to be a blessing for them. Driven from their Texas City home by the storm, the Beans went to Don's hometown of Clarksville. There they found out about "The Fiberglass Animal," a company owned by Burt Holister that specializes in making fiberglass mascots for high schools. Burt eagerly accepted the challenge of making the strange mascots the Beans wanted for their East Texas "team."

Armed with the pictures the Beans gave him, Holister built wooden frames, constructed the bodies, and then added details such as heads, tails, feet, and scales. The results are just marvelous. This fiberglass artist may have never seen a dinosaur, but his renditions are as authentic as any paleontologist's who never saw a dinosaur either. Since no one knows what color the creatures were, Holister was left on his own. He chose earth colors, because they seemed logical, but any animal that large hardly needed camouflage.

During the Triassic Period the dinosaurs only grew to 10 or 15 feet long and ran rather like ostriches with side toes

Yvonne Bean's favorite pet in her strange menagerie is her triceratops.

on their hind feet. By the Jurassic Period, some of the big reptiles had taken to the air. The Beans' collection covers both periods of geologic time.

The stegosaurus was Holister's first dinosaur. The plated clumsy ten-ton lizard once clomped around the swamps eating plants. Even his *two* brains only totaled two ounces. The Beans have composed a poem for the old pea-brain:

> If one brain found the pressure strong,
> It passed a few ideas around.
> If something slipped his forward mind,
> T'was rescued by the one behind.

The Beans included in their collection the fan-backed dimetrodon and the smilodon, or saber-toothed tiger, as well. When the struthiominus, the egg-stealing dinosaur, was delivered, the duck-billed creature holding his stolen egg looked all the world like an outerspace football player ready for a touchdown dash.

Yvonne's favorite dinosaur is the three-horned triceratops who weighed eight tons when full grown. If you want to see what the only ferocious herbivorous lizard looked like as a baby, just stroll along to the dinosaur eggs exhibit. The actual eggs were first found in Mongolia in 1923 by Roy Chapman Andrew's expedition.

In the gift shop is all sorts of dinosaur memorabilia: stuffed brontosaurus toys, dinosaur model kits, books, and anything lovers of "terrible lizards" could want.

To create an even more authentic environment for their weird animals, the Beans plan to add something new each year. Jurassic insects will fly and crawl with their dinosaur companions, and the ginko trees will bloom again—all in a special place in Texas.

How They Played the Game

More than 120 world-renowned Texas athletes are honored in the Texas Sports Hall of Fame.

When it comes to the world of sports, Texas is truly a state of champions. Many sports greats are still running for touchdowns, batting in home runs, and setting records on every type of playing field. But, the past is filled with hundreds of superb Texas athletes who are honored in a fantastic museum in Grand Prairie. One of the greatest athletes in Texas history is also remembered in her own special museum in Beaumont.

Texas Sports Hall of Fame

401 East Safari Parkway
Grand Prairie 75050
214-263-4255
Hours: Summer: 10–9
Winter: 10–5
Admission

Old used golf clubs, beat up football helmets, scuffed riding boots, and other old sporting equipment aren't usually worth a second glance, but when they belonged to the likes of Babe Zaharias, Doak Walker, and Willie Shoemaker, they take on a very special aura indeed.

In the world of sports, Texas practically bursts with heroes, and at the Texas Sports Hall of Fame, all are remembered and recognized. Even the most avid sports fan may not know about Ad Topperwein (see "Fabulous Flora and Fauna"), but in the early 1900s, Ad could outshoot any marksman on record. Not only was Ad an artist with bullets for a paintbrush (Ad shot rapid-fire outlines of cowboys and Indians in sheets of tin), but for 10 days he blew the hell out of 72,500 small wooden targets and missed only 9. Well, nobody's perfect.

The Texas Sports Hall of Fame is the first of its kind in the United States and the result of a 30-year fund raising effort by the Texas Sports Writers Association. The first member elected was the great Tris Speaker (see "The Last Inning") of baseball fame, and five new members are chosen each year. Biographical sketches of the members and descriptions of their particular sports achievements are presented on handsome display panels in the museum entry. On hand for the museum's opening were more than 40 of its honorees including Bobby Layne, Doak Walker, and Monty Stratton.

Great moments in Texas sports history are continuously screened in the Hall's four theaters. In the football stadium you can cheer Texas A&M's upset of vaunted Centre College and the birth of A&M's eternal "Twelfth Man." Or, you can watch the 1979 game between the Dallas Cowboys and Washington Redskins when the Cowboys won the Eastern Division title, 35–34. Also on film is Kevin Haney's 77-yard touchdown in the last two minutes of the game when TCU smashed Tulsa 24–17.

If you feel you need some professional help with your favorite sport, Ernie Banks passes along his tips on the art of bunting, Slater Martin improves your basketball ability, and Jimmy Demaret tells the secret to successful putting. Many more hints from the pros of just about every game are yours electronically. All you have to do for this free advice is press a button.

Touch and be a part of past sports history. Begin in the 1800s and walk, sit, or stand on various sports surfaces from Astroturf to a real high jump landing bag. All memorabilia, such as the first Heisman Trophy to Davey O'Brien and Earl Campbell's jersey, is displayed in the appropriate time period with backdrops, props, and music from the era of the heroes' fame.

More than 120 Texas athletes with names familiar to every American are immortalized in the Hall. Though not everyone will remember Bruce Bauer, the tennis champ in 1930 who played on everything but water, the names of Kyle Rote, Don Meredith, Lee Trevino, Darrell Royal, Sammy Baugh, Tom Landry, and Rogers Hornsby are recognized throughout the nation. You can match wits with sports computers, try to kick the soccer ball past the shifty goalie, or try to beat the lowest time to date on the computerized hand-to-eye coordination challenge.

This non-profit museum uses its proceeds for research, scholarships, special grants, and facilities for the underprivileged and handicapped. So, the small admission fee not only guarantees you hours of pleasure, but helps other sports enthusiasts as well.

"Babe" Didrikson Zaharias Memorial Museum

Interstate 10 and Gulf Street Exit
Beaumont 77704
409-838-6581
Hours: 8–5
Admission free.

To describe Babe's career requires every superlative in the jargon of just about every sport. This incredible athlete was a master of coordination in every game she played. The great Babe was declared Woman Athlete of the Year in 1932, 1945, 1946, 1947, 1950, and 1954. No other sports figure has received this honor as many times.

Mildred Ella was born in Port Arthur in 1911, the sixth of seven children of Hannah and Ole Didriksen of Norway. In elementary school this little girl could run faster, jump higher, hit harder, and throw farther than any other kid, boy or girl. The family moved to Beaumont, and Mildred changed the spelling in her last name. She later earned her nickname because her athletic prowess was on a par with another famous "Babe."

This female Babe also became an American legend. As a young woman, she won two gold and one silver medal in the 1932 Olympics, setting Olympic and world records in the 80-meter hurdles (11.7 seconds) and establishing an Olympic standard in the javelin throw at 143 feet 4 inches. Babe was forced to accept the silver medal in the high jump because an official objected to her use of the "western roll," and this still remains one of sportsdom's most foolish decisions.

To earn her place on the Olympic team, this 5-foot 7-inch, 105-pound sensation won the National Women's AAU single-handedly, one of the greatest individual achievements in the annals of sports. In competition with 200 of the nation's finest athletes, Babe took 5 and tied for 8 events. To make this accomplishment even more spectacular, Babe saw her first track meet in 1931 in Dallas while employed by Employers Casualty Insurance, and a year later this amazing woman was on the Olympic team.

While having no formal early training in track and field, Babe was an outstanding basketball player in high school and a three-time All-American with Employers Casualty. Even through Babe went on to national fame in diving, softball, baseball, tennis, and rollerskating, it was on the links that Babe preferred to make her mark.

Golf was one of Babe's later interests, and she became one of the top women golfers in sports history. The premier amateur, Babe rose to become the leading professional. As an amateur, Babe captured 17 tournaments in a row. After winning the U.S. Amateur in 1946, this great golfer became the first American to take the British Women's Amateur in 1947. During the LPGA's first 6 years, starting in 1948, Babe was the leader with 24 victories and the top money winner for the first four years. Her spectacular career continued with one trophy after another.

After turning to her career in golf, Babe fell in love and married a wrestler named Theodore Vetoyanis who had changed his name to George Zaharias.

Babe became ill in 1953, and the superb golfer was diagnosed as having cancer. She fought back, and probably no other facet of Babe's life emphasizes her determination and will to win as does her triumph in the U.S. Womens Open in 1954. Touring the course painfully, at times almost in tears, this indomitable athlete established a record of 12 shots as the largest margin of victory in this event.

Two years later the magnificent Babe lost a battle she could not win. One of the greatest athletes of all time was dead at age 45. Babe is buried at Forest Lawn in Beaumont with the famous quote "It's not if you win or lose, but how you play the game." There is no denying that Babe played the game very well indeed.

Beaumont has remembered its favorite daughter with a small museum built in the circular design of the Olympic rings. All the memorabilia displayed here is merely a third of her trophies: the rest are with her husband. The gigantic key on exhibit was presented to Babe by the City of Denver in 1947, and a commemorative stamp was issued in September of 1981. Many photographs and paintings portray Babe in her moments of triumph, and her shoes, clubs, and Olympic medals are on display. Even some of her harmonicas are part of the exhibits. (As talented as Babe was on the links, she could only play a few songs.)

The Babe Zaharias Open was started in Beaumont in 1953, and proceeds are used to support this museum. This is the only museum in Texas honoring one single sports figure, but the greatest woman athlete of the twentieth century is more than deserving her own special memorial.

One of the greatest athletes the world has ever known is honored with her own museum. (Photo courtesy of Greg Crow.)

See You in the Funny Papers

The funnies have been around a long time, and this purely American form of humor delights readers across the nation. Some comic creations are such a part of the American way of life that their personalities have become very real, with all sorts of people identifying with their favorite characters.

Cartoon strips have become more politically oriented in recent years, but back in those "good old days" good guys and bad guys were clearly defined. The hero fought against gigantic odds, but always won. Life was tough, but not hopeless. Two of the most beloved fighters for justice have found a permanent home in Texas.

Popeye doesn't have far to go for his magical spinach in Crystal City, the winter garden of Texas.

Popeye Statue

Chamber of Commerce
Crystal City

> "I yam what I yam and that's all I yam."
> Popeye

In the predominately Hispanic town of Crystal City, the patron saint is a one-eyed sailor with hypertrophied forearms who acquires super physical powers from handy cans of spinach.

Popeye first appeared to battle injustice in 1929 when Elzie Segar created his enormously successful character. The secret of Popeye's amazing strength was the stringy slimy vegetable that had arrived in England about a century before Queen Elizabeth I.

Known to the Arabs as *isfanaj*, this tender green plant was a rare delicacy for the British wealthy. Stumbling over the odd Arabic name, the British called the vegetable "spinach." Segar chose this vegetable rich in vitamins and minerals as his symbol of power because of his daughter Marie. Marie said, "When I wouldn't eat anything, the doctor said to give me a bit of ground up spinach, and I loved it!"

In southern localities spinach is grown chiefly as a winter crop, since cuts can be made 40 to 50 days after the seed is sown. Crystal City's "winter garden" temperature and soil were a perfect combination for Popeye's "natural fix." Frozen food was unheard of, and spinach was the green fresh vegetable shipped to the North. During the Depression, kids flabbergasted their parents by demanding the elixer popularized by their hero, Popeye, and production in the South increased one-third. Grateful spinach producers shipped Segar a case each week.

Popeye's creator died in 1938 at 44, but he left behind a comic character in America's heart right up there with Mickey Mouse. Segar's daughter said that her father thought of Popeye as his alter ego and a real person. This cartoon translation of the "natural man" so dear to Rousseau can barely read, swears like the sailor he is, and is totally ignorant of proper manners—but his heart is pure.

Segar's highly original Popeye was the first action-humor strip in continuing episodes in the newspapers. The cartoonist's enduring characters became a part of the American vocabulary. Alice the Goon with her hairy forearms talks in an oscilloscope language. "Jeep" is Eugene, a magical gremlin of the fourth dimension who eats orchids and pops up with aid for Popeye. Both jeep and goon have since taken on additional meanings, and perhaps you have forgotten these words originated with Popeye.

Wimpy, the mooch extraordinaire and hamburgerholic, eternally popped his shirt buttons into the waiting mouth of an ever-present featherless chicken. Poopdeck Pappy, the unworthy father of the hero, was there along with the beanpole fickle girl friend, Olive Oyl. Olive's many escapades prompted Popeye to observe wisely, "Wimmen is a myskery."

Swee'pea, the salty dog's adopted son, never grew past the crawling stage—but what can you expect from a gift sent by the Demonian people? Swee'pea was an object of worship for the Demonians, because the seven moles on his back resembled a pair of dice.

Along with all the good characters, the forces of evil were legion. Bluto was forever lusting after Olive Oyl (though heaven only knows what he saw in her), and the Sea Hag and innumerable vultures brought on Popeye a huge demand to gulp down his super-charged veggie. The squint-eyed hero got a lot of opportunities to punctuate his sentences with "@#$%¢&*."

Even though kids adored this blunt and completely natural hero, King Features handed down an ultimatum, "Stop Popeye's brutality and stop his swearing and make him respectable." Segar grumbled that it would be easier to make Olive a sex symbol, but he did tone down Popeye's cussing and fighting. Even though Popeye became less violent, he maintained his philosophy, "If ya think yer doin' right ya deserves credick, even if yer wrong."

In 1936 the citizens of Crystal City began a Spinach Festival, and in 1937 their patron saint arrived via a huge ship floating down Main Street. The festival continued until 1941, but was never resumed after the war. Popeye still stands at City Hall, looking rather amazed to find himself so far from the ocean. If the famous sailor could speak, no doubt he would say, "Well, blow me down!"

Alley Oop and Dinny

Fantasyland Park
Iraan

Not far from Iraan, ancient dinosaur tracks are frozen in stone, and in downtown Iraan, the most famous dinosaur of them all is frozen in cement. There are all sorts of weird pets, but only Alley Oop had a pet dinosaur. Alley Oop's Dinny was so popular it became the symbol of Sinclair Oil Company. (See "When Dinosaurs Roamed the Land.") Sinclair is as extinct as dinosaurs, but Dinny still lives in the memories of avid comic strip lovers.

In the mythical land of Moo, King Guz ruled with such ineptness his recalcitrant subject, Alley Oop, had to take matters into his own hands. When clubs were the "ultimate weapons," Dinny was an invaluable asset to Alley in his prehistoric vendettas against injustice.

If life in Moo began to pale and grow tiresome, Alley and his friends merely stepped into Professor Wonmug's time machine and zipped off to any century their creator, V. T. Hamlin, desired.

Alley had a sweetheart, Oola, who looked like a cave woman version of Miss America. Alley spent an incredible amount of time fighting over his sweetie, but at least he had the decency not to drag Oola by the hair.

Named for its benefactors, Ira and Ann Yates, Iraan's only moment of glory had been when the Yates #1 blew in about 1932. The largest producing oil well in the North American continent had sprayed the entire town a thick greasy black. But by 1965, the town realized it needed a boost to its economy and civic pride.

Barney Ayers was hired for the generous salary of one dollar per year to promote this town with the quirky name and to organize a chamber of commerce. Ayers found out that V. T. Hamlin had worked in the oil fields around Iraan before going on to fame and fortune with his brainchild, Alley Oop. Ayers told the mayor, "I'm going to build Iraan a dinosaur." This project was a bit vague, as Ayers' knowledge of dinosaurs was a bit vague. However, with a picture of Dinny, the determined Ayers designed a model from wire hangers welded together by the high school shop class.

In 6 weeks, Ayers had a 15-foot-high 65-foot-long Dinny. An oil well supply company supplied a 14-foot steel beam backbone and a 10-inch steel neck beam. With sucker rods, wire mesh, cement, and the help of local construction workers, Dinny was soon viewing his new arid home wondering what happened to all the swamps and bogs he was used to.

The 40-ton Dinny was unveiled in 1965 to a crowd of 3,000 fans, including V. T. Hamlin who flew in for the occasion at his own expense. A museum was built and a huge sign donated by Marathon Oil was hung over the gate to "Fantasyland." The sale of Alley Oop ashtrays, pennants, balloons, matches, and of course top hats helped finance the upkeep of the park. In 1967 Alley himself, complete with high silk hat and cigar, joined his beloved Dinny. On Alley's special day a dance and barbeque celebrated his arrival, and a Queen Oola and Miss Stone Age were chosen from local beauties.

Plans were made to add King Guz's Palace, a statue of the lithesome Oola, Dr. Wonmug's Time Machine, the wiley Grand Vizer, and Guz himself, but somehow they never made the Iraan version of the Kingdom of Moo. Barney Ayers moved on to Longview as pastor of the First Christian Church, however, Ayers' offspring, Alley and Dinny, still delight anyone who will take the time to make the detour off I-10 to Fantasyland.

Dinny and Alley make Iraan's Fantasyland Park a photographer's delight.

Heroes—of a Sort

In a state where the land and the legends are larger than life, it takes a lot of heroism to reach hero status. But, with all of its diversity, Texas has heroes for everyone. Not all are immortalized in marble and granite; a few have been remembered in a unique way in this unique state.

R. G. LeTourneau Museum

LeTourneau College Memorial Student Building
2100 S. Mobberly Ave.
Longview
Hours: 9–9 Mon.–Sat.

 R. G. LeTourneau is the classic example of the Horatio Alger rags-to-riches hero. This giant of a man literally moved mountains to become a multi-millionaire, for R. G. LeTourneau was one of the greatest inventors of earth-moving equipment that ever shoveled around the old earth's hard crust.

On the small campus of LeTourneau College stand some antiquated devices that baffle the casual visitor. These awkward looking machines are some of the first equipment LeTourneau invented in 1922. They were found in California and brought to the school their creator established.

When you think of the "school of hard knocks," you could not find a better graduate than LeTourneau. He suffered a broken neck in a racing car accident, was saved when a bucket of gasoline was accidently thrown on a grease fire, and survived a head-on automobile collision. The crash shattered his hip socket, fractured his pelvis, crushed his foot, broke the bones in one leg to splinters, and caused extensive internal injuries. The doctors did not bother to operate at first, as they felt their patient was hopeless.

LeTourneau survived all of these physical setbacks, for he possessed a deep and abiding faith in God. This genius of an inventor had eloped with his 12-year-old bride when he was 24. Their first baby died with influenza after World War I, and God spoke to LeTourneau, telling him that he had been working for material things instead of spiritual wealth. The words were few, but the meaning ran deep in the sad young man. From then on R. G. LeTourneau worked for the Lord.

This "mover of mountains" began his career as a "lead-burner" in a power plant. After leaving school in the eighth grade, LeTourneau worked for a while in a gold mine and took a correspondence course in mechanics. His first successful invention was a hot rod. He drilled a hole on the exhaust pipe just ahead of the muffler. When the valve opened, the trumpeting effect was shattering. One day he was called to repair a tractor which had a defective scraper. If the scraper had been in perfect working condition, LeTourneau might never have become a multi-millionaire.

The fascination with the scraper was a turning point in the inventor's life. LeTourneau knew that he "wanted to move dirt. Lots of dirt." He acquired his own tractor and rigged it to generate electric power to the scraper. Next he came up with his own scraper, "The Gondola." Hard times were still ahead, but LeTourneau summed up his winning philosophy with "You will never improve unless you blame yourself for the troubles you have."

By World War II, LeTourneau had moved a lot of dirt, but his equipment really had to move mountains for U.S. troops. Everywhere on the battlefronts, the big machines moved in to construct airports and roads. On D–Day, LeTourneau bulldozers stormed pill boxes, buried fire slits, smothered gun crews, tore up dragon's teeth and gun emplacements, and sliced through the hedgerows of Normandy. One bulldozer easily did the work of 1,000 men.

After the war, America had to remake the world, and LeTourneau went back to the drawing board. Looking for a steel mill site, he found in Longview the perfect setting for LeTourneau Technical Institute Christian College.

At 65, this genius sold his empire to Westinghouse with the agreement he would not compete with them for five years. Those five years were some of LeTourneau's most productive years. He cleared jungles in the Amazon, dug a deep water port in Vicksburg, and kept on designing equipment. LeTourneau faced every challenge with "there are no big jobs, only small machines."

When the "Mover of Mountains" turned 70, the mountains began to quake for LeTourneau was back in the earth-moving business. A stroke cut the mountain man down, and LeTourneau was dead at 80. He died with more than 200 unfinished inventions in his files.

The LeTourneaus had six children, and his "child bride" was Mother of the Year in 1945 and again in 1969. Portraits of this dedicated couple hang at the top of the stairs in the museum at LeTourneau College.

Deeply religious, LeTourneau made many speaking engagements all over the world for his church. The story is told that R. G. wanted to fly during a storm to a speaking engagement and admonished the pilot, "The Lord will get us there." The pilot retorted, "Well, Mr. LeTourneau, you and the Lord call me when you arrive."

A firm believer in tithing, LeTourneau felt, "You can never outgive the Lord." To prove his belief, he gave 90 percent of his fortune to the church and his God and still died a multi-millionaire. As LeTourneau said, "It is not how much of my money do I give to God, but how much of God's money do I keep for myself."

Many models of LeTourneau's inventions, many awards, scrapbooks, and photographs of his multitudinous services to his country and his God are on display. Also, on a small table are a worn and battered pair of hightopped black shoes. LeTourneau loathed new shoes and wore his old ones literally to shreds. These are big shoes, for this was a big man—truly a mover of mountains.

Douglas MacArthur Academy of Freedom

Howard Payne University
Brownwood 76801
Phone: 915-646-2502, Ext. 406
Tours: 11, 1:30, 2:30, 3:30 Mon.–Sat.,
Sun.: afternoon tours only
Admission free

"I shall return." These three words stirred American patriotism during World War II as much as "Remember the Alamo" stirred Texas revolutionists. Even though Texans remember their slogan, few know who first said it (Sidney Sherman, a lieutenant colonel at the Battle of San Jacinto), whereas "I shall return" was on the pages of history as soon as General Douglas MacArthur said it when forced to retreat from the Philippines. MacArthur became a symbol of democracy during a time when patriotic symbols were highly cherished.

General MacArthur did return to the Philippines, of course, and during the Korean "police action" he was recalled from his command by President Truman. MacArthur wanted to carry the defense of Korea past the limits set by the Joint Chiefs of Staff and defied their decision. Many, many Americans applauded the General for his actions, and he was given a hero's welcome when he returned to the United States. After his retirement, MacArthur allowed his name to be used for the new Academy of Freedom concept at Howard Payne University.

Howard Payne's Academy of Freedom has been identified as a church, a cathedral, and a memorial. In a sense, it is all of these and yet much more—it is a classroom with a goal to "establish an intellectual environment which will nurture understanding and reflective study of the spiritual, economic, social, and political problems of contemporary society. The Academy's program is to make the terms of freedom and liberty meaningful and real."

Completed in 1890, the building of native rock is very impressive. Its old walls have listened to the tenants of Presbyterians, Methodists, and Episcopalians. Since 1953 the Baptist College of Howard Payne has offered a four-year liberal arts degree in its classrooms. Students proudly proclaim Howard Payne as a college "where everybody is somebody."

Greeting visitors as they enter the Academy of Freedom is an eight-foot bronze of General MacArthur wading ashore at Leyte, October 20, 1944. It was sculptured by Waldine Tauch of San Antonio, who studied under Dr. Pompeo Coppini. The artist said, "This one will be my masterpiece." Dr. Tauch's imposing work was financed by Texas school children.

The impact of the Hall of Christian Civilization with its 33-foot mural is overwhelming. For five years Charles L. Sweitzer of Charlotte, North Carolina, painted the enveloping cycloramic version of man's relationship to God.

Awesome 15-foot statues of the Egyptian Pharaoh Rameses II flanked by tablets of hieroglyphics guard the entry in to

General Douglas MacArthur welcomes visitors to the inspiring Academy of Freedom. (Photograph courtesy of Howard Payne University.)

the Mediterranean Hall. The Egyptian exhibit symbolizes the search for freedom in the Decalogue and the Law given by Moses. The influence of Athenian democracy is portrayed in a model of the world's most perfect building, the Parthenon.

The Magna Carta Hall is set in a Medieval castle to emphasize the European contribution to American freedoms. A mural depicts the signing of the document that gave Englishmen their first burst of hope for concepts such as limited government, trial by jury, and the belief that the law must be respected by high and low alike. The entrance, walls, and cubicles are overlayed with cut stone, and oaken beams span the ceiling. Embroidered replicas of the banners of the knights who forced bad King John to sign the Carta hang from the walls.

The artist, Osborne Robinson, was so prepared when he arrived to paint the mural, it only took one month. It was customary in 1215 to portray the patron in art works, so Robinson painted in Dr. Guy D. Newman, president of Howard Payne. Robinson even included himself in the scene wearing Mexican apparel.

In man's quest for freedom, the most hallowed of all American political shrines is Independence Hall. In this room on July 4, 1776, Congress adopted the Declaration of Independence, and the American nation was born.

This room is the most authentic reproduction in existence of the original Independence Hall in Philadelphia. The space is only three-quarters of an inch shorter in width than the original. The original blueprints for the old Assembly Hall were only discovered recently, exposing errors in the reconstructed hall in Philadelphia. Only at the Academy and at Ford's Greenfield Village in Michigan are historically correct rooms.

After a tour of the replicas of historical rooms, a change of pace is offered by the General Douglas MacArthur Room.

Graduating first in the class of 1903 at West Point, the General probably held more military titles and received more decorations than any American fighting man in our history. Here are the two highest war decorations awarded by a grateful nation—the Congressional Medal of Honor and the Distinguished Service Cross. It is interesting to note that MacArthur's father also received the Medal of Honor during the Civil War, and it is believed that this is the only case of a father and son having both been awarded this distinction.

The most popular items in the collection are General MacArthur's world-famous personal symbols: the battered, gold-braided cap with the "scrambled eggs" design on the bill, his sunglasses with the case inscribed with his name and five tiny stars, and the world renowned long-stemmed corncob pipe. Other items include gift swords, flags, photographs, and many personal documents.

It is not solely Douglas MacArthur, general, that the Academy honors, it is Douglas MacArthur, inspired citizen, scholar, educator, athlete, dramatic writer, and statesman that is revered in the MacArthur Room. This great American is an example for all future generations of the meaning of the words "Duty," "Honor," "Country."

Essentially, these halls dramatize the background and meaning of the American way of life. One theme threads its way through all of the rooms—man's epic crusade for freedom. Each room depicts an important victorious confrontation in this eternal struggle.

Fire Museum of Texas

702 East Safari Blvd.
Grand Prairie
214-263-1042
Hours: 9–5
Admission

Since Prometheus defied the gods and gave man the gift of fire, mankind has had to figure out ways to put it out. Kids have always wanted to be firefighters when they grew up. The excitement of the firetruck racing against time, sirens howling, and red lights flashing was all so thrilling. Even in adults, there is still the little kid that yearns to jump in his car and dash off to gawk at the raging inferno.

Fortunately, some kids never lose their dream of becoming professional firefighters, and thousands more give their time as volunteer firemen, risking their lives for little or no remuneration whatsoever. In Texas 80 percent of the firefighters are volunteers.

On the State Capitol grounds stands a monument to these gallant men. Standing in his distinctive hat and holding a small child, this statue honors all volunteers who died in the line of duty. Many names are engraved along with the name of the fatal fire. The 27 who lost their lives in Texas City in 1947 (see "Disasters") are remembered as are those of the Dumas-Sunray fire in 1956. This petroleum tank farm fire began in a 15,000 barrel tank. The 50-foot

When old firetrucks retire, they go to the Fire Museum of Texas.

flames ignited three other tanks, and a fireball was seen for 40 miles. Of the 19 men who died immediately, 15 were volunteer firemen.

The general public is often unaware of the unsung heroism and dedication of their fire department—until it is their home or business that is blazing. Back in the "good old days" just because you had a fire did not necessarily mean the truck would come racing to your rescue. Back then you had to pay for your own fire company, and your building had the marker of the fire company you supported. If there was no marker, then there were no firemen at your fire.

No tribute could ever adequately honor the Texas firefighter, but the Fire Museum in Grand Prairie does a wonderful job. This non-profit museum depends on gate receipts, donations, and many, many hours of volunteer work. Opening in March of 1978, the museum almost went up in smoke because of financial problems, but as the curator put it, "An angel came and put out the fire." It is hoped, the Fire Museum's guardian angel will continue to hover overhead.

Children's eyes glow when they enter this huge room, but age doesn't matter as everyone loves firetrucks, particularly vintage firetrucks. Mostly on loan, the trucks are from Texas fire departments that treasure their equipment, and all are in excellent condition. One of the prize exhibits is an 1878 truck that extinguished fires in Houston until 1965. Originally horse-drawn, it was motorized in 1914.

The miniature firetruck, or "The Little Engine That Could" was donated by the Pharr Volunteer Fire Department. Fireman J. W. "Bill" Gross spent 2,000 man hours working on the truck with its Austin engine and parts. For years, Bill was a hit at parades and festivals all over Texas. This fireman of 25 years donated all of his proceeds to charity.

A really unique exhibit is a German "truck" dating back to the mid-1800s. A team of 12 men operated this antique. Eight volunteers jumped into leather harnesses and pulled their "truck" while another rode to operate the brake, and the other three ran behind to make up the bucket brigade. Several archaic "pumpers" complete the collection.

Photographs of firemen, fires, and fire departments from many years ago line the walls. A great deal of fire-fighting equipment, including a blanket that was held for trapped victims forced to leap from the flames, is part of the exhibit.

You can also compare modern equipment from all parts of the world with that used in Texas.

Firefighters used to use "bugles" to communicate instructions over the noise of the blaze and the crash of collapsing buildings. Often a silver bugle, beautifully engraved, was presented to a fireman for heroic deeds or longevity of service. Several of these treasured awards are in the museum showcases.

Fire prevention movies are shown in a theater donated by the Huntsville Fire Department, and the Texas Forestry Association created a woodland scene with a babbling brook. Standing tall in the midst of the trees and grass, Smokey Bear cautions visitors about the dangers of forest fires. A small home is loaded with fire hazards and you are challenged to locate the potential dangers.

To top off your tour of the museum, you get just what you've always wanted—a ride in a real fire truck. What a thrill! The lights whirl red and gold, the engine roars, and you can make the siren scream. What more could a kid ask for—no matter how old you are!

Monument to Texas Taxpayers

Stephens County Courthouse
Breckenridge

Standing in eternal tribute to the lowly hard-working taxpayer is the ornate doorway of the the 1883 red sandstone courthouse for Stephens County. Carved in its columns are the names of the architect, county judge, and three of the four commissioners. The fourth commissioner's name was omitted because he objected to the cost of the construction.

If he objected to the 1883 courthouse, he would have been in a state of apoplexy over the next one. During the oil boom of the 1920s, the old courthouse was torn down to make way for progress, and the taxpayers had to come up with construction funds once again in 1926. The 1883 portal was left to remind the citizens that the 1926 courthouse may soon crumble to dust as well. (It is not noted how many commissioners' names are inscribed on the 1926 columns.) Oh, well, courthouses may come and go, but taxpayers never die.

Police Museum

Houston Police Academy
17000 Aldine-Westfield Rd.
Houston 77073
713-230-2300
Hours: 9–4 Mon.–Fri.

Officer Danny Hare is mighty proud of Houston's Police Museum, and he deserves to be, for Officer Hare is a one-man museum staff. To begin a museum tour, you may have to call Officer Hare from an old police call box in front of the entrance. This Gamewell box

Uniforms of "Houston's finest" from years ago are displayed at the city's Police Museum. (Photograph courtesy of Houston Police Museum.)

came from the corner of San Jacinto and Congress. These call boxes were used from 1916 to the 1980s. An officer had to call in every hour, and if a policeman was needed, either a bell or horn on the box would sound.

The first exhibit is a 1970 Harley police motorcycle. This three-wheeler was not too popular with the force, but kids love to sit on the bike.

A terrific pictorial history of the Houston Police Department lines the museum's walls. In 1900 Houston was still a cowtown, but the City Marshall's office became the Police Department, and J. C. Blackburn, Houston's first chief. He had under his command 46 dedicated men to protect 45,000 citizens. Normal duty was a 12-hour shift, 7 days a week. There were no pensions, no overtime, and no sick leave. If an officer didn't work, he didn't get paid.

The first uniforms were navy blue with a white stripe down the pants copied from the English uniform of Sir Robert Peel's "bobbies." In addition to handcuffs, a club, etc., the officers had to carry around their own ink well and pen. No, not as a weapon of defense, but for writing warrants if they had to wake up a judge in the middle of the night. Until 1928, a policeman's gun had to be concealed.

Badges used to be hand-engraved silver dollars. Some badges were very ornate and patterned after the round Mexican silver dollar badges of the Texas Rangers. On top of all this glory, officers earned $60 a month, and this salary remained in effect for four decades.

In 1910 the HPD acquired its first patrol car. That car and two motorcycles made up the entire traffic squad. The mounted police and later the motorcycle police were always an elite group, and saw to it that the 8 mph speed limit was enforced. Their green uniforms with black bow ties were worn until World War II.

Many of the old uniforms are on display. Eva Jane Bacher was the first woman officer in 1918, and in 1920 the first woman detective. After Eva Jane no more women were on the force until Jo Singleton in 1956. Jo's uniform was a skirt made from men's pants and a man's shirt. She carried her pistol in her purse and did not go out on the street. In the late sixties the ladies wore a "mini-skirt" that came up to their knees. Finally, in 1978, women went through the same training program as men and wore the same uniform as male officers.

One display is four cases of the weapons taken from suspects during one eight-hour shift. A sawed-off shotgun, a zip gun that shoots .32 and .22 caliber bullets with a rubber band, several .22 rifles, "throwing stars" made from lawnmower blades, nails, belt-buckle knives, pen guns, brass knuckles, and Saturday night specials are just a few examples of the lethal hardware collected.

Other display cases contain weapons used by law-enforcement officers ranging from a model 1894 Winchester saddle gun to a 1921 Thompson submachine gun. The Riesing submachine gun on display was issued in 1941 because of fear of a Japanese invasion of Galveston, and never fired on

duty. It is not uncommon for police to carry military arms, as they are cheaper.

Here at the HPD Museum you can sit in a police car, turn on the sirens and the "bubble machine" lights and feel just as though you are speeding madly to the scene of a crime. A police helicopter hovering near the ceiling reminds you that the HPD's helicopter squadron is the largest patrol division in the county. Other exhibits describe the demanding duties of the SWAT team, and extensive information is presented on rape prevention and drug abuse.

A somber note among the exhibits is an album of officers killed in the line of duty. One of the worst years was 1982 with four officers dead. On the bright side is a bulletin board with letters from kids who have visited and loved the museum.

Officer Hare has many plans for his police memento rooms including an authentic cell and a written history of the HPD. Meanwhile, Hare's terrific efforts to portray Houston's Police Department at its finest is well worth the time and effort.

Texas Underground

During the gold rush days and silver booms Texas was just a place to pass through on the way to the mother lodes of the Rocky Mountains. If the land did not produce precious metals, no one cared what else was buried beneath the soil. So, all the glamor and glory of the gold fields bypassed Texas completely, and its people had to settle for herding cattle up the Chisholm Trail for excitement. Several decade later, Texas' boom towns made the Gold Rush pale in significance. Black gold replaced yellow gold, and Texas had more oil for the taking than anyplace else when Spindletop blew in the twentieth century.

First Oil Well in Texas

Five miles east of FM 266
Oil Springs

The story of the immense wealth stored underneath Texas began early in 1859. A Virginian named Lyne T. Barret was convinced that oil was beneath the surface of Nacogdoches County. Barret became the perfect example of the old saw "For want of a nail . . ."

because had he been able to acquire equipment, Barret would have drilled the first producing oil well in the world. Instead, in August of that year, the honor went to Pennsylvania.

Finally, in 1866 Texas' first wildcatter used crude tools made by a blacksmith and drilled 106 feet and struck oil. While not exactly a gusher, Barret's well did produce ten barrels a day. After capping the well, Barret went to Titusville, Pennsylvania, and made an agreement with the Brown Brothers. Returning to Texas with Barret was the experienced oilman, John F. Carll.

Carll and Barret drilled an 80-foot dry hole, and the Pennsylvania group withdrew their support of Texas' first strike. The Yankees had a sure thing underway up North, and Nacogdoches was too far from a profitable market. Barret never drilled another well.

A revived interest in the oil spring at Nacogdoches began in 1886 when E. F. Hitchcock brought in a well flowing 250 barrels from only 70 feet. Even though this bonanza quickly went dry, about 90 more wells were drilled in the Oil Springs field, and Texas became an oil producing state. The first steel storage tanks in Texas were erected and still stand near the discovery well. By 1890 the field was deserted, drilling was finished, and the springs were left to seep in a forgotten forest.

If you go out to Oil Springs today, be sure it hasn't rained for a long time, for that red East Texas mud becomes impassable. Some pumps are again producing after the energy crisis, but the site of Texas' first oil well is just a pipe in the ground oozing black oil water and a historical marker that has served as a target for pot-shots. Lyne Taliaferro Barret has been remembered with an incredibly tacky monument on the campus of Stephen F. Austin State University just across from the Old Stone Fort. In a ceremony on September 30, 1966, the Honorable Ben Ramsey, chairman of the Railroad Commission, dedicated the plaque "to honor the man who opened a prosperous century for this state."

Lucas Gusher Monument

Gladys City Boom Town
409-838-8122
Hours: 1–5 Fri., 9–5 Sat.
Admission
Beaumont

Spindletop Museum

Lamar University
University Drive and US 287 South
409-838-8122
Hours: 1–5
Admission free
Beaumont

Prior to January 10, 1901, Beaumont, meaning "Beautiful Mountain," was a dinky lumbering town named for a slight elevation southeast of town. Since that January day, Beaumont became known as "the city of oil." Not only was the destiny of Texas changed, but also the destiny of America, for that slight elevation was "Spindletop," the Brobdingnagian oil gusher.

The name "Spindle Top" originated before the Civil War, because heat waves shimmering on the crest of a rise gave it the appearance of a spinning top. As St. Elmo's fire was often seen dancing in the moonlight, Spindle Top was the perfect setting for ghost stories.

Pattillo Higgins, a young Beaumonter, had studied geology and decided the little hill was actually a vast oil reservoir. On a Sunday afternoon picnic, Higgins even stuck a cane into the ground and ignited the escaping gas to the delight of the children. He named his Gladys City Oil Company for a seven-year-old member of the group. However, poor Pattillo struck dry hole after dry hole and became the brunt of local jokes and was ridiculed as "the millionaire."

Finally in desperation, Higgins ran an advertisement for a backer in an engineering journal. There was only one reply, but that was enough. The response came from Antonio Luchich, a graduate of the Austrian Naval Academy who had Americanized his name to Anthony Lucas. Lucas shared Higgins' conviction, and yet was advised by experts he would never strike oil at Spindle Top. Only Dr. William Phillips of the University of Texas offered encouragement and put Lucas in touch with Guffey and Galey who had reaped such golden rewards in Corsicana.

Galey arrived in Beaumont, chose the site, and hired the expert drillers, the Hamill brothers. At 1,020 feet the bit hit a crevice, and the drill stem seemed about to break. The stem was pulled and 700 feet of pipe lowered into the hole. Mud began spurting to the surface when suddenly, 6 tons of pipe went shooting through the air and broke into pieces. Deep within the bowels of the earth, a deafening roar burst

Gladys City, boomtown of Spindletop, thrives once again for visitors who want to relive those exciting days. (Photo courtesy of Greg Crow.)

forth, and at 10:30 A.M. mud, gas, and oil awoke from its millions of years of sleep and poured over Texas. Lucas gasped, "A geyser of oil! A geyser of oil!" The gigantic strike was less than seven feet from the spot Higgins said it would be. When "the millionaire" was told about the gusher, he calmly replied, "Don't you remember that I've been telling everyone for more than ten years this would happen?"

Prior to Spindletop (now one word), there had been only one other such gusher—in the Baku field in Russia. Overnight thousands of sightseers, speculators, promoters, fortune hunters, and "boomers" poured into Beaumont. Six trains arrived daily from Houston as gawkers stook in awe of 100,000 barrels of crude a day pouring forth into a lake of oil. No one knew how to cap the well, and finally the Hamills invented a valve apparatus that had to be moved by teams of mules over the hole. Special goggles, masks, and earplugs were invented for protection from the oil and the ear-splitting roar that never abated. At last, after nine days and one million barrels of black gold, the screaming monster was silent.

Higgins' dream metropolis of Gladys City became an ugly sprawling nightmare. Clapboard shanties, filth, and mud shared the space with 285 rigs. Out of more than 600 new oil companies, Texaco, Gulf, Mobil, and Sun survived. Spindletop had become Swindletop.

The Lucas Gusher alone out-produced the entire state of Pennsylvania, and with the next five gushers, more oil flowed from Spindletop than came from the rest of the world combined. The boom was short lived, however, for in ten years overproduction created a ghost town. With the development of new petroleum technology, Spindletop boomed once again in 1926. Now, massive chemical complexes and refineries dominate the landscape around Beaumont, Orange, and Port Arthur.

The twentieth century was born at Spindletop, for petroleum products revolutionized industry and transportation. The United States emerged the wealthiest nation in the world. To commemorate this event, the Lucas Gusher Monument was dedicated in 1951 with a 58-foot granite obelisk topped with a Texas Star. Erected on the original site of the geyser of oil, this National Historic Landmark had to be moved to the Lamar University campus due to soil subsidence.

Adjacent to the Lucas Gusher Monument is a reconstruction of Gladys City, a Beaumont Bicentennial gift. The little "town" is jammed with derricks and is delightfully authentic. The only things missing are the mud, the brawling saloons, and the con artists.

The Spindletop Museum is in a small yellow brick building behind the Lamar University Educational Service Center. The displays for such an important historic event are quite meager, but the old photographs and a few early drilling bits are interestingly presented by the museum's curator, David Hartman.

Discovery Well of the Permian Basin

Santa Rita #1
Big Lake and Austin

When Coronado encountered the vast desolate plains of West Texas in his search for Cibola, the fabled Seven Cities of Gold, little did the great conquistador dream that the greatest fortune lay buried beneath his feet. But, Coronado had no way of knowing that his trek took him over the remains of an inland sea with the hidden treasure of oil. This endless land that convinced the arrogant conquistadors that the Indians could have it forever is now acclaimed as one of the greatest oil regions in the world. The Permian Basin is still made of those same endless plains, but now the desolation is dotted with oil wells and processing plants.

Santa Rita #1 was named for the Patroness of the Impossible for many good reasons. Rupert Ricker persisted in acquiring leases on the University of Texas lands in spite of being told they would be worthless. Next, the well was spudded-in only minutes before the expiration date of the drilling permit on January 8, 1921. (As for the legend that the rig broke down and that determined the site, it is only a tall Texas tale.) To add to all the other impossibilities, Carl Cromwell had to drill until May 28, 1923 before the Permian Basin's first well came in at 3,055 feet. But, because these men defied the impossible, West Texas was transformed into a land of oil derricks and millionaires.

A replica of this famous well is in the city park in Big Lake, and the original lady stood on the University of Texas campus in Austin. However, the original burned, and the Santa Rita #1 you see today in Austin is also a replica. Called "the oil well that talks," a continuous recording telling the story of the discovery drones through the day. Unknowing passengers in cars stopping for the traffic light are startled to hear a voice from nowhere talking about an oil well.

The University of Texas will let the well talk all it wants to, for since 1924 the school has received more than $1.2 billion in royalties making UT the most richly endowed school in America.

Big Lake's replica of the Santa Rita #1 represents the underground wealth of the Permian Basin.

Edgar B. Davis Memorial

Luling Chamber of Commerce
Luling

For years, everyone who came to Luling commented on the horrendous odor of sour gas that permeated the area. Visitors may have complained about the smell, but the people of Luling loved it, just as they loved the man who discovered the Luling Field.

When Edgar B. Davis arrived in Luling he was a millionaire twice over. With his brothers, Davis had made a fortune in a shoe manufacturing company in Massachusetts. At 35 the young millionaire had a nervous breakdown, and sailed around the world to rest. In Sumatra, Davis became intrigued with the idea of breaking the Dutch and English rubber monopolies, since the newly invented automobile needed an endless supply of the raw stuff.

After returning home, Davis played golf with a man who was treasurer of the U. S. Rubber Company. A deal was struck, and the retired millionaire was back in harness. Returning to Sumatra, Davis revolutionized the tropical jungles with his rubber plantations. Where the Dutch went with boots and the English went in puttees, Davis wore low quartered shoes, stepped over hooded cobras, and was never bitten. Nor did Davis ever contract malaria or become ill.

It is estimated that this brilliant entrepreneur received about $3,500,000 for his efforts. Of that amount, more than $1 million was returned to Davis' employees in the form of gifts. The kindly benefactor planned to retire and take life easy once again.

Meanwhile, in the southern part of Texas, forces were at work that would bankrupt this shrewd Yankee. Edgar's brother, Oscar, had invested $75,000 in some Texas oil leases, and asked Edgar to go down to Texas and have a look at all of those dry holes being drilled. He arrived to find a miserable town and an even worse oil syndicate. Advised to get Oscar's money back (if he could) and go home, Edgar stayed and bought out the syndicate himself.

After returning everyone's money, Edgar renamed the company The United North and South.

After 6 dry holes, Davis was almost broke. As he started his seventh well, the oil business was about to defeat a man who had made millions elsewhere. When the owner of some property objected to a well being drilled there, Davis skidded his rig about a mile before "something" told him to halt. On a hot August afternoon in 1922, Davis and two friends were watching the Rafael Rios #1 from an open car when suddenly, a black column began rising from the rig. The Luling oil field was born.

Rafael Rios #1 turned out to be a dud and only produced 150 barrels, but Magnolia Petroleum paid Davis $500,000 in advance for a million barrels of oil. By 1924, the new oil mogul was producing from other wells 57,000 barrels a day. Davis sold out to Magnolia for more than $12 million, and in 1926 that was the biggest oil deal Texas had ever seen. Fifty years later, 139 million barrels of oil had flowed from the Luling Field.

When millionaires spend their money, it is often for luxurious possessions. At age 53, Edgar B. Davis had millions to burn, but this strange New Englander recognized something that escapes many of the wealthy—an obligation to those who helped make his fortune. Davis announced two picnics (one for whites and one for blacks) on June 5, 1926. After 15,000 guests from all parts of the world consumed more than 20,000 pounds of barbeque, drank an endless amount of soft drinks, and smoked 100,000 cigarettes, Davis announced that all members of his organization would share in his new wealth. In three brief sentences, Edgar B. Davis gave away $5 million to his employees and associates.

There was even more for the community which had made Davis a rich man again. He built a country club for white citizens and one for blacks, both endowed with upkeep funds. Another million established a model farm to encourage diversified farming over a one-crop (cotton) economy.

One wonders what possesses a man like Edgar B. Davis. Instead of enjoying his new wealth, the millionaire started drilling again. Every effort was a dry hole, and in four years, Davis had lost everything including his fabulous mansion. After he moved into a tiny tenant house on the Luling Foundation Farm, Luling showed its fierce affection for its benefactor in a peculiar way. When Davis could not regain his home, it was mysteriously wrecked. The town seemed to feel that if Mr. Davis could not have his home, no one else could either.

Four years later, Edgar B. Davis was once again bringing in new wells. In 1951, after 32 years of wildcatting in one of the toughest businesses in the world, Davis died at age 78. He wrote in a stockholders report " . . . success means a large financial gain, not only to ourselves but to almost everyone within this broad radius. I have faith in God for the future." The funeral rites were read by pastors from the Baptist, Christian, Episcopal, Methodist, Presbyterian, Catholic, and Seventh Day Adventist churches, and by four black ministers.

Edgar B. Davis, great humanitarian, rests under the oaks where his beautiful home once stood. In its place is the fully equipped Edgar B. Davis Memorial Hospital. Luling's pumps are still producing, and the town has even cleaned up its terrible smell. At the chamber of commerce a metal rig is dedicated to Davis' memory along with a bell from the old Luling Foundation Farm. His simple epitaph engraved on a plain granite tombstone reads "A man of faith."

The Permian Basin Petroleum Museum

1500 Interstate 20 West
Midland 79701
915-683-4403
Hours: 9–5 Tues.–Sat. 2–5 Sun.
Admission

In 1975 President Gerald R. Ford opened one of the most unusual and informative museums in the United States in Midland. Midland is the center of the Permian Basin oil business, even though, ironically, no oil has ever been discovered in Midland County. Here at the Permian Basin Petroleum Museum a group of private citizens have developed a stunning tribute to the petroleum industry.

It takes more than five hours to read and experience every display and exhibit in this marvelous museum. To really enjoy all of the attractions, you should make several visits. Even if you don't know the first thing about geology or oil production, these exhibits make learning simple, fun, and interesting. There are no "hands off" signs, and you can

The importance of the oil industry, past, present, and future, is brilliantly displayed at the Permian Basin Petroleum Museum. (Photograph courtesy of Permian Basin Petroleum Museum.)

turn dials and push buttons, using not only all five senses, but also your mind.

In one area you walk through the ancient Permian Sea that covered Texas about 230 million years ago and see the 200,000 different plants and animals that evolved into precious fossil fuel. A multi-media map introduces you to the origins of oil and gas, describing drilling procedures and explaining what the museum is all about. Games let you test your knowledge of the industry. For example: Crude oil is extremely flammable. True or False? The answer is false, for most crude will extinguish a lighted match.

The West Wing stresses the "people history" of the region before and after oil was discovered. A collection of branding irons from ranches in the Permian Basin (which includes 54 Texas counties and 4 New Mexican) are displayed, and a panorama of photographs of nearby Wink portrays the growth of a typical oil boomtown. In addition, a Hall of Fame honors outstanding achievers connected with the development of the oil industry.

The pumping unit in front of the building was donated by various companies, and the cable-tool rig, the Santa Rita #2, is the oldest surviving rig from the Permian Basin's early fields. Out in the "Oil Patch" past the parking lot is one of the finest and most complete exhibits of antique drilling equipment in the country. Plaques explain each old relic some of which are still operable.

The museum prides itself on being "A Museum for Tomorrow" and stresses how the oil industry's successes or failures will affect your tomorrows. So, if you want to know what the future holds in store, the Permian Basin Petroleum Museum is one of the best places to find out.

East Texas Oil Museum

Highway 259 at Ross
Kilgore 75662
214-984-1445
Hours: 9–4 Tues.–Sat., 2–5 Sun.
Admission

The World's Richest Acre

Main and Commerce
Kilgore

Daisy Bradford's farm was extremely reluctant to give up her riches to Dad Joiner. Since August of 1927 with two dry holes, Joiner's luck had been all bad. Still, Doc Lloyd, the geologist, was optimistic. Joiner's Hard Luck #2 showed oil and gas, but the hole had failed to produce. With the third try, the rig skidded 200 feet down a slope, and Joiner said, "This is as good a place as any. Let's drill here." Finally on September 3, 1930 (the Historical Marker says October 3) oil went over the top of Daisy Bradford #3, and the East Texas oil boom was on.

That eventful Friday had been an exhausting day for the drilling crew as 2,000 spectators had watched their vain efforts. Late in the afternoon, the reluctant Woodbine for-

A classic example of overdrilling was Kilgore's World's Richest Acre. (Photograph courtesy of East Texas Oil Museum at Kilgore College, Kilgore, Texas.)

mation broke loose and blew oil over the crownblock. The crowd went wild, and East Texas rocked and reeled with the onslaught of the "boomers."

In December the Lou Della Crim #1 put Kilgore on the map, and Longview offered $10,000 to the producers who would bring in the first well within 12 miles of its courthouse. When the Lathrop #1 tapped the 140,000 acre reservoir of Woodbine sand, the great East Texas oil field emerged as a giant among oil deposits.

Columbus Marion Joiner sold his oil interests to an entrepreneur named H. L. Hunt, and retired from the chaos he had created. Hunt emerged a billionaire.

East Texas absolutely bloomed with derricks. Kilgore boasted of "The World's Richest Acre," with 1,100 wells within the city limits. One was even drilled through the marble floor of the Kilgore bank. The rigs were not removed until the sixties, but a replica impresses you with the magnitude of the oil strike. On 10 lots, 24 wells were owned by 6 different operators. On the small derricks within the replica of this fabulous acre are the names of the wells and their owners. From this one-acre plot saturated with oil, two and a half million barrels of crude were produced. Kilgore's little acre was wealthy indeed.

To commemorate this "Granddaddy of Oil Fields," on the fiftieth anniversary of the Daisy Bradford #3, the H. L. Hunt Foundation opened the East Texas Oil Museum. As you open the doors of this Texas treasure, the pipe wrench handles will take you back to those rip-roaring boom days when East Texas was a sea of oil. A huge mural of "Dad" Joiner, a soft-spoken Bible-quoting man in his seventies standing with the 300-pound "Doc" Lloyd also in his seventies and Daisy Bradford herself greets you inside.

The lobby has memorabilia from an East Texas school, a church, and also some classic old cars of the era including a

Model A Ford driven until 1981 by a little lady in her eighties.

Be prepared for a moment of sheer amazement when you push the swinging doors into Boomtown, U.S.A. A real Main Street, filled with the eternal sea of cloying, thick muck, has bogged down four big mules and an antique truck and car.

You can wander along the plank walks and browse among life's little pleasures at the General Store or take the kids to a real drugstore for refreshments. The Gusher Gazette will sell you a newspaper for a nickel while the editor calls in the story "Troops Are in Kilgore." (In 1931 martial law was declared in East Texas as overproduction had glutted the market, and oil sold for an unheard of 15 cents a barrel. The Hot Oil Act finally restored law and order in this money-mad town.)

A nickelodeon throbs with big-band tunes, a blacksmith pounds his anvil, making oil rig tools, and the barber jokes with his customers. You sort of expect Clark Gable, Spencer Tracy, and Claudette Colbert to come marching up the street with their hands full of oil leases.

An elevator takes you to the "center of the earth" to explore the Woodbine sand that made all this entertainment possible, while Professor Rockbottom explains the geology as you descend. Don't worry, you won't be gone long, for it's a very fast elevator.

The highlight of this wonderful museum is the movie, *The Great East Texas Oil Boom*. Old historical film clips really tell the exciting story in scene after scene of drilling, dry holes, gushers, and *mud! mud! mud!* At the end of the movie, the floor begins to shiver and shake, a deep rumbling is heard, and another Daisy Bradford #3 prepares to burst through the theater floor.

Joe Roughneck

Pioneer Park
Texas Highway 64 West
Henderson

City Hall
Conroe

Boonsville

 In the oil industry, workers speak in their own particular jargon, and a lot of words have been added to Webster's since Spindletop. Drilling for oil is called "making hole," and the apparatus so necessary for the drill stem is a derrick. The word "derrick" reached the English language in a rather gruesome way. It seems that the executioner of the Earl of Essex, the beloved of Queen Elizabeth, was named Derrick. Derrick's heavy blow with the ax was so poorly placed on Essex's neck that the beheading required two more horrible whacks.

Admirers of Essex almost killed the clumsy axman, but Derrick was rescued and lived to perform scores of executions. His career advanced to include hangings, and he pulled the noose on so many doomed souls that Derrick's name became synonymous with the gallows. When a hoisting apparatus was invented that resembled the dreaded instrument, the machine came to be known as a derrick.

At the Spindletop Museum in Beaumont is a detailed explanation of oil patch terms. A "boll weevil" is a green worker because he was often fresh from the farm. A "roustabout" is an unskilled worker, and the skilled laborer, is called a "roughneck." A roughneck is expected to work under any conditions and perform hard labor as much as every day for an entire month. "There's some things a roughneck won't do, but there ain't nothing he can't do" is a truism this hardworking man has earned. A roughneck can perform basic electrical engineering, mechanics, pipe fitting, and operate any part of a rig. Yet, at the unemployment office, a roughneck is listed as unskilled labor.

When Lone Star Steel expanded into casing and tubing for the oil industry, they needed a gimmick. L. D. Webster worked out sketches with a Dallas advertising man, Don Baxter, and the cartoon character Joe Roughneck was created. This fabled figure of the oil patch first appeared in Lone Star's ads, then on bronze plaques awarded to rugged individualists who had roughnecked around the rigs. Creators of the salty subject say R. E. "Bob" Smith, one of the promoters of the Astrodome, was the model for Joe. Another story is that the patron saint of the Roughneck Clubs was designed by Torg Thompson who gave him a jaw squarely set to denote determination, a nose flattened as a souvenir of the rollicking life in a boomtown, eyes soft with kindness and generosity, and a mouth with a trace of a smile. Joe is rough and tough, sage and salty, capable and reliable, shrewd but honest.

There are three Joe Roughnecks today honoring the industry. One is in Boonsville, another in Conroe, and one in Henderson. The Conroe statue commemorates George William Strake who brought in the 19,000-acre Conroe field and became the first oil millionaire in Houston. His fortune was estimated at one to two hundred million dollars.

Just a few miles west of Henderson near the original site of the Daisy Bradford #3 in a Texas roadside park stands a joint of steel pipe from the one-millionth ton produced by Lone Star Steel Company. Encased in the pipe are 100 shares of Lone Star stock designated as a college scholarship fund. Also buried are letters from President Eisenhower, Senator Lyndon Johnson, Speaker Sam Rayburn, Governor Price Daniels, and many others. A Bible donated by E. B. Germany, president of Lone Star, rests in the pipe. All of these endowments were placed in the time capsule at the State Fair of 1956, and the monument was dedicated on March 22, 1957 "to the men who visioned an empire, dared to seek it and discovered it in the East Texas Oil Field."

On top of the pipe stem is mounted a life-size bust of the dynamic symbol of the oil and gas industry, Joe Roughneck, who will stand guard over the articles until A.D. 2056. Joe's bust was originally cast in bronze, but was especially cast in iron by the Lone Star Foundry for his vigil. The stock will be administered by the National Bank of Dallas and the East Texas Chamber of Commerce and should be worth approximately $1 million.

Governor John Connally acclaimed Joe as "a kind of composite spirit of hard-working men who made Texas and the nation world leaders in petroleum production." Meanwhile, just over the rise is the chugging of an old gasoline engine at the Daisy Bradford #7.

Billionth Barrel of Oil

Snyder

Standing beside a Paul Bunyan-sized pump in Scurry County is a gold barrel of oil—a monument to the last Texas oil boom. In 1948 the Canyon Reef formation was struck at 6,000 feet, and this huge field of 85,000 acres contained an estimated 4 billion barrels of "Texas tea." Snyder experienced the last of the "boomers," and emerged from a sleepy ranching community into a big-time oil town.

On the twenty-fifth anniversary of the rich discovery, Scurry County produced its billionth barrel of oil. The town celebrated with a Boom Town Follies that included honored guests Governor Dolph Brisco, Ken Curtis (Festus of *Gunsmoke*) and Nelson Eddy and Jeanette MacDonald. A barrel contains 42 gallons, and W. A. Vestal, a consulting engineer, calculated the second billionth barrel will not be produced until the year 2020.

The Western Company Museum

6100 Western Place
Fort Worth 76107
817-731-5100
Hours: 8–5 Mon.–Fri.
Admission free.

While Eddie Chiles, chairman of the board of The Western Company, might tell you he is mad, you won't be mad at all after a visit to The Western Company Museum. Every exhibit in this fine museum is shiny, new, and well done, highlighting every facet of the petroleum industry. You can take a course in astronomy, geology, chemistry, physics, oceanography, paleontology, philosophy, history, or economics and never move more than a few feet.

A gigantic display of beautiful photographs of the earth's solar system and other astrophotography greets you as you enter. Fossils more than 250 million years old tell the story of oil's formation, and an absolutely gorgeous aquarium portrays life in tropical seas. You can see the interaction of tectonic, seismic, and volcanic forces and how hydrocarbons are affected by the porosity and permeability of rock formation.

The Western Company specializes in acidizing, fracturing, and cementing for the oil industry, and has expanded into service and well drilling for offshore rigs, making this a

"Eddie" Chiles may be mad, but you won't be when you see his petroleum industry museum. (Photograph courtesy of The Western Company Museum.)

truly international company. This large corporation moved from its original location in the Permian Basin to Fort Worth in 1959. The museum is located on the first floor of the corporate headquarters.

Authentic displays trace the development of oil field technology, beginning with cable and rotary methods of "making hole." The multimedia presentations include rig sounds, motion, light, cinema projection, and photomural backgrounds. With cine-robots, three generations of the Williard family bring the petroleum industry to life. "Grandpa" stands by his primitive rig in Corsicana in filthy oil-smeared overalls and tells just how it was back in the beginning. Years later, Williard's grandson is in charge of an offshore rig drilling in 1,200 feet of water.

As for the future, Western predicts it will become a multi-billion dollar corporation by the turn of the next century because of the critical need to find and produce more petroleum and natural gas. These fuels are expected to provide 75 percent of the world's energy well into the twenty-first century.

Should H. E. "Eddie" Chiles' prediction come true, Texas will continue to lead the nation as it has since 1928 as its number one oil producer. In 1980 alone, Texas drilled 19,253 wells of which 27.8 percent were dry holes, and more than $1.5 billion literally bit the dust. But, from 1866 until 1980, Texas' gigantic oil fields produced 46 billion barrels of crude from 124 of its 254 counties. Don't you know Lyne Taliaferro Barret would be astounded to know that the prosperous century he began has gone far beyond his wildest expectations.

Thurber Smoke Stack

Thurber

Before the black gold of Spindletop changed America forever, another black gold powered the nation's industrial might—bituminous coal. In 1886, William W. Johnson developed the tremendous deposits of this source of energy in Erath County, and Thurber was a thriving city of coal miners. Johnson sold out to Texas & Pacific Coal Company in 1888, and Thurber became the classic example of a company town. Texas & Pacific owned the land, both its surface and underground.

Thurber was also a totally unionized town, and is believed to be the first in the United States. It was also one of the first towns in the world with complete electric service. Of the 10,000 inhabitants, 17 nationalities were represented, and most spent the majority of their time in the tunnels.

Yet, Thurber boasted an opera house with 655 seats, and the Metropolitan Opera performed on its stage. Among the town's distinguished visitors was John L. Lewis, who arrived in his private railroad car on May 1 each year when a strike was called. Lewis left every May 31 when the strike was settled. A visitor of a different sort entirely, Wallis Warfield Simpson, spent the summer in Thurber with her grandfather, Colonel Robert Dickey Hunter, a leading capitalist.

Thurber acquired another industry other than coal when it went into the brickmaking business. Every brick street left in Texas today probably has some products with "Thurber" etched on their surfaces. But, even the brick industry could not save Thurber. On October 27, 1917, the death knell tolled for the town. In the nearby Ranger Field, McClesky #1 blew in, and the company became the Texas & Pacific Coal and Oil Company. Coal was soon dropped from the title, and by 1921 there was nothing left to unionize. In 1933 Thurber was totally abandoned.

Still standing over 127 million tons of coal is the smokestack used by the power plant that electrified the town. It is now a monument to a ghost town, and a restaurant occupies the building that was the old drug store.

Every ghost town has a ghost, and if you happen to see a pretty young girl walking the forgotten old streets of Thurber, singing in a foreign language, just pause, and she will fade away as completely as the town.

Helium Monument

Tourist Information Center
2701 I-40 East (Nelson Street Exit)
Amarillo 79101
806-373-1122

Monuments are usually built for something or someone rare and unusual, but Amarillo's citizens have erected a monument to one of the most common elements in the universe. Dedicated in 1968, this metal tripod balancing a rod pointing skyward, commemorates the one hundredth anniversary of the discovery of helium. Sir Joseph Lockyer found this noble (meaning it does not combine with other elements) gas while studying the sun's light during an eclipse. Sir Joseph then invented the word helium from the Greek *helios*, or sun.

Most of the world's helium comes from five natural gas fields in the United States, and one of the largest was discovered in Amarillo in 1929. Since it will not burn, helium has replaced hydrogen in balloons. This odorless,

Amarillo's strange Helium Monument is actually a time capsule of life in Texas in 1968.

colorless gas also maintains proper pressure in rockets, and divers use a combination of helium and oxygen in their tanks. It also makes you sound like Donald Duck when you breathe it.

Even though helium is the most common of elements, it is one of the strangest of all liquids. It conducts heat extremely well, yet it expands instead of contracting when it cools.

The four time columns of the monument are filled with about 4,000 items indicative of life in 1968. All are sealed in a helium atmosphere. One column will be opened in 25 years, one in 50 years, one in 100 years, and the final column in the year 2968. At the small museum in the tourist bureau are display cases of what the people of 1993, 2018, 2068, and 2968 will marvel at. Detergent boxes, bedroom slippers (bedroom slippers?), roller skates, Corning Ware, Elizabeth Arden cosmetics, light bulbs, chewing tobacco, Kent cigarettes, a Sears catalog, and an 8-mm movie and projector.

In the 1,000-year column is a bankbook for a $10 savings account, which will be worth $1 quintillion (at 4 percent) in 2968. The money will go to the U.S. Treasury.

Salt Palace

Grand Saline

"When it rains, it pours."
Morton's Salt

This famous slogan does not refer to Houston's weather, it is the trademark of Morton's salt. Salt grains are hydroscopic and absorb moisture from the atmosphere, resulting in a gummy mess. Morton added small quantities of stuff like sodium aluminosilicate, tricalcium phosphate, etc., to their salt and damp weather no longer deters their product from being sprinkled on your food.

Salt has been essential to man and animals ever since there were men and animals. Ned Neanderthal did not have to look for salt deposits to get his daily requirements, because his staple diet was raw meat, and the natural salts were not lost by cooking. When Ned began to eat vegetables and cereal and boil his meat, the addition of NaCl became of great importance to his good health.

Ancient cultures usually included salt in their offerings to the gods, and covenants were ordinarily made over a sacrificial meal in which salt was a necessary element. The preservative qualities of salt became a fitting symbol for an enduring compact. There are also many references to salt in the Bible, and we all know what happened to Lot's wife.

Not only was salt rare and costly centuries ago, it was thought to have magical powers. The Roman general, Pompey, began a superstition that endures today by throwing salt over his shoulder for luck. Salt was also sprinkled on food the Romans suspected might contain poison. So potent was this belief in salt's protective powers, it left a permanent mark on language. When in doubt about a statement, you are likely to say, "I'll take that with a grain of salt."

Our vocabulary is heavily sprinkled with different meanings for salt. Sailors are "old salts," crusty people have "salty" personalities, and others are "the salt of the earth." A Roman soldier received a part of his pay in the form of a salarium, or an allowance for the purchase of salt. A soldier who did not earn this small allowance was "not worth his salt."

As every shopper knows today, salt is just about the cheapest item on the grocery shelves, and it is an ingredient in practically every food sold. Salt is so prevalent that too much salt can cause the body to retain water and build up tissues that make the heart work harder. Now special sections in stores offer salt-free products for customers with health problems.

Tiny little Grand Saline has been supplying Texans with salt for a long, long time. Perched on top of a mountainous salt dome, the Indians came here to harvest this hot trade item until John Jordan arrived in 1845 to start his own salt factory. That perservative was mighty necessary for deer and buffalo meat. Now, a huge modern Morton's Salt Plant digs into the bowels of the earth for its principal source of income.

The shaft to the mine is only 750 feet deep, but the salt runs 20,000 feet into the earth. Production started in 1930 on the same level the miners are still working on now. This "room-and-pillar" mine is set out like a checkerboard, and each room is 75 feet wide by 25 feet high at stage one. At stage two, a process called benching takes 75 feet of floor space out, but the dome is so solid, the ceiling needs no support.

At one time tours were conducted through the mine, and banquets held deep within those 100-foot rooms. None of this is permitted now, because caterpillars "muck out" salt, which is blown free by a well-planned explosion. A driller makes holes for explosives, and jeeps career around the vast rooms. The mine's ceiling is pitch black from the machinery exhaust.

Sitting beside Highway 80 is Grand Saline's Salt Palace. Don't look for an edifice on scale with Windsor Castle; just look for a one-room building of grayish translucent blocks covered by a metal awning. Inside are salt cartons, rock salt, bags of salt, salt shakers, and just about everything salty Grand Saline could think of. Of course there is an annual gala Salt Festival which should not "be taken with a grain of salt."

Water Museum

San Antonio Water Board
1000 Commerce Street
San Antonio
512-225-7461
Hours: 7:45–4:30 weekdays
Appointment only: Ask for Customer Service
Admission free

> "Till taught by pain,
> Men really know not what good water's worth."
> Lord Byron

 A museum to water? Pure water is becoming a worldwide concern, but has it already become so rare it is now in a museum? Well, not really.

In a restored 1860 house next to the San Antonio Water Board are a few mementos of the city's early water supply with funky fire hydrants and pieces of wooden pipe wrapped with wire. When the wood was saturated, it swelled and filled the cracks. But, mostly the museum contains diagrams of the Edwards Aquifer. An aquifer is a water bearing rock or underground stream of pure water, and the total amount stored in the aquifer is usually unknown.

Several displays of ancient acequias (irrigation canals) complete the exhibits, and about the most interesting fact about the Water Museum is that it is the only one of its kind. One is sufficient.

San Antonio's Water Museum is located appropriately at the Water Board offices. (Photograph courtesy of San Antonio's City Water Board.)

Show Biz

The stars really are big and bright deep in the heart of Texas. Some of the world's greatest performers claim the Lone Star State as their home. Monuments or museums have yet to be built to all of them. Van Cliburn, Scott Joplin, Farrah Fawcett, Janis Joplin, Mac Davis, and Willie Nelson lack their own monument but a few of the famous have been remembered in symbolic ways.

Bob Wills Monument

Highway 86
Turkey

"Bob Wills is still the king."
Waylon Jennings

 The list of songs written about Texas is about as long as the list of books written about the state. Texas A&M students thrill to the "Aggie War Hymn," U.T. alumni drawl out "The Eyes of Texas Are Upon You," and "The Yellow Rose of Texas" is the most popular girl in the Lone Star State, but the entire country sings along with "Deep within my heart lies a melody, a song of old San Antone. . . ." Waylon Jennings is absolutely right, "Bob Wills did more for Texas and our kind of music than any other musician."

The "King of Western Swing" and the originator of this unique swing style of music was christened James Robert Wills in 1906 by his fiddle-playing father. Jim Rob's first instrument was the mandolin, but when he switched to a fiddle, Jim Rob also switched to Bob.

Bob departed the prairies of Turkey, Texas, when he was in his early twenties. He hit it off on radio station KFJZ as a member of the Light Crust Doughboys. Fortunately, Bob was fired, but unfortunately it was due to excessive drinking and his inability to get along with the Doughboys' leader, W. Lee (Pappy) Pass-the-Biscuits O'Daniel.

After parting with the Doughboys, Bob took his banjo-playing brother, Johnnie Lee Wills, and vocalist Tommy Duncan and formed the legendary Texas Playboys. For 24 years Wills' "Ahhhh-ha" was as popular as "Remember the Alamo."

The Texas Playboys became an institution on station KVOO in Tulsa. This swing band with country overtones proved extremely popular with its miscellany of ballads, blues, and jazz. Horns and fiddles vied for front line positions, and the combination was a roaring success.

In 1940 the greatest country classic of them all rocked the charts and sold past the million mark. "San Antonio Rose" was just one of the 500 songs Bob Wills composed,

and his others sold in the millions as well, but none would surpass this all-time masterpiece.

Wills was always extremely successful, but bad health destroyed this great talent when "the King" was in his early fifties. After two heart attacks, Bob's band leading days were over even though he had a few limited appearances and recordings. In 1968 Bob Wills was admitted to the Country Music Hall of Fame as well as the National Cowboy Hall of Fame.

Strokes followed the heart attacks, and yet Bob fought back and appeared at functions in a wheelchair. Finally, a massive stroke resulted in a year-and-one-half coma until on May 13, 1975, the king was dead. Before Bob's final stroke, the hometown of this great bandleader commissioned Bill Willis of Granite, Oklahoma, to design and erect a monument to a king who ascended the throne of country-western music. Willis made a model of his idea and arranged to take it to Bob for his approval. Willis said, "I'll never forget the expression on Bob's face when he saw the model and his big grin of approval."

The finished product honoring Bob Wills is an eight-foot tall red granite base with etched figures of Bob with his fiddle and cigar, his war record, his movie career, and a list of his hits. Right up there with "San Antonio Rose" is "Spanish Two-Step," "Maiden's Prayer," "Faded Love," "Ida Red," and "Time Changes Everything." Atop the granite is a huge aluminum shaft with a double-sided fiddle. When Bob Wills Day is celebrated the last Saturday of April, the shaft rotates, and strains of all the famous Bob Wills songs waft through the streets of Turkey. For information on this celebration, contact B. D. Williams (806-423-1033).

Today, Bob Wills is a Texas hero. His music is as popular as ever, and Wills' influence is acknowledged by countless artists. There are serious contenders for Wills' Texas crown, but as Waylon Jennings so rightly put it, "When you cross that old Red River, boys, Bob Wills is still the king." Ahhhhh-ha!

Rangerette Showcase

Physical Education Complex
Kilgore College
Broadway at Ross
Kilgore 75662
214-984-8531
Hours: 10–11, 12–4:30 Tues.–Fri., 2–5 Sat.–Sun.
Admission free

 When the referee blows the whistle for halftime, football fans across the nation get set for a performance of marching bands, flags, anthems, fight songs, mascots, and the stars of the show—the drill team! As the pretty young girls march on the field smiling and twirling, the crowd breaks into resounding applause.

Fans sometimes don't realize the extent of work that goes into gaining the privilege of wearing those cute little costumes and dancing across the football field. All the spectators see are routines of precision and split-second timing done with grace and ease. Those long arduous hours of practice are forgotten.

Drill teams are a tradition with large high schools and colleges now. They are expected and planned as part of school programs, and specially trained drill instructors are hired. For the girls, becoming a drill team member is the equivalent of being chosen by a select sorority, and you have to be of high moral character and a fair student to remain in this elite corps. Infractions of strict conduct codes can result in instant dismissal and disgrace.

Mommies plan from the cradle for their daughters to achieve drill team membership. Gymnastics, baton twirling, dance lessons, the perfect smile—all are part of a girl's preparation for the drill team tryouts.

This truly American phenomenon all began in 1940 at Kilgore Junior College when a brilliant woman, Gussie Nell Davis, brought show business to the gridiron. She and her Kilgore Rangerettes set drill team standards that are now copied throughout the nation. Gussie was given the task of attracting girls to Kilgore Junior College, getting girls to participate in sports, and keeping fans' attention at halftime. This mastermind of show business exceeded beyond anyone's wildest expectations.

For ten years this "living art form" was the only college precision dance team in the United States. Since then, every school worth its football team has a drill team.

The Kilgore Rangerettes have performed at the Cotton Bowl since 1949, and after football season, they tour the world, dancing their way behind the Iron Curtain. The thousands of engagements include television, conventions, movies, parades, and variety club performances.

Every year 130 or more dedicated girls apply for the 31 available spots. An intensive ten-day training period is conducted in August before the final members are chosen. In the corps are 65 girls—5 officers, 48 girls on the line, and 12 substitutes. Rangerettes must always answer, "Yes, Ma'am," and "Thank you, Ma'am" to constructive criticism, but the most important rule is, "A Rangerette is always in class."

Transportation costs are so staggering nowadays that the Rangerettes travel in smaller groups of 12 to 16. For major performances, the 100 piece Ranger Band accompanies the group. After all, how can the girls dance their famous highkicks without music.

Gussie died in 1979, and the Rangerettes are now directed by the talented Deana Bolton. At the Rangerette Showcase, a lounge area pays tribute to its founder with many of Gussie's personal mementos and a large portrait of this fabulous lady donated by a former Rangerette.

Also at the Rangerette Showcase are displays of numerous costumes and props, plus hundreds of photographs and newspaper clippings. The girls have been photographed with celebrites all over the nation. A wall collage recognizes numerous college organizations that have played a part in Rangerette history, and tribute is paid to Kilgore citizens who have aided in their rise to prominence. The best exhibit, however, is the movie *An American Phenomenon*, depicting the rewards of being one of Red Grange's "Sweethearts of the Nation's Gridirons."

Few ex-drill team members go into show business as a career. Most prefer to accept the excellent training in self-discipline, good study habits, cooperation, and health as reward enough.

With their white Texas hats perched precariously to one side, white tasseled boots, red shirts, and short flared blue skirts, the Kilgore Rangerettes have danced their way into the hearts of all America. Even a state as big as Texas could not keep them all for its own.

Mary Martin as Peter Pan

Weatherford Public Library
Weatherford

The "boy who never grew old" was vibrantly brought to life by a marvelous lady who will never grow old in the eyes of her millions of fans. Mary Martin is the superstar of superstars. But, of all her fabulous hits on stage and screen, Mary Martin will probably be best remembered and loved as Peter Pan.

In Sir James Matthew Barrie's charming story, Peter Pan lures the three Darling children to Never-Never Land where they encounter Indians, mermaids, pirates, and Lost Boys. Favorite characters such as Nana, Captain Hook, and Tinker Bell share adventures with Wendy, Michael, and John Darling. Much of the popularity of the story is due to the play rather than the book, *Peter and Wendy*, because in the book Barrie intrudes too often with grown-up comments and is too prone to heavy-handed observations on life.

The star of the play was born in Weatherford, but was turned down for a part in a Billy Rose production for Fort Worth. Mary Martin still became beloved all over the world. Even the great Billy Rose could be wrong.

Mary Martin's first big hit was *Leave it to Me* in 1938 followed by *One Touch of Venus* in 1943. In 1946 there was *Lute Song*, and then the unforgettable *South Pacific*, which ran on Broadway for three years. *Peter Pan* made its debut in 1954, and was only surpassed by the super spectacular *Sound of Music* in 1961. Songs from these musicals were sung over and over again, and many are as popular now as the day they first enchanted audiences.

The famous hair that she has washed so many men out of is now a cap of silver gilt curls, and Miss Martin is constantly active with television talk shows and other appearances. When she came to Austin for the "Famous Women of Texas" exhibition, Mary Martin put on her white lynx coat which is part of the exhibit and sang her record-breaking hit "My Heart Belongs to Daddy."

Weatherford's favorite daughter is now honored with a delightful five-foot four-inch bronze statue of the superstar singing "I Gotta Crow" from *Peter Pan*. The sculptor, Ronald Thomason of Weatherford, even borrowed her Peter Pan costume from the Metropolitan Museum for authenticity. Thomason, named Texas Artist of the Year in 1974, was personally requested by Mary Martin to do the statue, and the delightful art piece was unveiled July 4, 1976.

The image of Mary Martin is now elevated on a concrete base as she stood on stage with feet spread apart and hands on hips, exuberantly crowing her song. Thomason only worked with the live Miss Martin on a few occasions, but when she saw the statue, she wrote:

"How was it possible for you to have Peter's feet flat on the ground and give the impression of flight—that strength that I always felt within all the years I played that Magic Spirit—it just—oh to find the word—inspired? James Barrie must have been sitting like the sprite he was, whispering in your ear with Glee!"

Miss Martin's love of acting was inherited by her famous son, Larry Hagman, better known as the conniving J. R. of television's *Dallas*. As for Mary Martin, she will always endure as that Magic Spirit to all of her worshipful fans.

Buddy Holly "Walk of Fame"

Lubbock Memorial Civic Center
Lubbock

"Buddy Holly had soul. He'll never die."
Janis Joplin

 During the late fifties a musical genius hit the recording studios. In just 18 months, Buddy Holly had 9 smash hits. Years ahead of his time, you wonder what Holly's talent would have created had he not died in 1959 at age 23 in an airplane crash.

Charles Hardin Holly was born in Lubbock in 1936 with a natural aptitude for music. At 12, with a $45 Fender guitar, this shy, skinny youth with crooked teeth and a reedy voice was developing his incredible style. By high school, Buddy and his friend, Bob Montgomery, had a regular spot on radio KDAV, singing and playing country music.

One of the big influences in Buddy's life arrived in Lubbock in 1956. Elvis Presley and Colonel Tom Parker met the young musician, and there was even some talk of Parker taking over Buddy's and Bob's careers. Nothing ever came of the idea, and Presley signed with RCA.

Decca picked up Holly as a solo, but no fame resulted from the recording sessions. With two losers "Blue Days, Black Nights" and "Modern Don Juan," Decca hated "That'll Be the Day," and it was back to Lubbock for Holly. Fortunately, Buddy took the song to a little recording studio in Clovis, New Mexico. Calling his band "The Crickets," the song was released on Coral records. From then on, Buddy Holly and his Rockabilly Crickets were nationally recognized as one of the hottest new talents in the musical world. "That'll be The Day" turned gold almost overnight.

Drummer Jerry Allison married a girl named Peggy Sue, and her name became immortalized as Holly's first solo hit. From coast to coast and overseas, The Crickets soared to superstardom. Some critics claim The Crickets turned out the "best of rock 'n roll ever made." Holly was the first artist to go beyond the classic 12-bar rock 'n roll and established the tradition of the guitar-based self-contained white rock group. Old hillbilly and black music combined with Elvis brought about the full development of rock.

In 1959 The Crickets made a grueling tour of the midwest. In order to take a little rest, Holly, Waylon Jennings, and Tommy Alsup decided to charter a plane from Mason City, Iowa, to Fargo, North Dakota. The Big Bopper, J. P. Richardson, asked Jennings for his seat, and Richie Valens, who had just had a big hit with "Donna," flipped a coin with Alsup for his seat. Valens won . . . or lost.

Americans forgot about The Crickets, but Paul McCartney remained a Crickets fan. The Beatles took their sound and entomological name from them, and McCartney bought the publishing rights to Holly's songs from Norman Petty in 1976.

There is hardly a group today that does not owe part of its style to Buddy Holly. In recognition of his great talent, Lubbock has built a memorial to Buddy Holly called the "Walk of Fame." This beautiful park will someday honor people from West Texas who have made significant contributions to the entertainment industry. The person honored will have their name and contribution placed on a bronze plaque embedded in the cement. Welcoming them is the heroic eight-foot, six-inch statue of Buddy Holly sculptured by Grant Speed of Lindon, Utah.

Hondo Crouch

Luckenbach

"Let's go to Luckenbach, Texas,
With Waylon and Willie, and the boys. . . ."
Waylon Jennings

 Waylon and Willie have long since departed Luckenbach for Las Vegas, Hollywood, and the White House, but Luckenbach "where everybody is somebody" still remains.

Everybody is not very many, and a census of three is not uncommon, for Luckenbach is basically just one incredibly run-down old barn with a bar that looks

The great "Imagineer," Hondo Crouch, still resides in stone in Luckenbach, where everybody is still somebody.

like "Junk City, U.S.A." However, Luckenbach's charisma did not begin when it was a trading post in 1849. The six resident German immigrants had built nine buildings and two outhouses that had absolutely no charm whatsoever.

In 1976 Luckenbach had even less buildings, but it was world famous because of one man, Hondo Crouch. "The Crown Prince of Luckenbach" was a rancher, philosopher, artist, poet, musicman, and Texas folk hero. Hondo called himself an "Imagineer," and was truly one of the funniest men in Texas.

For 15 years Hondo had a theater troupe that was sort of a Hill Country "Laugh-In." They played to packed houses even though Hondo intensely disliked memorizing lines and practicing.

The "Imagineer" dreamed up the innovative Luckenbach World Fair, and in 1976 staged the Non-Buy-Centennial as a protest against the commercialism of the nation's two-hundredth birthday. More than 50,000 people attended the production. Though invited, the Prince of Wales and Elizabeth Taylor declined to come and share armadillo chili on the halfshell.

Hondo died in 1976, and Nashville lowered its flags. *Time* listed his passing in "Milestones," and his death pre-empted a scheduled appearance on the *Tonight* show. Hondo's oldest child called him a gentle man, a poet, "a talking treasure" with genuine love expressed in unexpected ways.

"The Mayor of Luckenbach" was eulogized by the famous. Cactus Pryor stated, "He was a character because he chose to be a character, because people like character and Hondo liked people. He was a significant human being who saw life quite clearly through those sparkling Texas eyes and decided it needed to be made happier for people."

Representative J. J. Pickle wrote, "Long after the affairs of state have been settled, Hondo's name will be remembered above the legislators and judges...because he was just plain folks."

"You should have seen Hondo
when he did 'Luckenbach Moon.'
I was lucky.
I did."

Willie Nelson

"He didn't care who came to pick
Or set upon his couch
'Cause everybody's somebody
In the heart of Hondo Crouch."

Rick Beresford

A small bust of this poet, humorist, philosopher, and gentle man stands in the town Hondo made so famous. The people still come to pay homage, and Luckenbach is still a mecca for blossoming musicians. Even though its magical mayor is gone, the town of Luckenbach lives on.

The British Connection

Even though a Texan might speak English in England an Englishman would have a hard time understanding a Texas drawl. But, if you want to make a visitor from Merrie England feel right at home in Texas, take him to the Globe Theater in Odessa and the Browning Museum in Waco. And even an Irishman could establish contact with the "old sod" up in Shamrock and kiss a sliver of the Blarney Stone. With the "gift of gab" he would wax eloquent over these Texas tributes to its British heritage.

Globe Theater of the Great Southwest

2308 Shakespeare Road
Odessa 79761

"All the world's a stage,
And the men and women merely players...."
William Shakespeare

The actor who spoke those lines in the sixteenth century had no idea they would endure more than 400 years and the author would be acclaimed as the greatest playwright that ever lived. As most actors, he was probably wishing he had a larger role and hoped the "groundlings," who only paid a penny for the play, would not throw rotten vegetables at him for his performance in this comedy.

Being an actor was hazardous work on the Elizabethan stage. Not only were the groundlings a rag-tag rabble, but

The Bard of Avon would feel right at home in Odessa's replica of the Globe Theater. (Photograph courtesy of Globe of the Great Southwest.)

the spectators in the prized three-tiered gallery seats also came well armed with ammunition for actors who did not suit their tastes. Some of the audience even sat *on the stage* and offered their "comments." The pressures to put on an academy award winning performance in every play must have been intense, especially in Elizabethan times.

As women were barred from the stage, men had to play all feminine roles. Also, there were no breaks in the play such as acts or intermissions. These conveniences were added later, long after Shakespeare's time (probably to make the action easier for students to understand). When the trumpeter blew his three blasts to announce the opening of the play, the performance did not stop until the final lines.

Costumes were very elaborate, and color was important to express the moods of the characters. However, Caesar died not in a toga, but in the Renaissance clothes of the day. Although extremely elaborate, no costumes had any relation to the actual time period of the historical setting.

Props were very realistic, and Hamlet had to be very careful in his death scene not to actually kill actor Claudius. During a performance of a play entitled *All is True*, the Globe burned from cannon wadding that set fire to the roof. (The Globe was quickly rebuilt.)

In Odessa, many of the original features of the Globe have been preserved. The idea behind the Globe of the Southwest began more than 25 years ago when a student brought a model of the original Globe to his English class. The student commented to his teacher, Mrs. Marjorie Morris, that it would be exciting to have a real Globe in Odessa. That casual remark fired the imagination of this dedicated teacher, and she set to work with a vengeance to make the Globe a reality.

After copious research and personally soliciting donations and grants, Mrs. Morris's dream came true, and the flag flew from the turret announcing, "The play's the thing!" (*Hamlet*, II, ii, 633). The new Globe seats 318 (groundlings are no longer allowed). Because of the unique octagonal shape and the primary building materials of wood and plaster, the acoustics are absolutely perfect.

Some things are different from the Renaissance theater. The 1,800-square-foot stage is thrust into the audience to create an intimate actor-audience relationship as it was in Shakespeare's day, but it is no longer on the trestles that

made possible another favorite Elizabethan sport—bear baiting. Also, the roof is permanent now, whereas the pit for the groundlings in the original Globe was open to the elements.

A country-western "Opree," as well as many other outstanding dramas, is performed in the Globe. If William could get used to the sight of his beloved theater way out in West Texas, he might still be a little surprised to hear the "Cottoneyed Joe" coming from within its walls. Still, he would probably be delighted with this tribute on the Odessa College Campus.

Armstrong Browning Library

Baylor University
Box 6336
Waco 76706
Hours: 9–12 2–4 Mon.–Fri., 9–12 Sat.

 The nineteenth century produced some of the finest poets in British literature, including Coleridge, Wordsworth, Bryon, Keats, and Shelley. Among these greats were Robert and Elizabeth Browning whose love story has endured through the ages.

Remember the story of the Pied Piper of Hamlin who lured the rats from the infested town? When the ungrateful citizens refused to pay up, the piper then enticed the children to follow his melodies into a mountain. This delightful Browning poem came to life in 1924 on the campus of Baylor University. A Baylor music student dressed in a red and yellow costume and playing a flute strutted gaily through the Quadrangle while 400 children in rat costumes emerged from behind bushes, trees, and buildings to follow the piper around the corner of Burleson Hall. As the piper retraced her steps, the "rats" had become children and disappeared a second time (but not into a mountain).

The cause of this unique pageant was a brilliant teacher named A. J. Armstrong. Dr. Armstrong had the rare gift of teaching, and he brought to his students his love and admiration for Robert and Elizabeth Browning.

Armstrong arrived in Waco in 1912 as chairman of Baylor's English department. This educator considered himself nothing but a teacher. In 1948 Dr. Armstrong told a *Time* reporter, "If I had ten migrations of the soul, I'd want to be nothing more than a teacher." Affectionately known as "Dr. A.," he pinned notes to his lapel, gave grades of "minus 50," dealt out horrendous assignments, and never listened to class bells but his classrooms burst at the seams with eager students dying to be called "Daughter" or "Kid" by Dr. A.

Dr. A's version of Browning's "Ah, but a man's reach should exceed his grasp, or what's a heaven for?" was "Don't be colorless; be somebody! If you've done the best you can and you're not J. Pierpont Morgan, the Virgin Mary, or the Guardian Angel, don't worry!" Well, Dr. A certainly practiced what he preached, and this master teacher was far from colorless. His admiration for the Brownings resulted in one of the most beautiful tributes to poetic

The Pied Piper lures children into the mountain in one of the Browning Library's beautiful stained glass windows.

In the Elizabeth Barrett Browning Salon the walls are painted twice to achieve the precise shade of green that was her favorite color. Near the center of the room is the escretoire on which Elizabeth penned, "How do I love thee? Let me count the ways." Her figure appears in each window, always dressed in green.

The Foyer of Meditation holds eight 17-foot levanto marble columns quarried in Italy and shipped intact to Waco. A small alcove at the end of the Foyer houses Harriet Hosmer's cast of the "Clasped Hands" of the two poets. Elizabeth was in her late thirties when she eloped with Robert, and they were married only 14 years before her death. They often sat holding hands on the porch of their Florence home, Casa Guidi.

Dr. Armstrong remarked often, "If we can create a place where young people can meditate on great thoughts and by that means give the world another Dante, another Shakespeare, another Browning, we shall count the cost a bargain." Let us hope that great thoughts will also give the world another Dr. A.

Blarney Stone

City Park
Shamrock

Once upon a time, God looked down from heaven and decided the earth was too drab and cheerless; it needed more beauty and gaiety and laughter, so He created an isle and painted the trees the green of an emerald and the grass the green of an apple and the hills the green of precious jade. The result of His handiwork was the Emerald Isle of Ireland.

It is a shame the Great Creator did not chose the site for all of that beauty in the high plains of the Texas Panhandle. He could have done wonders for the scenery there. At the turn of the century a homesick Irishman named George Nickel did the best he could with the barren wastes and named his post office Shamrock for the luckiest green thing ever found on the face of the earth. Nickel's luck was bad, however, and the mail was delivered only a few times before he was burned out. The town was nearly called Exum (ugh!) or Percell 13 years later, but the new postmistress insisted the original name remain.

In 1938 a Shamrock bandmaster, Glenn Truax, envisioned the town capitalizing on its Irish name, and with the help of the Booster Club, the first St. Patrick's Day Festival was reeled off with a few thousand people and 12 bands. By the thirty-sixth St. Patrick's Day, 15,000 visitors were on hand to honor "the wearing of the green."

On the Saturday closest to March 17, the entire town of Shamrock turns into leprechauns and claims to hold the largest Irish celebration outside of Ireland. Even the newspaper turns green for the occasion. Miss Irish Rose is chosen from lovely colleens, the Texas governor makes a speech, a fiddler's contest is held, and banquets, dances, and a parade add to the festivities.

genius in the world. The Armstrong Browning Library was completed in 1951 at a cost of more than $2 million.

Dr. A had presented his Browning collection to Baylor in 1918. Maintained by the Carroll Library, by 1924 it was distinguished as the world's largest on the two poets. Armstrong financed his acquisitions with tours of the world and also by booking such personalities as Caruso and Sandburg to appear at Waco Hall.

Armstrong began to dream of a structure as inspiring and magnificent as the great buildings of Europe for his Browning memorabilia. Pippa's statue on the front lawn welcomes visitors to Armstrong's dream come true—the Armstrong Browning Library.

The imposing portrait dominating the entrance hall of Robert Browning was painted by the Brownings' only son, Pen. Robert and Elizabeth lived a romantic love story. The famous lovers were forced to elope to escape Elizabeth's domineering father, and lived in Florence, Italy. Elizabeth died there, but Robert is buried in Westminster Abbey. Dr. Armstrong visited Pen in Italy, and after Pen's death, the expert located more Browning pieces for the museum.

The arrival of the library's first stained glass window depicting Robert Browning's "The Pied Piper of Hamlin," was the occasion for Dr. A's 400 "rats." Since this first stained glass window, 50 more have joined it, depicting the Brownings' works. Only two windows in the Library remain to be created in stained glass.

For the student of the Brownings' works, the Library contains more than 2,000 original letters and manuscripts written by the famous poets. First edition volumes, the Brownings' personal books, and many secondary materials make this a researcher's paradise. The more romantic visitor can admire the gold locket Robert gave his wife on their first anniversary, or a lock of Robert's hair.

Not only does Shamrock remember the Emerald Isle on St. Patrick's Day, but the city carries an important piece of the homeland all through the year.

You no longer have to go to Blarney Castle in Ireland, climb 120 steps to the battlements, empty your pockets, lie flat on your back, hang onto two iron bars and have your ankles held by strong arms so you can lean backwards to kiss the Blarney Stone. Since 1959 you can just go to the Elmore Park in Shamrock, casually lean over a concrete cylinder, and press your lips to a sliver of the famous symbol embedded there. From County Cork to County Wheeler, the Blarney Stone has come to Texas.

According to the legend, the Blarney Stone was brought to Ireland during the Crusades in 1446. This 9-inch-deep, 4-foot 1-inch-long by 1-foot-1-inch-wide block of limestone was the rock Jacob used as a pillow when the vision of the golden ladder appeared to him.

To kiss the stone will bring you luck as Francis Mahoney so aptly put it in 1835:

> "There is a stone that whoever kisses,
> Oh! he never misses to grow eloquent,
> 'Tis he may clamber into a lady's chamber,
> Or become a member of Parliament."

Well, faith and begorra, it 'tis no blarney you will find a pot of gold at the end of Shamrock's rainbow whether it's St. Patrick's day or not.

Beloved Critters

You always expect a Texan to love his horse and dog, but how about an alligator and a horned toad? One thing about the Lone Star State, it loves its critters!

Ottie

Lufkin

Everyone knows about the Lone Ranger's horse, Silver, Tom Mix's Tony, Roy's Trigger, and Dales' Buttercup. But, one enduring old mare never made the big time.

Ottie never pulled down the wall of a jail to save her human friend from an unjust imprisonment, nor did Ottie ever have to run for aid for a wounded cowboy star. Ottie did not even do tricks for applause. All this wonderful horse did was work.

The owner of this marvelous mare was C. N. Humason, one of Lufkin's early fire chiefs, mayor, churchmen, and ice cream store owner. This 1896 version of the Good Humor Man hitched his Ottie to the first ice cream wagon in Lufkin, and was eagerly welcomed everywhere he went with his delicious refreshments. His horse, Ottie, also pulled the hearse to the cemetery and led the funeral procession.

Ottie also tried to be first to arrive at hundreds of fire alarms. Humason said of his devoted horse, "She went through twelve buggies, fourteen sets of harnesses, two hundred shoes, and one ten-cent buggy whip."

When Ottie went to the Great Livery Stable in the Sky in 1918, she was 44 years old. During her last six months, Ottie was tenderly fed and watered. Finally, the family doctor was called to give her chloroform so that she might pass on in a peaceful sleep.

Ottie was gently wrapped in a heavy duck tarpaulin and laid to rest near the Glendale Cemetery where she had gone so often carrying others to their final rest. No marker was erected on Ottie's grave, so Humason had a small plaque placed in the family plot bearing the inscription:

Ottie

Mar. 22, 1874
Mar. 24, 1918
Aged 44 Years
A faithful old mare

Big Al

Lone Star Steel Corporation
Lone Star

Everyone gets misty-eyed over Smokey Bear, Bambi, Old Yeller, Black Beauty, and other sentimental stories of faithful and beloved animals. But, in Lone Star, it was indeed a sad day when Big Al no longer patrolled the swamps he had inhabited for so many years. Usually, 'gators just end up as handbags, belts, and shoes, but not Big Al. This 12-foot alligator rated a special funeral and tombstone.

About all there is in Lone Star is the huge Lone Star Steel Company. This industrial giant is proud of the fact that the ecology of the area has not been destroyed by the plant's heavy production, so when the "company pet" died, Lone Star honored his memory with an appropriate send-off.

Big Al had patrolled the waters around the steel mill for at least 20 years, but his favorite haunt was west of the mill and below the dam. Photographers tried in vain to capture Big Al on film, but the camera-shy 'gator never even gave them a crocodile smile.

Down through the years Al's size was estimated between 10 and 15 feet. Finally, a few years before the 'gator's death, a Lone Star photographer captured the big beast slithering into the water, and his extraordinary 12-foot length was verified.

Big Al was found dead from natural causes in the channel he loved so well in 1978. Al's age was estimated as between 75 and 100, which is not unusual for alligators. Lone Star Steel decided to hold reptilian rites for their mascot as befitting his faithful service in the company's waters.

The funeral was held at 1 P.M., April 28, which did not leave time for Big Al's relatives to crawl up from Louisiana for the services. L. D. (Red) Webster, vice-president of advertising, opened the rites with, "Friends, we meet to euogize the long life of a giant alligator, whose presence for many years has supplied us with countless stories, and whose passing brings a sense of regret to all who so frequently made him the subject of tall tales based on fact as well as fiction."

Then, the eulogy was delivered by the Reverend Don Carson, pastor of the Lone Star Church of Christ with: "We are not here simply to bury an alligator, for that would be ludicrous. . . . Man has a responsibility to wildlife, for we should respect what God has created. Sometimes we haven't kept up our end of the deal."

A special honor guard then lowered the 12-foot casket into a hole twice the size of usual graves as taps sadly echoed over the East Texas hills. Big Al was toasted at his wake with Gatorade, and then the employees went back to work.

The huge 'gator is gone, but he will never be forgotten. A bronze alligator rests on his grave along with a plaque describing Al's contribution to Lone Star Steel: " . . . preservation of an atmosphere in the mill area that will continue to promote the growth of our abundant wildlife, flora and fauna, fishes, and fowl."

At the unveiling of the monument in 1979, two Big Al $1,000 student scholarships were awarded to outstanding offspring of Lone Star employees, and "Son of Al," a mere 7-foot 150-pound 'gator donated by the Tyler Zoo was set loose. Rev. Don Carson was on hand to christen "Sonny" with water from the plant lake with the admonishment, "Mind your manners as did Big Al, and always keep a great distance between thee and me."

Sonny now patrols the Lone Star channels, pausing to grab a snack from the abundant food supply. Happy and content, Sonny may just outgrow and outlive his famous predecessor.

Buried with full military honors, Reveille III joins I and II at Kyle Field. (Picture courtesy of The Eagle—Bryan and College Station, Texas—*Photographed by Peter Leabo.)*

Reveille I, II, III

Kyle Field
College Station

Aggie jokes are a Texas tradition, but it is no joke that Texas A&M has more school spirit than any other Texas college or university. Nor is there any question they have one of the finest marching bands, not only in Texas, but the United States. But the pride and joy of the football team and the school is their mascot, Reveille.

Reveille I was just a mutt that adopted A&M. The dog's antics and sheer delight in performing with the band at halftime started a cherished piece of Aggie showmanship. When Reveille I went to run with former Aggie bands in Aggieland heaven, there had to be another Reveille. Reveille II was a pure bred collie as was Reveille III and now Reveille IV.

When Reveille III joined I and II, the Aggies decided to have a funeral for its beloved mascot of nine years. This symbol of the Twelfth Man tradition was laid to rest at the north entrance to Kyle Field following a brief, moving ceremony. Histories of Reveille I, II, and III were read to the huge crowd by Company E-2 commander Mike Clark. The unit is responsible for the care of the Aggie mascot. A eulogy to Reveille III was given by Corps Chaplain Mike Marchand.

Reveille IV sat restlessly with her master, Bob Vanderberry, during the ceremony. As the Singing Cadets sang "Auld Lang Syne," the maroon and white draped casket was carried slowly to a place beside those of the previous two mascots. Reveille III now rests in the hallowed spot facing the scoreboard of Kyle Stadium, so all former mascots can see when the Aggies are scoring, and their spirit become a part of each victory.

It sort of makes you wonder what kind of send-off is in store for Bevo and Shasta (the University of Texas and University of Houston mascots, respectively).

Old Rip (1897–1929)

Eastland County Courthouse
Eastland

On the top ten list of "Amazing Things in Texas," Old Rip has to get star billing. This incredible horned toad's story has far more skeptics than true believers. Even though the little fellow made the headlines in Ripley's "Believe It or Not," he was named for another Rip, the one who slept 120 years.

Old Rip did not sleep 120 years, but for a lizard that rarely grows more than 4 ½ inches long, 31 years is a real long nap. Old Rip's broad, flat, spiny skin made him look somewhat like a toad, but it's those sharp-looking spines all over his body that keep tender-mouthed predators from completely eradicating horned toads.

When disturbed, these prehistoric looking beasts' blood pressure forces blood to the cavities in its scabby head, which spurts out the corners of its eyes. Most horned toads are senior citizens at six, but Old Rip defied all the horned toad statistics in the world.

One bright sunny day in 1897 the cornerstone for the new Eastland County Courthouse was being dedicated. The Justice of the Peace, Ernest Wood, saw his son playing with a horned toad, and suggested the harmless little reptile be placed with the Bible and other traditional cornerstone paraphernalia.

Being buried alive is certainly not a pleasant way to end one's life in this world, and Old Rip decided he wasn't going to give in to a town's whims. For years, this tiny creature literally lay in limbo until a new courthouse was needed. In 1928 a crowd of people showed up at the demolition ceremony to see what happened to "Old Rip." Judge Ed Pritchard removed the Bible, and underneath it sat "Old Rip." The judge gave the little lizard a shake, and Old Rip snapped to life.

Naturally, after 31 years of entombment, a resurrection of this sort made Old Rip a celebrity. He toured the country and even played the White House for President Coolidge. Either the stress of fame or just plain old age was too much for Old Rip. He died of pneumonia after a short year of glory, but Eastland at least gave him a really fancy coffin and tombstone. Rip is still at the courthouse, but this time he is stuffed and encased in glass in his plush velvet-lined box. Who knows, maybe when Eastland tears down this courthouse. . . .

The Lone Prairie

The coyotes still howl, and the wind still blows free on the vast grasslands of Texas. Barbed wire, paved roads, and power and telephone lines have brought civilization, but they have not stopped the eternal unrelenting wind. In a way, it was the wind that tamed the prairie and made the ranchers' and sodbusters' lives bearable on the High Plains.

World's Tallest Windmill

Littlefield

Butler, Star, Halladay, Eclipse, Aermotor, Samson . . . these heroes of West Texas are almost dead now, and few people recognize their names, but no invention contributed more to settling Texas than the windmill. The lone prairies of West Texas would have stayed lonesome a lot longer if Daniel Halladay had not come up with his 1854 invention of a self-regulating windmill. Paddle-shaped blades pivoted, or feathered, as the wind increased, pumping the precious water to the surface. By the 1870s, these manmade marvels were hailed as a "national blessing," and railroads installed them at 30-mile intervals to water down the iron horses.

Steel windmills fanned the breeze in the 1880s, but there were a lot of home-made varieties turning those pumps as well. In a land without landmarks, the windmills became signposts for cowboys and travelers. When electricity wiped out these stalwart heroes of the plains, most were dismantled or left to rot.

The world's tallest windmill is a replica of the 132-foot monster on the Yellowhouse Division of the XIT Ranch. The original was toppled by winds in 1926, and this replica was erected in 1969. This towering structure provided water for thousands of cattle, and it had to be tall to reach the winds of the level plains. Wind activated the fan atop the tower, which in turn cranked a pump lifting water out of the ground.

Out on the plains around Spearman, J. B. Buchanan has a wonderful antique collection of these old workhorses, and the Panhandle Plains Museum in Canyon has a great display on windmills. Also, an experimental wind energy station outside of Amarillo is now supplying electricity, the force that had put an end to the windmill.

Ranching Heritage Center

The Museum of Texas Tech University
Fourth Street and Indiana Avenue
Lubbock 79409
806-742-2442
Hours: 8:30–4:30 Mon.–Fri.
Admission

Out in West Texas early settlers on the great plains had to have a lot of stamina to put up with the weather, the Indians, and just downright loneliness. The only building material available for shelter was the land itself. A sod house might be lovely in the spring with its roof a riot of colorful prairie flowers, but a heavy rain could easily cave in that same roof. Also, all the rodents and insects that made the grass their home never left just because it became the pioneer family's house.

At the Ranching Heritage Center you can trace the evolution of ranch homes from this primitive sod beginning to the elegant Victorian mansion. This excellent museum of more than 20 historic ranching structures is a unique tribute to the endurance of early pioneers.

Each building is meticulously restored, even down to the furniture and the outhouse in the rear. Berms visually block modern surroundings from the historically landscaped settings, and the "greenhorn" can see what the home on the range really looked like. The trail over these 12 acres takes you through 100 years of Texas ranching history.

Not only are authentic homes nestled here among the berms, but the barns, bunkhouses, cabins, windmills, and ranching tools are displayed just as they appeared so long ago. No ranch was complete without a blacksmith, and here is one all ready to shoe the horses before the roundup. Even the famous Matador Ranch's office is intact. Built with foreign capital, this huge empire encompassed 400,000 acres.

Special events are staged and re-enacted at the Ranching Heritage Center. You can watch "pioneers" make lye soap, or a smitty shoe horses. You can taste sourdough bread as it comes from the oven, and see butter form as a churn beats it into shape. The art of shearing a sheep is demonstrated, and the wool is spun into thread, and then woven into fabric. Beautiful hand-made quilts in all of the old-time designs are available for purchase.

Cogdell's General Store has all sorts of wares reminiscent of pioneer life such as branding irons, lye soap, and even those cardboard fans that were early-day airconditioning.

This museum is more than just a preserve of old buildings, it also records and interprets the social and business culture of the ranching industry from its Spanish origin in Old Mexico to its spread northward throughout Texas and all of America's rangelands.

At the Ranching Heritage Center you can see just how lonesome the prairie was for Texas pioneers. (Photograph courtesy of Texas Tech University Museum.)

Welcome to the Jet Age

Once upon a time the symbol of speed, wealth, and power in the United States was the train. Americans loved trains, and great fortunes were amassed by railroad tycoons. Instead of the "company jet," the Vanderbilts, Morgans, and Fisks had opulent railroad cars or even entire trains, in which to conduct their affairs. A presidential train rather than Air Force One took the nation's leader to his destination.

Throughout the country, a train's route either made a town or destroyed it, for the life-blood of the nation ran on its rails. With the demise of the passenger train, a way of life came to an end. Once-magnificent hotels near the station become deserted wrecks as did train stations that were once a community's pride and joy. Buildings stand desolate and rotten, magnificent engines rust away in forgotten obsolescence, and cars stand abandoned by the rails they once rode. As the country's railway system fades into oblivion, one wonders what the future holds in store for the mighty jets, complex airports, and Interstate highways.

Atalanta Railroad Car

Austin Street
Jefferson 75657
214-665-2513
Hours: 9–5
Admission.

A New York editorial described Jay Gould, Daniel Drew, and Jim Fisk as "foul hyenas who when their prey was full rotten . . . came to sink their jaws into the carrion." Yet, Texas owes one of those foul hyenas a great debt, for because of Jay Gould, one of the most beautiful little towns in the United States is preserved in Jefferson, Texas.

The story is famous of how Gould predicted the "end of Jefferson" in the register of the Excelsior House for the town's refusal to *give* him the land to bring the railroad to Jefferson. (See *A Guide to Historic Texas Inns and Hotels* Lone Star Books, Houston, Texas.) Jefferson's booming steamship trade gave the town the confidence to resist the tycoon's demands. When the Great Raft on the Red River was destroyed (see *Traveling Texas Borders* Lone Star Books, Houston, Texas) and the paddlewheelers became obsolete, one of the largest cities in Texas became one of the deadest cities in Texas. Fortunately for tourists, Jefferson became a sleepy hamlet caught in a time warp.

The foul hyena who brought Jefferson to its knees was a frail consumptive millionaire with the look of a frustrated poet. But, there was no poetry in Jay Gould's soul, only greed. Gould, Fisk, and Drew had decided to defeat a formidable opponent, Commodore Vanderbilt. They chose the Erie Railroad as their battleground. Through Boss Tweed, Gould and his conniving partners bribed legislators to the tune of $1 million. Their investment resulted in Vanderbilt's losing the "Erie War." But the war of the tycoons was not over. Gould then replaced old Dan Drew as president of the Erie Railroad and made Fisk vice-president.

As a result of the "Erie War," Gould emerged as a master manipulator of railroads. The Erie itself was so crippled, it did not pay a penny of dividends for 69 years on common stock.

Gould's next venture was an attempt to corner the gold market. His partner in crime was none other than Corbin, President Grant's brother-in-law. Grant finally got wise and stopped Gould, but not before he had already sold his gold shares and had created a Wall Street disaster. The financial genius was 33 years old and racked by tuberculosis.

After the Crash of 1873, the most brilliant part of Gould's career began with his acquisition of the Union Pacific, Kansas Pacific, Denver Pacific, Missouri Pacific, and Central Pacific Railroads. But, trains were not Gould's only possessions; he also owned Western Union and the *New York World*.

Gould died in 1892 at age 56. His deliberate mismanagement of whatever he touched resulted in a $77 million fortune with his estate worth twice that amount. Historian Stewart H. Holbrooks says, "Gould's drive came from the same source that drove Genghis Khan and Napoleon Bonaparte."

For the moguls of the post-Civil War period, in addition to palatial mansions and lavish parties, certain appurtenances were obligatory. Yachts were very popular, but a private railroad car was a necessity. Gould owned several opulent private cars, and his finest was the 250-foot, $50,000 Atalanta, named for the goddess of speed.

Somehow, the Atalanta was abandoned in Texas, and the members of the Jesse Allen Wise Garden Club of Jefferson salvaged the old wreck that has become one of Jefferson's favorite tourist attractions. Beautifully refurbished, this "palace on wheels" contains a sterling silver washbasin, exquisite lace curtains, and pictures of Mrs. Gould and the Gould mansion in Tarrytown, New York.

In a truly ironic touch, this symbol of Jay Gould's wealth is preserved by the town he tried to destroy.

Age of Steam Railroad Museum

Fair Park
Washington and Parry
Dallas
214-361-6936
Hours: 11–5 Sunday only
Admission

During the 1960s a group of locomotive enthusiasts in the Dallas area became concerned over the rapidly disappearing railroad of the preceding decades. After much planning, the Southwest Railroad Historical Society was formed to preserve the rail history of Dallas. With cooperation from the State Fair of Texas, the railroad industry, and many other concerned parties, the Society established the nostalgic Age of Steam Railroad Museum.

You begin your trip through the Golden Era of Railroads by boarding the rear platform of the "Texland," a private

Steam no longer billows from the old engines, but you can still climb aboard on the "Big Boy."

care built in 1900. The "Glengyle" was constructed in 1911 as an experiment in bedroom cars.

In an age of three-hour coast-to-coast flights, it is difficult to think in terms of days spent on a train for the same distance. At the peak of the Pullman company's operation, it had 5,000 cars like the "Goliad," a 1926 twelve-section open sleeper with upper and lower berths that contained a drawing room and powder rooms for both "He" and "She."

Also on display are three steam locomotives, a "Big Boy," a Frisco 4501, and a Russian Decapod. The Russian engine was one of only 25 built in the 1940–41 period. All except eight museum pieces have been put to the torch.

The *pièce de résistance* is a Dallas railroad station built in 1903 saved from the wrecking crew. A sign advises passengers that Dallas' altitude is 459 feet, and the population is 42,638. A hand-operated trolley car stands near a mailbag hanger used in the days trains carried the mail or you bought an expensive air mail stamp.

If you would like to contribute your time to this non profit organization, the address is 7226 Wentwood Drive, Dallas, 75225. Every effort is greatly appreciated.

The Center for Transportation and Commerce

The Strand at Twenty-fifth Street
Galveston 77550
409-765-5700
Hours: 10–6
Admission

Don't let that long dull title turn you away, this is a wonderful museum in spite of its unexciting name. Whistles toot, bells clang, smoke billows from engines, and you "All Aboard" for the days when the country's economy revolved around the railroad.

Galveston's Victorian depot of 1875 has been marvelously restored to house memorabilia from the Steam Age. As you enter the station yard, an old Baldwin Prairie 2-6-2 locomotive looks just like it did when it was new in 1925. It was called the Wobbly-Bobbly-Turnover & Stop instead of the Waco, Beaumont, Trinity, & Sabine because it derailed so often. When the old relic was located for the museum, a tree was growing through the cab.

An 1885 fire engine stands ready to race to a local fire, and a caliope awaits magic fingers to make the steam whistles toot a song. You can explore 35 railway cars on the Center's 4 tracks, including every type of carrier from 1890 to 1930. Here are rare freight cars and opulent private cars such as the "Anacapa" that hosted President Eisenhower and his opponent, Adlai Stevenson.

Inside the depot's waiting room restored to its art deco ambiance is a really unique exhibit. Thirty-nine life-sized travelers are poised in a moment from 1932. Using a 1932 Sears Catalog, artists Elliot and Ivan Schwartz dressed and posed live models for their unique art form. Models were wrapped in wet plaster, and the results are startlingly beautiful and impressive. Frozen in time, some will even let you

Frozen in time, an old gentleman of 1932 waits for the train to pull into Galveston Station. (Photograph courtesy of The Center for Transportation and Commerce.)

listen to their conversations as they talk about where they are going and other delightful details of their lives.

The history of Galveston is told in light and sound from its discovery in 1528 by Cabeza de Vaca to the terrible disaster of 1900. The dioramas and "pop-up" figures tell the Galveston story in a delightful way.

This grand museum is the culmination of a dream for Galveston by Mrs. Mary Moody Norther, director of the Moody Foundation. More than $4 million was committed to the accummulation of the steam age mammoths. A fifth track stands empty awaiting the Old Interurban which provided the rail transportation between Galveston and Houston.

Today, when the only railroads that operate in the black are those on the Monopoly board, it is wonderful that their history is being preserved, and Texas is grateful to the Moody Foundation for its gift.

Shrimp Boat Monument

Brazosport Harbor Channel on Texas 288
Brazosport

Her name is *Mystery*—such a glamorous name for such an unglamorous lady. Her origin was only a cypress swamp, and her maker a bayou boat builder named S. Klonaris.

This was a gal built for strength, reliability, and hard work, and she fulfilled her role to perfection for she went farther out into the Gulf, fished deeper waters, and caught bigger shrimp than any other shrimpers around. The new lady in town was then "top of the line."

Delivered to the Trawling Company of Berwick, Louisiana, in 1940, the boat's first owner named her *Mystery*, because it was a mystery how they were going to pay for her.

Mystery pushed her way through the Gulf waters bringing home about 3.5 million pounds of shrimp. The queen of the line was the first shrimper to carry a radio telephone, and she was the envy of the Gulf Coast. *Mystery* was unable to retain her royal title, however, for boats of steel with the modern innovations of freezers and refrigeration were making their appearance. Finally, tired and battered with all salvageable fixtures removed, *Mystery* was left to rot at the Brazosport dock.

When the Brazosport Chamber of Commerce decided to erect a monument to the area's shrimping industry, *Mystery* became a queen again. Moving day was momentous. Her masts had to go because of utility lines, and the trailer's centerbar sagged to about a half inch off the dock's surface, and it took hours to move a scant half mile, but she made it. Now, completely restored on dry land, *Mystery* was then "dedicated to the men and boats who pioneered the shrimping industry and made Brazosport its capital." A Coast Guard official closed his records on *Mystery* with the word "Dismantled."

Elissa, "The Tall Ship for Texas"

Galveston Historical Foundation, Inc.
P.O. Drawer 539
Pier 22
Galveston 77553
409-763-1877
Hours: 10–6, closed Tues.
Admission

This beautiful lady with the beautiful name was christened in 1877 in Aberdeen, Scotland. Constructed by the master shipwrights, Alexander Hall and Son, *Elissa* was a credit to her builders. Even though the iron barque's magnificent sails had long since been replaced by engines, a deckhouse, and bridge, *Elissa* was still very much afloat over 100 years later.

Elissa was a miracle of rediscovery, and salvaged from the verge of total destruction in a Greek scrapyard. Purchased for $39,000, more than 13 months were spent making her seaworthy for tow. When *Elissa* reached her permanent home in July of 1979, the project was financially prostrate.

While under repair in Greece, *Elissa* was placed on the National Register of Historic Places, the first object ever to be honored while outside the limits of the United States. A grant from the National Trust ensured her trip to Galveston.

So much had to be done, and the story of the restoration of *Elissa* is a volume of details, problems, and success. The National Maritime Historical Society dedicated an entire issue of *Sea History* (Fall 1979) just to the story of *Elissa* from conception to finish.

Many more grants came forward to finance the great lady's new look. The Galveston Historical Foundation's director, Peter Brink, laid down the first rule of fund raising,

"The sailing ship is perhaps the most beautiful thing men have ever built. . . ."

"If they gave before, ask for more." The Moody Foundation came through again for *Elissa*. Expert workmen arrived from all parts of the country, and a 70-member volunteer crew supplemented the regular crew. *Elissa's* 430 tons made her a manageable project, and she is absolutely typical of the old workhorse sailing vessels of the nineteenth century.

Teak stairs, woodburning stove, 26,000 feet of new rigging, masthead, gleaming decks, fiber rope, and stark white sails from Scotland complete one of the world's best maritime restorations.

Today, when you see the beautiful lady with her sails unfurled riding the seas again, she looks as lovely as she did when she left Alexander Hall and Son so many years ago. As Walter Rybka, restoration director, said, "The *Elissa* restoration is an opportunity for Texans to share in preserving America's maritime heritage. . . . The sailing ship is perhaps the most beautiful thing men have ever built with their hands, a work of art as well as a tool."

The Pate Museum of Transportation

US Highway 377 (Between Fort Worth and Cresson)
Cresson
817-332-1161
Hours: 9–5, closed Monday
Admission free

The Pate Museum of Transportation is filled with eclectic displays of how man traveled other than by walking. As you enter the grounds, Victorian elegance is preserved in the 1914 "Sunshine Special's Ellsmere." The interior of this rail car is lovely with its rich mahogany paneling, and it was used to transport U.S. Presidents.

Other exhibits include helicopters, Saber jets, Shooting Stars, Flying Bananas, tanks, missiles, and Apollo and Gemini training capsules. A Navy Minesweeper Boat 5, one of the very few sea-going vessels displayed inland, nudges shoulders with a London double-decker touring bus.

Texas has several fine antique automobile museums in San Antonio, Houston, and Kerrville, but even though old car museums are not very unusual, The Pate has some rare vehicles, including a 1904 Schacht with its solid wood body and 12 ½ horsepower motor.

A big black clunky 1950 Russian Z.I.M. is as obsolete as the American Studebakers, Frazers, and Packards that accompany it. One car you will never see in any other exhibit is a nondescript 1962 Checker, Cab. This old Cab #36 was the one used by Lee Harvey Oswald on that fateful day in Dallas. Bill Whaley drove Oswald to 500 North Berkley. Due to traffic, 30 minutes after the assassination, the cab was only 4 blocks from the crime. The fare was one dollar, but Oswald only paid 95 cents.

After a tour of the museum, get out your picnic lunch and sit a spell. The Pate has lovely grounds, and visitors are welcome to enjoy them.

This Air Force helicopter is one of the many aircraft displayed at the Pate Museum of Transportation.

World War II— The Big One

It was a terrible time.
It was a wonderful time.
It was a time to remember.
Author Unknown

Just ask any American over 50 where he was on December 7, 1941, and he will answer without any hesitation at all. The impact of the Japanese attack on Pearl Harbor shattered the nation so thoroughly that decades have not erased the memory of that "Day of Infamy."

Texas' contribution to those heroic years was tremendous. Not only was the Supreme Commander of the Allied Forces born in Denison, but Dwight D. Eisenhower also became President of the United States. Texans switched their battlecry from "Remember the Alamo" to "Remember Pearl Harbor," and her volunteers were legion. One of Texas' most famous volunteers received every combat decoration offered by the U.S. Army plus the Croix de Guerre with Silver Star. This Congressional Medal of Honor winner was born Audie Leon Murphy in 1924 near Kingston, Texas. The nation's

most decorated soldier died in an airplane crash in 1971 and is buried at Arlington National Cemetery. At the Confederate Research Center in Hillsboro, some of Audie's memorabilia is on display.

With all the flat land in Texas, it was natural that air bases found an ideal site in the state. Kelly Air Force Base in San Antonio is the oldest military air training base in the country. It was named for George S. M. Kelly, the first American pilot killed in a military plane. Brooks Air Force Base, also in San Antonio, was built during World War I, and its Hangar 9 is the oldest surviving military hangar in Texas. A small aviation museum is open there from 8 to 4 during the week.

U.S. Army Air Defense Museum

5000 Pleasanton Road
Fort Bliss
Hours: 9:00–4:30
Admission free.
915-568-5412

After the heroic air games with the Red Baron during World War I, the future of aircraft was secure. However, as soon as the airplane became a military weapon, other artillery had to be developed to shoot it from the skies. The only museum to anti-aircraft weapons and equipment is at Fort Bliss. Wouldn't old Geronimo's eyes bulge if he could see all the missiles, guns, searchlights, and sound locators around the fort where he was once imprisoned. Inside the museum are maps, dioramas, and displays tracing the development of anti-aircraft weaponry. From a 40-mm gun used in Bougainville in 1944 to the futuristic "Redeye," a short-range, man-portable, shoulder-fired infrared homing missile system, you can see how sophisticated warfare has become.

Flying Tiger Museum

U.S. 82 West
Paris 75460
Hours: Contact Sammy Burchinal

 In 1975 Issac Newton Burchinal, Jr. made the Wall Street Journal with a report on his unique flying lessons. If you missed World War II, you could still take a ten-hour course in a PT-17 Trainer or in an AT6 Trainer. Fighters and bombers took 4 hours, and you could learn Burchinal's "seat-of-the-pants" flying for $2,550 per course. The instructor encouraged his students with statements like "You better hug your wife better'n you pull on that wheel or you're in miserable shape." Or, he might scream, "Quit drivin' and start flyin'!"

Burchinal's grand old gals were the stars of the movies *The Great Waldo Pepper*, *Midway*, *Catch-22*, and *Baa Baa Black Sheep*. You can still see these great performers at the Flying Tiger Museum. Prices have gone up for those who care to indulge in a bit of Walter Mitty nostalgia. It costs $150 per hour for the PT-17, $600 for an F8 Saber Jet, and $800 for a spin in the B-17 Flying Fortress. Also, if you yearn for the wild blue yonder in one of these relics, you better hurry, for they are all for sale.

Confederate Air Force Ghost Squadron

Rebel Field
Harlingen 78550
512-425-1057
Hours: 9–5 Mon.–Sat. 12–5 Sun. and Holidays
Admission

"Hitler built a fortress around Europe, but he forgot to put a roof on it."

Franklin Delano Roosevelt

 The second "war to end all wars" had been over 12 years, yet a small group of ex-pilots kept in touch through their shared love of airplanes and flying. One airman had bought a war surplus P-40 Warhawk, the first truly modern American fighter plane, in 1951. (A few Warhawks got in the air at Pearl Harbor, and Chennault's Flying Tigers flew them in China.) To add to their one-plane air force, the pilot friends began a search for a P-51 Mustang, reputed to be the greatest fighter of the war, and in 1957 they found one in El Paso.

The group originally only intended to keep the Mustang in good shape, and formed a loosely defined flying "club." Others began to join, and one member jokingly painted Confederate Air Force on the P-51's fuselage. One and all were instantly commissioned "colonels."

After an F8F Bearcat was acquired, interest in the old aircraft began to spread. In 1960 the "colonels" decided to create a collection—but where? No surplus planes were in existence, and official indifference and official destruction had almost obliterated the greatest air fleet ever built. From January 1, 1942, until December 31, 1945, the United State's built 275,245 aircraft and 733,760 aircraft engines. In one year alone, American industry equalled the war production of all the Axis nations combined, and the enemy had had a 10-year lead! Fifteen years after V-J Day, almost all were lost. The CAF became a group with "a large cause;" to halt thoughtless destruction of these symbols of America's finest years.

Today, 50 Wings of the CAF are in the air with 13,000 members all over the world. Of the 77 aircraft at Rebel Field, there are 49 different airplanes. This resolute group of dedicated men not only salvaged American planes, but the enemies' famous fighters as well.

The most well known German fighter was the Messerschmitt Bf 109, a standard Luftwaffe single-seater preferred by German aces. The Heinkel He 111 proved deadly in the Spanish Civil War, but was vulnerable to the RAF Spitfires and Hurricanes. Every bombing raid lost one Heinkel in four. The museum's Japanese Zeroes are actually expertly crafted replicas using AT-6 Texans and Vultee BT-14 Valiant frames.

When Winston Churchill said, "Never in the field of human conflict have so many owed so much to so few," he meant the gallant men of the Royal Air Force. More British Spitfires rolled off the assembly lines than any other Allied warplane.

Along with the P-51 Mustang, the enemy's most feared opponents have become legendary. The P-47 Thunderbolt ("the jug") was so reliable all its leading aces survived the war. With its two engines, the P-38 was the plane that accomplished one of the most celebrated missions of the war. It flew 30 feet above the ocean for more than 500 miles to shoot down Admiral Isoroku Yamamoto, the mastermind of Pearl Harbor, at Bougainville.

In an F4F Wildcat, Edward "Butch" O'Hare single-handedly saved the *Lexington* by shooting down five out of nine Japanese bombers in six minutes. The hero of this incredible feat was the first American of World War II to be awarded the Medal of Honor. All of the Grumman cats are here at the CAF, not only the Wildcat, but the F6F Hellcat and F8F Bearcat.

One of the rarest CAF aircraft is the Sikorsky R-4B, the world's first production helicopter, and the only helicopter to serve in World War II. It was found in rural Ohio tamely dusting crops.

"Without the B-17," said Carl Spaatz, wartime chief of staff, "we might have lost the war." Of all the great American planes, none were more celebrated than the Boeing B-17 Flying Fortress. Designed in 1934, it was in production in 1938. Its strong construction and heavy armament made it a mainstay of the Air Force.

The military designation of the DC-3 is the C-47 Skytrain. Called the "Dakota," "Gooney Bird," and in Viet Nam "Puff, the Magic Dragon," the C-47 was the standard air transport for all Allied Forces. These reliable and versatile planes can still be found winging through the atmosphere as corporate aircraft and in charter services. The CAF uses it as the transport for the CAF's parachuting exhibitions.

On August 6, 1945, a lone B-29 Superfortress, the *Enola Gay*, flew over Hiroshima. It had a 3,700 mile range and could carry 12,000 pounds of bombs, but on this deadly flight, one bomb was enough. The pilot of this command is an honored guest each year at the CAF AIRSHO, and Paul Tibbets' somber and level voice relates dropping the first atomic bomb. This superfort of the CAF was found in California being used in Navy ballistic missile tests.

There is more to the museum than just old airplanes. World War II uniforms of both the Axis and Allied troops are on display. A Hall of Honor is set aside for Air Force Medal of Honor winners and aces. A Norden bombsight, once so super-secret, it was never left in the bomber, is on exhibit. If a plane were forced down, an explosive mechanism destroyed the bombsight.

Many other World War II antiques are still airborne, and the CAF presents its "finest hour" the first weekend of every October with its AIRSHO. Another famous "colonel," Tennessee Ernie Ford, narrates the stirring tales of the AIRSHO's featured attractions. One thrilling re-enactment is the bombing of Pearl Harbor. It is called "Tora, Tora, Tora" (Tiger, Tiger, Tiger), the Japanese code words for its surprise attack.

If you would like to become a CAF "colonel," membership in this splendid organization is open to all who share its beliefs. Your mythical commander is Jethro E. Culpepper who has served in every war since 1776. Maintained by private donation without any state or federal grants, you will be helping preserve a portion of America's military aviation heritage.

Iwo Jima Monument

Marine Military Academy
Iwo Jima Boulevard
Harlingen

One of the most glamorous units of the Armed Forces during World War II was the Marine Corps. Their rigorous training and versatility in warfare made the Marines a very elite force, and that tradition endures. It was the Marines that immortalized one of the most stirring monuments to great American heroism.

In the closing months of the War in the Pacific, U.S. troops had recaptured most of the territory taken by Japan during those bleak years of 1941 and 1942. Still remaining was a minute dot on the map 660 miles south of Tokyo—

One of America's finest moments is captured in the stirring Iwo Jima Monument.

Iwo Jima. Mount Suribachi dominated the tiny island as a major target, there were almost insurmountable problems in securing it from the Japanese.

On February 19, 1945, the 4th and 5th Marine Divisions landed on this stepping stone to the Land of the Rising Sun. By February 23 the bloody climb to Mount Suribachi had begun. At mid-morning soldiers thrilled to a small American flag waving valiantly from the peak. C. B. Gathwright had taken a piece of iron pipe for a flagpole, and from it flew the Stars and Stripes he had carried in his pocket.

That same afternoon, a second larger flag was raised in victory by five marines: Sgt. Michael Strank, Cpl. Harlon H. Block, Pfc. Franklin R. Sousley, Pfc. Rene A. Gagnon, and Pfc. Ira Hayes. The sixth man was the Navy's Phm. 2/c John H. Bradley. This poignant moment in history was captured forever when news photographer Joe Rosenthal caught the flagraising in an inspiring Pulitzer Prize winning photograph. When the picture was released, sculptor Dr. Felix W. de Weldon, then on duty with the U.S. Navy, was so moved he constructed a scale model within 48 hours. This model became the symbol for the seventh and final war bond drive.

After the war ended, Dr. de Weldon labored nine and a half years to build a working model from molded plaster. The bronze casting took another three years, but on November

10, 1954, the 179th anniversary of the U.S. Marine Corps, President Eisenhower dedicated the magnificent monument at Arlington National Cemetery.

In 1981 Texas received the treasured gift of the original working model of this marvelous statue from Dr. de Weldon. There were many reasons Texas was selected for this prized gift. Dr. de Weldon primarily wanted it placed at the Marine Military Academy to stand as an inspiration to the young cadets. Also, the street facing the memorial was already named Iwo Jima Boulevard, and the Valley's fairly constant temperature and humidity will preserve the casting. At the base of the flagpole is Cpl. Harlon H. Block, a Texan from Weslaco who later died in combat. Another great Texan's memorable quote, "Uncommon Valor was a Common Virture," was carved on the 11-foot high Brazilian black marble base. Fleet Admiral Chester W. Nimitz was from an old Fredericksburg family.

Shipping 130 tons of statue to Texas from Rhode Island was not an easy task. Governor Clements held a fund-raising dinner that brought in $120,000, and the Texas Motor Transportation Association offered to transport the gigantic shipment. Christened the "Freedom Convoy," 9 flatbed trucks plus an 18-wheeler with a crane rolled 110 pieces of the sculpture to Harlingen. This generous donation amounted to $65,000 in equipment, personnel, and fuel.

Dr. de Weldon came to supervise the reconstruction and the waterproof shellacking. Once the 90-foot masterpiece was in place, it received a bronze epoxy which dried the same color as the bronze casting at Arlington.

At the dedication, on a beautiful day in April, among the honored guests were Governor and Mrs. Clements and the widow of Harlon Block. Unfortunately Joe Rosenthal was ill and later died without seeing his photograph immortalized once again. Another stirring moment occurred when the ROTC cadets arrived from Austin, having jogged in a relay, with the 14- by 9-foot flag. As at Arlington, this flag is never lowered, but flies eternally, serving as a reminder to Americans of their finest years.

Lost Battalion Room

Wise County Courthouse
Decatur

 Another tribute to a National Guard unit is the Lost Battalion Room. In November of 1941 Battery F, Second Battalion 131 Field Artillery, 36th Division, had sailed from San Francisco under the code name PLUM. At sea when Pearl Harbor was attacked, the soldiers went on to Java. Captured in March of 1942, the entire battalion was held prisoner in Asia. They were used as forced labor for the Japanese Burma-Siam railroad and were the heroes of Pierre Boulle's book *Bridge Over the River Kwai*. Because the War Department would not (or could not) disclose information of what happened to the unit, the newspapers called it "The Lost Battalion," and here are mementos of their torturous ordeal.

The Admiral Nimitz Center

340 East Main
Fredericksburg 78624
512-997-4379
Hours: 8–5
Admission

"We inspire our youth by honoring our heroes."
Nimitz Center Motto

 Texas' greatest contribution to the Navy during World War II was Admiral Chester W. Nimitz, commander-in-chief Pacific. Commanding thousands of ships and planes plus millions of men, Nimitz wielded more power than all commanders in previous wars. This modest Texan never let his authority overshadow his humility nor his love of people.

Nimitz was born in Frederickburg in 1885, and his father died before his birth. Grandpa Nimitz became the most important man in Chester's life, and from him, the future admiral inherited his love of the sea and his philosophy of life:

"The sea—like life itself—is a stern taskmaster. The best way to get along with either is to learn all you can, then do your best and don't worry—especially about things over which you have no control."

Young Nimitz graduated from Annapolis in 1905, seventh in his class of 114. Early in his career he was court-martialed for grounding the destroyer *Decatur* in Manila Bay, but his future did not suffer from the incident. During World War I, Nimitz served as aide and chief-of-staff to the commander of the Atlantic Fleet's submarine force. When

The historic Nimitz Hotel is now a museum to one of Texas' most honored heroes, Admiral Chester W. Nimitz.

appointed "CinCPac," this brilliant commander was promoted over 28 admirals. The peak of Nimitz's career was the day he boarded the battleship *Missouri* and signed the Instrument of Surrender officially ending World War II on September 2, 1945.

When Nimitz was asked if the museum could be named in his honor, he agreed but requested it be dedicated to the two million men and women who served with him in the Pacific. A slide show portrays the life of this famous admiral and his leadership during the war. The building itself was a great part of Nimitz' early life, for his grandfather ran the Steamboat Hotel here and had hosted such guests as Robert E. Lee and U. S. Grant. (See *A Guide to Historic Texas Inns and Hotels* Lone Star Books, Houston, Texas.)

Adjacent to the Center is one of the loveliest gardens in Texas. The Garden of Peace was a gift from the people of Japan. Visit this treasure of tranquility with the admonition, "This garden is like a church. Enter and think good thoughts." Designed by Taketora Saita of Tokyo, it contains a replica of Admiral Togo's study which was built in Japan and reassembled here in the Garden of Peace. The Japanese historians consider Togo, Lord Nelson, and Nimitz the three greatest admirals the world has ever known. Even though Togo and Nimitz were adversaries, Nimitz returned his foe's Samurai swords to their ancestral home, and started a fund to restore the *Mikasa*, Admiral Togo's flagship. This serene classic garden is a symbol of the friendship and admiration of the two admirals and the two nations.

A block from the Nimitz Center is the Pacific History Walk. Enter through two anti-aircraft guns, and as you stroll through some of the world's rarest war relics, the story of the Pacific War unfolds. From Pearl Harbor is the wreckage of the first Japanese aircraft to drop bombs on American targets. "Val" sank more Allied ships than any other type of Axis aircraft.

Strange sounding names—Guadalcanal, Tarawa, Iwo Jima— became common words to Americans who had never heard of them before 1941. Here at the Pacific History Walk you can climb into the gun emplacements, sit in a camouflaged pit, walk the bridge of a submarine, and listen to tapes explaining the functions of the weaponry that made possible the recapture of those far-away islands. The walk ends with a replica of the atomic bomb dropped from the *Enola Gay* so many years ago, which changed the history of the world. It is astounding that so much destruction was packed in this strange device. The Admiral Nimitz Center truly honors "those who gave their lives and to all who offered their lives defending freedom."

Fort Hood

Killeen

Most of Texas' forts were originally built to fight Indians, but Fort Hood was a result of World War II. Established in 1942, by the next year 95,000 troops were in training. By the seventies, Fort Hood contained the largest concentration of armored power in the country and

the largest population of any post in the free world. Two museums honor Fort Hood's distinguished units.

The First Team
Building 2218 Headquarters Ave.
685-741-4198
Hours: 12–4 Sat. & Sun., 9–4:30 Mon.–Fri.
Admission free

The First Cavalry Division was activated in 1921 at Fort Bliss in El Paso. Until 1942 troopers patrolled the Mexican border, but had to turn in their horses for horsepower. This was the first unit to enter both Manila and Tokyo, so MacArthur dubbed them "The First Team." The Division's colors flew in Korea, and again in Vietnam, with valor and bravery.

Some of The First Team's traditions date back to the 1860s and 1870s. The song "Gary Owen" was first played at the Battle of the Washita River at the request of Lt. Col. George A. Custer. (See *Traveling Texas Borders*, Lone Star Books, Houston, Texas.) The bugle call "charge" ordered a headlong frontal attack, and the combination of the bugle call and song is now used to signal the audience to stand and to bring the troops to attention for the Division's ceremonies. In the museum are documents signed by Custer as well as shell casings from the battlefield of Little Big Horn.

Another display depicts the Buffalo Soldiers, black troops who performed so bravely during the Indian Wars following the Civil War. Also, here is a World War II machinegun nest, a Vietnam Room, and a Medal of Honor Room. The nation's highest award has been bestowed on 34 of The First Team's troopers.

Second Armored Division
Building 418—Battalion Ave. and Academic Dr.
Hours: 9–5 Mon.–Tues., Thurs.–Fri., 12–5 Wed.,
12–4 Sat. and Sun.

This museum is easy to recognize by the collection of armored vehicles surrounding it. Organized in 1940 after the successful invasion of Poland by Hitler's Panzer division, the group's first commander was Major General Charles L. Scott, who was almost immediately succeeded by Major General George S. Patton.

Patton put the division through intense and difficult training, including 600-mile marches, and the museum depicts the hardships of those training days. However, before the war was over, Patton's men had completed two amphibious landings and seven major campaigns. This war machine captured 95,000 enemy prisoners, liberated 22,500 Allied prisoners, and received numerous citations.

Among the war memorabilia are letters to and from General Patton and an extensive array of weaponry displayed in life-sized war settings. A collection of video tapes of a brief history of the division, the film *Patton*, and modern weapons in current use can be viewed.

Thank You, Mr. Bell and Mr. Edison

"You've come a long way, baby." There is no doubt about it, Ma Bell is not the girl she used to be, and the old lady celebrated her one hundredth birthday on March 7, 1976. Wouldn't Alexander Graham Bell (or Don Ameche, for those of you who remember the movie) be pleased to pick up a Mickey Mouse telephone, dial anywhere in the world and say, "Come here, Watson, I want you."

Texas has three telephony museums, and each has exhibits of just about all of the innovations that made Mickey possible. However, at the rate of telephone sophistication, it won't be long before Mickey will be obsolete as well.

Mo Spradley Telephone Museum

216 1/2 Van Buren
McGregor 76657
817-840-3482
Hours: Appointment only

Mo Spradley and his son, Little Mo, never intended to go into the museum business. It all started when Frank Ross retired as president of Southwestern Bell Telephone Company and wanted to find a home for his antique phone collection. Mo and Little Mo could not resist the temptation. After a year of restoring these old telephones dating from 1889 to 1948, the Mo Spradley Telephone Museum opened its doors.

Mo thought it was a joke when he got a call from Universal Studios to help them with a film they were making starring Sissy Spacek. But, the studio was dead level serious. The script for *Raggedy Man* called for a smalltown telephone operator in the 1940s, and Universal needed Mr. Spradley to set up the working switchboard of the correct age and design. Mo was also an expert on how the switchboard served as a key to the entire community and how "central" knew everybody's business.

Mo already had most of the equipment, and loved helping with the movie. The Spradleys thought Sissy Spacek one of the nicest people they had met and were her guests at the World Premier. So, the next time you see *Raggedy Man*, one of the movie's unseen stars is Mo Spradley of McGregor.

One unusual phone is ideal for parents with teenagers in the house. Called the Hush-a-phone, it was invented in England in 1927. You could talk into the mouthpiece without anyone but the party at the other end hearing your conversation.

There is an 1891 version of "call waiting." If someone called while you were already talking, a button dropped. Then, you could call back the operator and ask who had called you. Also, the "call forwarding" system was to just

ring up central and tell her where you would be if you got any calls.

A German phone would drive some telephone users crazy, for it was metered and kept an account of the time the caller talked. What was even worse, back in the early days of the telephone, McGregor had two phone companies. So, everyone had to have two telephones and remember who subscribed to which phone company.

The Spradleys still have a lot of old telephones waiting to be repaired, but they keep working and adding to the building at the back of their home, which displays their collection. They do not sell or swap any of their collector's items, nor do they repair other antique phones.

No value can be placed on a private museum such as the Spradley's, and the owners have no idea of its worth. As Mrs. Mo said, "We just think of the historical value. If nobody comes to see it, it isn't worth a penny to us."

E. H. Danner Museum of Telephony

General Telephone Company of the Southwest
2701 S. Johnson Street
San Angelo 76901
915-944-5306
Hours: 8–5 Mon.–Fri.
Admission free

A telephone is such an integral part of life, it is difficult to realize that there was a time when placing a call was a historic event. This amazing invention was thought of as far back as 1664 when Dr. Robert Hooke wrote of a device he had developed for conveying sound. In 1840, the physicist Sir Charles Wheatstone was credited with first using the word "telephone." In a touch of irony, 20 years later John Reis demonstrated an instrument in Frankfort which he called a telephone, but the contraption only transmitted musical sounds and individual letters. Because he failed to tighten one screw, Reis missed inventing a transmitter which would have carried the voice.

The E. H. Danner Museum, named for the president of General Telephone, is a small collection of telephone antiques, but it is privileged to have one of only two models known to still exist of the original five models of the Gallows Frame Telephone invented by Alexander Graham Bell. Voluminous court records prove that not everyone agreed that Bell was the Father of the Telephone, and it took a ruling of the Supreme Court to award Bell the title.

Several old pay station telephones are in the collection. One is an 1890 wall cabinet not made by the Gray company as most pay stations were in those days. Also, authentic in every detail, a Kellogg switchboard will show you what happened when you rang "Central" in 1910. A mortician named Strowger built the first dial phone because he was convinced "Central" was giving his business to competitors.

While you are in San Angelo, if you have an antique phone that needs restoring and modified for today's dialing, call Otis Levere at the House of Telephones (915-655-4174), and Otis will create a beautiful usable instrument for you.

Big Bend Telephone Museum

P. O. Box 1024
Alpine 79830
915-837-3393
Hours: 10–12, 2–4 Mon.–Fri.
Admission free

Not all telephone companies have to answer to Ma Bell. There are over 1,600 independents, and the Big Bend Telephone Company was established in 1960 with Neville Haynes as its president. When Haynes learned that the Brad Smith collection of antique phones were up for sale, he decided Alpine needed a telephone museum.

And what a beautiful museum it is! Occupying one large room of the Big Bend's offices, the museum conveys every phase of the development of the telephone. A model of the first phone Bell invented is a gift of the Bell system, while not far away is a model of the first satellite in space.

A magnificent conference table is a masterpiece of woodwork. It is made of square redwood telephone poles, which were installed in 1890 for the Southern Pacific Railroad. The poles used for the table top weigh 850 pounds and came from the telephone line running between Alpine and Marfa. This portion of the line was built by Chinese laborers who were imported from the Pacific Coast.

A rare 1878 model was constructed only two years after Bell's patent. It has two transcribers, one to talk through and one to listen through. One transcriber has a silver bracket, and the other a brass to make it easy to distinguish which transcriber to use. The telephone came from an abandoned monastery in the Mexican state of Chiapas. Don't you wonder who the fathers "rang up?"

Another rare antique is an 1897 Federal Telephone and Telegraph Company fiddleback wall telephone, one of the few made of metal. It gets its name from the case shaped somewhat like a fiddle. One other special phone is a Montgomery Ward wall telephone used in hotels. For some reason, it did not retail well and had a limited production.

Do you remember when phone calls were a nickel? There is a Western Electric brass candlestick phone with a five-cent coin box, circa 1918. But, the museum is not limited to just rare, old, or unusual telephones. There is a telegraph pole with a unique ceramic insulator, probably the only such insulator in existence. A tin-plate phone booth came from Marfa, and a porcelain phone booth from Langtry. Old phone directories have their place as well, and the 1926 Austin phone book had a whopping 79 pages.

A 1905 switchboard is a classic example of the wizard with cords and buttons that made a high priestess out of the local central operator. Usually "Central" was a woman, but this 1905 switchboard was operated by John Bradford who ran a general store in Pumpville.

Several cases display "lovely jewels of the poles" or insulators. After much experimentation, the telephone and telegraph industries settled on molded glass for the standard insulator. Usually aqua or blue-green, insulators can also be green, amber, or even clear glass. Literally millions of these pieces were manufactured during the 1850–1900 era, and few changes have been made in their design since. However, underground cables, microwaves, and satellites have made insulators prized collector's items.

Every marvelous treasure in this museum has been carefully restored, and a great deal of the credit goes to Charles Lightsey, general manager. As wonderful as the museum's exhibits is its dedication:

> "This Telephony Museum has been established to commemorate our forefathers—pioneer men and women—whose vision, courage, and fortitude transformed a frontier wilderness into a prosperous and civilized land. Despite untold hardships those early settlers endured, leaving to their descendants a legacy of regional pride.

> Remembering their isolation and yearning for access to communication we gratefully dedicate this collection of telephone art to those who have gone before, and to the pioneer spirit that still lives in the people of the Big Bend.

Antique telephones line the walls at the Big Bend Telephone Museum.

Texas Broadcast Museum

1701 Market Street
Dallas 75202
214-748-1112
Hours: 11–4 Wed.–Fri., 11–5 Sat.–Sun.
Admission

The Texas Broadcast Museum is a garden of Gramophones with the horns sprouting like blossoms. Perhaps there are so many old phonographs in this plethora of nostalgia, because they were the first things Bill Bragg collected. As Jenny Bragg said, "Everyone kept telling us that we had so many old Gramophones we ought to start a museum, so we did."

WOAI still spins those golden oldie platters at the Texas Broadcast Museum.

Now there is a lot more to the Texas Broadcast Museum than just old Gramophones. The Braggs began their museum with 17,000 records, some so thick they look like black pizza dough, but devoted fans have donated another 15,000 platters. All those old discs still produce sound and music, so you could hear all 32,000 of those "golden oldies" if you had a few hundred hours to spare. Begin spinning on an 1896 Columbia Q phonograph, then try the tones of a 1905 German Pigmyphone.

When KDKA in Pittsburgh broadcast the presidential election returns on November 2, 1920 (Harding won), the radio changed the world forever. Millions of Americans tuned in, and by 1927 they could plug the "crystal set" into the electrical socket. The "cathedral," or "tombstone" model was the nation's number one best seller in the early thirties, and during an era of despair and depression, radio was *the* entertainment for Americans. People still remember when you could walk around the block on a summer Sunday night and never miss a word of *Amos and Andy*, and you didn't have to have a portable model.

If you would love to go back to those pioneer days of radio, or if you have a secret desire to be a disk jockey, both wishes can come true at this funky museum. WOAI, the first radio station in the area, donated its entire broadcast setup to the collection. WBAP even broadcast from this 1938 equipment at the 1980 Texas State Fair, complete with the sound effects of the thirties and forties. You, too, can sit down, flip the switch, pull the mike in place, and broadcast as you may have yearned to do. Your message won't make it to the satellites, but the other museum visitors will be delighted to applaud. Liberace even got his start in radio, and KSKY has provided their old studio organs where the maestro played without benefit of candelabra.

Over in a corner is the famous Jot 'em Down Store. If you were around in the thirties, you certainly knew the two famous tenants of this establishment. Full of down-home advice, the two bucolic wits, Lum and Abner, entertained devoted fans on their weekly show. This stage set has been authentically reproduced, even to the wiring used in the thirties.

The guitar in a place of honor once played the all-time hit "Rock Around the Clock." Yes, that is Bill Haley's guitar along with his gold and silver records.

The huge boxes about the size of a Wurlitzer are early TV sets. When TV first began to mesmerize viewers, the picture was about the size of a Kodak colorslide, but in black and white. The picture kept getting bigger, but so did the sets. A "portable" took two very strong men to "port" it. Also, a necessity for every TV owner was a special TV light. All sorts of dire predictions came out about what would happen to your eyes unless you watched television with the proper light (all obviously a propaganda pitch of lamp manufacturers), but TV was so new that everyone bought that malarky and dutifully purchased a "TV Lamp."

As with early radio shows, all television programs were broadcast live. Back in those days, watching commercials was wonderful. Indestructible chairs cratered, desserts ran oozy and gooey, brand X often turned out better than the advertised product, and teeth did not blind you with sparkling brightness.

Live dramas enthralled audiences, not so much for their actors' talents as to see who would muff their lines, and how they recovered. Comedians such as Milton Berle, Bob Hope, and Sid Caesar ad libbed incredibly funny jokes, and it was impossible to censor their talent.

Communication to mass audiences is always graced with a touch of magic, and here at the Texas Broadcast Museum, you cannot help but be impressed with the technology that makes a transistor accepted as a way of life. If we have come this far since 1920, what do the next six decades hold in store?

Thank You, Mr. Bell and Mr. Edison   **75**

Hysterically Historical

One of the wonderful traits of Texans is their sense of humor. Sometimes it is intentional as with the World's Largest Jackrabbit, Strawberry, and a full-sized mule. Then there are instances where monuments just turned out to tickle your fancy, even though they originally had a serious purpose.

A "zero stone" really was important despite your tendency to equate it with absolutely nothing. An imposing obelisk with a jaybird perched on top may seem ridiculous, but it is actually a symbol of a major upheaval in Texas. So, before you giggle and snicker over some of Texas' monuments, there really is a reason . . . well, sort of a reason.

Monument to a Jaybird

Richmond

Richmond has a statue that is strictly for the birds, the jaybird, that is. Perched high atop a tall pedestal in downtown Richmond is a jaybird and around the base are the words:

> "Go, Stranger, and to the Jaybirds tell
> That for their country's freedom they fell."

No, you don't have to go out and commune with jaybirds, you can merely tell anyone willing to listen about the Jaybird-Woodpecker War.

As every history student knows (particularly those south of the Mason-Dixon Line), the South suffered horribly from the effects of Reconstruction. The word "carpetbagger" entered the vocabulary and the Ku Klux Klan burned crosses all over Dixie.

In Fort Bend County, the years 1888–1890 were particularly violent because of a feud between the two political factions, the Jaybirds and the Woodpeckers. The Jaybirds were composed of the wealthy population and regular Democrats, whereas the Woodpeckers were the northern sympathizers claiming to be Democrats.

The election of 1888 was conducted with much bitterness and hatred. J. M. Shamblin, the Jaybird leader, was killed, and his replacement, Henry Frost, was wounded. A mass meeting was held and certain scalawags were warned to leave town in ten hours. They left.

Texas Rangers arrived, and on election Day, the heaviest vote ever cast left the Woodpeckers in control. More killings resulted and on August 16, 1889, the two factions

Atop his giant stone perch, a jaybird symbolizes a Southern conflict.

fought the "Battle of Richmond." After 20 minutes of gunfire and 5 deaths, the Woodpeckers retreated to the courthouse. Governor Ross arrived, and his command of the situation resulted in the removal or resignation of all Woodpeckers.

So, Stranger, when you go to tell about the monument to a Jaybird in Richmond, you can say it is a Richmond version of a Confederate victory.

Thomas Cree's Little Tree

Highway 60 West
Panhandle

Johnny Appleseed never made it to the High Plains of Texas with his bag of seeds, so the Panhandle's version of this legendary character had to settle for a bois d'arc or Osage orange tree.

If you have ever driven the High Plains, it is still extremely easy to visualize the early days when the edge of the caprock to the Canadian River was a sea of grass. Nothing, but absolutely nothing, broke the horizon. There

Now a rotting stump, the first tree in the Panhandle was once a hardy bois d'arc.

was no water to make adobe, no rocks for stone houses, not a limb for timber, and no landmarks for travelers.

Early settlers could live in tents which blew away in the relentless high winds or dwell in their somewhat cramped and impossible-to-heat covered wagons. It was just best to use the only material available—sod. (See "The Lone Prairie.")

In 1888 Thomas Cree brought his young bride to his dugout home on a section west of Panhandle, Texas. The Crees settled down to the hard pioneer life but yearned for a shade tree. Unbelievers pointed out that if a tree would grow in this desolation, winds would have carried seeds here long ago. Undaunted, Cree set out to find a tree, and returned home with a scraggly little bois d'arc wrapped in burlap.

Cree planted his rarity at the edge of a buffalo wallow near the wagon trail to Amarillo, now the four-lane Highway 60. Drouth came, and Cree sold his claim for $50, a mere $8 less than the marker cost 75 years later. But, Cree's first tree became a thing to cherish. It wasn't the largest tree in Texas, nor did great people sit beneath its boughs, but early ranchers got their bearings from this tiny silhouette, and when the sturdy bois d'arc lived through nature's disasters, others ventured to plant a tree, too.

Today, the ranch homes of the High Plains are surrounded by lovely shade trees, and towns nestle under canopies of Chinese elms. In the spring of 1963, the Texas Historical Commission designated Thomas Cree's tiny monument as the first tree in Texas to receive a historical marker.

No, even the hardy bois d'arc could not survive the onslaught of civilization. Pollution in the air finally accomplished what blizzards, winds, tornados, and drouth failed to do, and Thomas Cree's tree is now a dead rotting stump.

Zero Stone

Fort Stockton Historical District
Fort Stockton

If you take the Historical Tour of old Fort Stockton, you will see a puzzling sign, "Zero Stone." No explanation is evident, but at one time, every survey of Pecos County used it.

The Pecos River was once the boundary line of an area so desolate it was the last wilderness to be opened to civilization. In this harsh land where everything grows spines, thorns, or horns, the Pecos River forms the eastern boundary of the county of the same name. Created out of Presidio County in 1871, Pecos County's 4,688 square miles or 3,000,320 acres sit on top of some the deepest gas wells in the world.

Now rich in gas and oil, Fort Stockton's main asset at one time was water. Comanche Springs was a major stop on the Comanche War Trail, and Cabeza de Vaca, who saw most of Texas before any other white man, sipped from its daily flow of 60 million gallons of water. Naturally, Comanche Springs was a prime site for a fort against the inhabitants who named it.

The Jesuits journeyed to the springs in 1845 and named this oasis St. Gall, but when the army arrived, the site became Fort Stockton. To survey the area in 1859, the survey party placed a zero stone to be used as the origin point for all local surveys, and the "zero stone" is still in place on the courthouse square. Don't confuse it with the granite slab standing upright; that is the World War I monument. The zero stone lies at the base imbedded in the ground.

Heart of Texas

Courthouse Square
Brady

On the courthouse lawn at Brady is a monument in the shape of Texas with a big heart in the center. Brady's claim as the "Heart of Texas" is not exactly accurate. You have to go 2 miles south of FM 502 on US 377, and another 5 miles northwest to get to the geographical center of our 267,339 square miles. For trivia lovers, Texas is 801 miles from north to south, 733 miles east to west, and comprises 7.4 percent of the nation's total area.

R.I.P.

Who's Who in Texas Graveyards

A statue larger than life is not for every mortal, nor is immortality easily achieved. The only monument most of us will ever get is a lowly tombstone.

Have you ever noticed that headstones are never sold as "tombstones" but rather as "monuments" or "memorials." Have you ever wondered what will be inscribed on your tombstone, or who will put it there? To be on the safe side, have it erected and your epitaph chiseled before you go as Shanghai Pierce did. If you don't, there is no telling what will end up on your final monument—if anything.

Texas has a veritable treasure trove of bizarre, beloved, and bewildering personalities resting in its soil. For "gravers" the Lone Star State is a bonanza of unique characters that ended up in Texas forever—although not all made that decision themselves.

Not all the interesting graves are the final resting places of famous Texas heroes, distinguished statesmen, or people who shaped the destiny of the world. Some did not even rate a tombstone, and some who did lost theirs to theft. But, all of these graves contain the bones of someone or something that created a bit of history in its own way. Maybe it was just by living longer, dying richer, or doing some heroic deed, but all have a special story to tell, and only by dying are they still alive.

Saints and Sinners

The good Lord knows the difference between good guys and bad guys, but sometimes He keeps it all to Himself. Through the ages the good and bad get all mixed up, and really rotten people become folk heroes. Legend and reality get so distorted with time, it is hard to separate the two. The pages of Texas' past are crammed with fast guns, fast talkers, a saint or two, a lot of sinners, and some who are a strange combination of both good and bad.

John King Fisher

500 Block of North Park Street
Uvalde

"This is King Fisher's road! Take the other!"

 This emphatic sign appeared on the Pendencia Road where it joined the Eagle Pass highway, and prudent travelers took the other. The time was the 1870s, the place was the Nueces Strip, and the man who installed the sign ruled a kingdom made possible only in a lawless Texas.

The problems in this area dated from the Texas Revolution when defeated Mexico had never agreed that the land from the Nueces River to the Rio Grande belonged to Texas. After the Mexican war, the territory became a veritable no-man's land called the Zona Libre (Free Zone), the Nueces Strip, and also King Fisher's Territory.

Border bandits harassed ranchers; Indians raided settlers; and GTT (Gone to Texas) desperados drifted in from a defeated Confederacy. Pioneers who yearned for law and order were a tiny minority. It was even common knowledge the Mexican government actually aided the bandits and Indians as revenge against their two defeats by the Anglos.

In a volatile area like the Nueces Strip, the groundwork was laid for the rise of a powerful leader. He appeared in the form of a handsome, fearless man riding a stallion named Yaller Lightnin.

King Fisher is proof of the theory that the times make the man. With his flamboyant silver-studded Mexican sombrero, black Mexican jacket embroidered with gold, crimson sash, and two silver-plated revolvers, King Fisher was lord of all he surveyed. He was also the scourge of the Texas border.

John King Fisher was born in Kentucky in 1856. He grew up in Goliad, and at 16 he was sentenced to 2 years in Huntsville prison for housebreaking, but was pardoned after 4 months. The young renegade moved into the Strip and was immediately hired by ranchers to protect their livestock from the endless raids by Mexican bandits and Indians. King quickly became adept at all cowboy skills, as well as the fast draw. At 17 King was appointed constable in Dimmitt County.

Fisher got so good at taking care of other ranchers' stolen horses and cattle, he decided to go in business on his own with unbranded cattle, or mavericks. Before King was out of his teens he was a leader of men and a power in this wild land.

Strange tales grew up about the youth and the number of men he had killed. One report related that King had shot a certain bald-headed man because he wanted to see whether a bullet would glance from a shiny pate.

By the mid-1870s even the untamed Nueces Strip was feeling the long arm of the law. Captain L. H. McNelly of Texas Ranger fame made it his goal to put Fisher behind bars. After McNelly's death, Captain Lee Hall took up the battle, but Hall was as unsuccessful as his predecessor. More than 20 indictments against the handsome outlaw were handed down—to no avail, for Fisher was acquitted of 6 charges, and 15 indictments were dropped for lack of evidence. King Fisher walked out a free man after years of work by dedicated Rangers.

Fisher did seem to reform, however. He moved his wife and baby girl to Eagle Pass and ran a livery stable. After a second daughter was born, King even gave up his saloon interest. Amazingly, the former outlaw then moved to Uvalde to become sheriff of Uvalde County where a third daughter was born. The King of the Strip became a devoted family man and as good a lawman as he had been an outlaw (or so the history books say).

The past returned to end King's foray into law and order, however. King's death scene is the stuff of a Hollywood script, and has so much drama, fact and legend become difficult to separate. On March 11, 1884, King

Fisher was in Austin where he met the murderer Ben Thompson. Some accounts say Thompson and Fisher were friends; other accounts question the relationship and say they were antagonists. Thompson had been acquitted 20 months earlier for the murder of Jack Harris, but Harris' friend, Joe Foster, swore to avenge Harris' death.

The story goes that King was trying to patch up the quarrel between Thompson and Foster, but another theory is that King merely brought Thompson in to Foster's dancehall and theater to set him up for the kill.

Regardless, when Foster refused to drink with Thompson and Fisher, Thompson was ambushed by Harris' friends, and Thompson was hit with 13 bullets and Fisher with 9. Fisher, a two-gun draw, only pulled one pistol and fired one shot. The verdict at Foster's trial was "justifiable self-defense." With marvelous dramatic irony, the one shot Fisher fired hit Foster in the leg, and Foster died of infection ten days later.

The King was dead at 30 and buried in a tear-shaped casket with the biggest funeral Uvalde had ever seen. A Mrs. Hannehan, the mother of an outlaw King had killed, on the anniversary of her son's death piled brush on King's grave, set it afire, and danced with devilish glee. In 1959 the grave and iron fence were moved across the street. The casket was opened, and reports say King was still remarkably handsome.

John Wesley Hardin

Concordia Cemetery
El Paso

"If you wish to be successful in life, be temperate and control your passions; if you don't, ruin and death is the inevitable result."

 These wise words of counsel were stated by a man who was never temperate, nor who ever controlled his passions, and ruin and death was the inevitable result; John Wesley Hardin knew exactly what he was talking about. He did live to age 41, which is a ripe old age for gunfighters, but he had spent 16 years in prison.

This son of a circuit-riding preacher was named for another circuit rider across the seas whose flaming spirit had forged the Methodist Church, but the American ended his career as the worst killer in the history of Texas. How terrible was the Reverend Mr. Hardin's boy?

Hardin's favorite targets were freed slaves, Yankee soldiers who enforced emancipation, Indians, and Mexicans. The young bigot claimed twelve notches on his gun before he had started shaving. In Abilene Wes shot a loud mouth who was stupid enough to say he didn't like Texans. Wes had a deadly cross-hand draw, grabbing for each gun with the opposite hand and coming up with two guns blazing.

In the summer of 1872 Hardin finally felt the taste of lead. As a sore loser in a game of tenpins, the posse put a bullet in his thigh, and Wes surrendered. A nervous deputy then shot him in the knee. In spite of his injuries, Hardin

John Wesley Hardin earned the title of Texas' Wildest Son with forty notches on his gun. (This figure is on display at the Southwestern Historical Wax Museum—see page 13.)

escaped from the Gonzales jail when a thoughtful friend brought him a saw.

Next, Wes moved to DeWitt County—good country for cattle and even better country for feuding. As a cousin of the notorious Taylors, Hardin had no trouble choosing sides in the bloody Sutton-Taylor feud. Naturally, the Taylors "won," as they killed more Suttons.

After six more years of doing little else but blowing other men's brains out, Wes settled down with his wife and baby in Comanche. He was 21 years old. Respectability was short-lived, however, when the sheriff from Brown County, Charlie Webb, tried to arrest him. Webb was Hardin's fortieth notch, and the one-too-many for the killer.

Texas then became too hot for its wildest son. A mob, sheriffs, the Pinkertons, and the Texas Rangers were on his trail, plus some fools who lusted for the $4,000 reward. Captured on a train in Pensacola, Florida, by a determined Ranger, he was hauled back to Gonzales for trial. Hardin had the gall to claim self-defense for shooting Webb and managed to get off with second degree murder and 25 years.

In prison, in between floggings, solitary confinement, escape plots, rebellions, and defiance, Hardin got a law degree and wrangled a full pardon. El Paso was his next and final stop.

Young John Selman, a policeman, threw Hardin's ladyfriend in jail. Wes got her out, but said some very unpleasant things about Old John Selman being the sire of a monstrous offspring. Old John took offense and threatened to kill Hardin.

The scene was the Acme Saloon. Wes was rolling dice with the bartender for drinks. He looked down and uttered his last words: "Four sixes to beat." At that moment a

bullet smashed into the back of his head. Old John was an excellent shot.

Ironically, an enemy of Wes' settled the score. Before Old John could plead self-defense in court, Old John was shot in a duel with George Scarborough. Later Scarborough died with his boots on in Arizona at the hands of "Kid" Curry. Being a gunfighter was tough work.

If you go to look for this Number One Texas killer, Wes lies near the walled section of Concordia Cemetery reserved for the Chinese coolies who built the railroad into El Paso.

Clay Allison

Orient Hotel Museum Grounds
Pecos

"He never killed a man that did not need killing."

 An epitaph like Clay Allison's justifies all sorts of murders and mayhem. But, the facts are that Clay Allison was a gunslinger with a mean, quick temper, an even quicker triggerfinger, and an addiction to alcohol. If anybody needed killing, it was Clay.

Captured during the Civil War as a Confederate spy and sentenced to death, Allison allegedly escaped by slipping his thin hands through the handcuffs. After he drifted west and bought a ranch around Mobeetie, he became known as "Clay Allison of the Washita."

Like most he-men of the West, Clay was a striking figure: Six feet tall with steel-blue eyes, he wore a black frock-coat, white shirt with shoestring tie, shining black boots, and a wide sombrero. Clay's idea of justice was exhibited when a quack pulled the wrong aching tooth, and Clay in retribution extracted four of the "dentist's" molars.

Allison's exploits with the bottle were famous in every bar. In the little town of Canadian up in the Panhandle, he

Clay Allison died with his boots on, but it was demon rum that put him under.

charged down from College Hill on a black horse shooting up the town, wearing only his hat, boots, and gunbelt. After Allison sobered up, he rode with his clothes on.

Up on the Red River, Clay met a declared foe, Chunk Colbert, for dinner. The two antagonists stirred their coffee with their gun muzzles, and as Chunk's right hand came off the table, Allison tipped his chair back and fired as he dropped out of Chunk's range. Colbert had a neat hole right between his eyes. Clay sat back down and finished his dinner with Chunk, even though Chunk had lost his appetite and couldn't get his face out of his food.

Another famous Allison duel to the death was fought with bowie knives in a large roomy grave. The winner shoveled the dirt and Allison handled as mean a shovel as bowie knife and sixshooter.

Well, the fast gun did not do Clay in; old demon rum was the winner. Riding to his ranch, roaring drunk, Allison fell out of his buckboard and a rear wheel broke his neck. One of the gunman's in-laws, John McCullough, was mighty glad, too, because Clay was coming out to kill McCullough for saying ugly words about him. The *Ford County Globe* gave the gunman a grand sendoff:

"Clay Allison knew no fear. To incur his enmity was equivalent to a death sentence. He contended that he never killed a man willingly but out of necessity."

Well, that's just Clay's opinion.

Diamond Bessie

Oakwood Cemetery
Jefferson

 Jefferson's Oakwood Cemetery contains 15,000 interments, but Jeffersonians, obviously tired of giving instructions to the site, have erected a big sign on one grave's iron fence—"Diamond Bessie."

Diamond Bessie was actually just plain Bessie Moore. As the inamorata of a diamond salesman, Abe Rothchile, Bessie was lavishly decorated with sparkling samples of Abe's wares. So, the rather colorless Bessie Moore became Jefferson's famed Diamond Bessie.

As the story goes, on the last day of the year 1876, Bessie and Abe went on a picnic. (It must have been a balmy New Year's Eve in East Texas.) Abe left town, and after his sudden departure, Bessie's body was found minus the goods that gave her the nickname. Abe was arrested and brought back to Jefferson for trial. Declared guilty after the first trial, there was a second trial, and Abe's verdict was just the same. But, the third time he went before the jury, lucky Abe was acquitted, but not before he had lost an eye in a scuffle with his guards.

As for indigent Bessie, the local people had to take up money to bury her, and a stranger erected the tombstone. There's nothing like a mysterious stranger to keep a legend alive. Bessie is much more famous in death than she was alive, for every spring during the Jefferson Pilgrimage the town performs the *Diamond Bessie Murder Trial*, and it is such a box office hit, you need to purchase tickets at least a year in advance.

Bessie is in the illustrious company of Sheriff Vines, who captured her alleged killer, as well as the numerous lawyers involved in the three trials. As Jefferson was once one of Texas' largest cities, Bessie's graveyard neighbors are noted state officials, merchants, bankers, railroad tycoons, and religious and cultural figures. (Nearby, antagonists Robertson and Rose (first names unknown) who killed each other, lie chained together with an iron post marking the common grave.)

Sam Bass

Round Rock

"Sam Bass was born in Indiana, it was his native home;
At the age of 17 young Sam began to roam.
Sam first came to Texas, a cowboy for to be—
A kinder-hearted fellow you seldom ever see."

From the Ballad

 Legend has it that Sam Bass was once a deputy sheriff. True, he did work for the sheriff in Denton, Texas, but as a hired hand. Sam was a race horse addict, and gambling landed him in so much trouble, he left for a better life of crime. Sam met up with Joel Collins, and the pair fleeced thousands of dollars from ranchers who had entrusted them to take cattle up the trail to Kansas. With their ill-gotten gains, their next stop was Deadwood, South Dakota, where the resident cardsharps took the two thieves to the cleaners.

Bass and Collins weren't the least interested in digging for all that gold around Deadwood, they wanted it without

Sam Bass breathed his last on his twenty-seventh birthday. (This figure is on display at the Southwestern Historical Wax Museum—see page 13.)

manual labor. Thus began a comic opera of the road as the undynamic duo began to rob the Deadwood coach. The first stage never even stopped in response to their command. The next did stop but was empty of passengers as well as gold. The third try was hardly a charm either, as the coach only yielded $30, and the tender-hearted thieves felt so sorry for the penny-poor passengers, they gave each $1 for breakfast. The pickings got even worse, with only a gold watch and $6 to show for their later efforts. Collins decided they should look for the greener pastures of train robberies.

Collins' idea was a smash at first, with $60,000 in brand new $20 gold pieces. If was a brief moment of glory, however, for Collins was soon struck down by the posse. Sam was luckier and went on to become the stuff of legends.

Back in Denton as a road agent, Sam fared as poorly as he had in his days in the Black Hills. Train robberies weren't lucrative, either. Bass's best haul was $1,280 that had to be split 4 ways. Two more iron horses yielded only $600. Sam was not destined for big bucks in his career.

Sam's fame rests more on his eluding capture rather than on his ill-gotten gains. Cove Hollow was an unpenetrable refuge near Denton, and the outlaw's capture was impossible. When Sam met his doom, it was through betrayal.

The Texas Rangers apprehended the Murphy brothers for harboring criminals, and made a deal with Jim that if he would help capture Sam, he could go free. Rangers described Jim Murphy as a "veritable Judas in every sense of the word." The veritable Judas joined the fugitives in Cove Hollow at a time when hands were solely needed, as Sam was starting a new venture. Having given up on coaches and trains, Sam had made the bank at Round Rock his objective. Poor Sam, he was fated to have even worse luck with banks. On the way to scene of the crime, Murphy managed to wire the Ranger, "We are on our way to Round Rock to rob the bank. For God's sake get there."

The Rangers got there, and the Bass outfit rode into the ambush. In the gunfire Bass was hit but managed to ride out of town. Later that night a farmer came into town with the news Sam was dying outside his cabin. The Rangers tried for three days to get Sam to name his confederates, but he refused. Finally with the words "The world's bobbing around," Sam Bass died on his twenty-seventh birthday.

Jim Murphy got his comeuppance as well. The charges were dismissed, but Denton had nothing but hatred for Jim. Some nights he was so terrified he slept in the jail. In less than a year, some medicine meant for his eyes found its way into Jim's mouth, and the traitor died in convulsions.

George "Machine Gun" Kelly (1897–1954)

Paradise

Machine Gun Kelly ended up in Paradise—the one north and west of Fort Worth. Poor George Kelly was the supreme example of the henpecked husband and was basically a big lovable braggart, who drank most of the rotgut booze he bootlegged. Kelly's tragic flaw was his

stupidity. Had it not been for his love of Cleo Coleman Shannon, George would have died just another forgotten drunk and certainly not a legend.

Cleo changed all that. In fact, the story of Machine Gun is really the story of Cleo, for it was she who created Machine Gun. By 15, Cleo had changed her name to Kathryn and had borne a child. Divorced at 17, Kathryn was well on her way to a life of sin in the bootleg business and in helping her mother run a "hotel" that was not interested in overnight guests. Another marriage to bootlegger Charlie Thorne lasted a stormy three years. Charlie could not stand the strain and died with a self-inflicted bullet in his head. His farewell message was, "I can't live with her or without her, hence I am departing this life."

Kathryn was not the type to sit around and mourn, and the same year hooked up with George Kelly, a small time punk. Big, pudgy, smiling, drunk George was about as vicious as the proverbial lamb. Kathryn really had her work cut out for her, promoting the bumbling George as a hardnosed, high-living, mean and tough bankrobber. In spite of the fact that George had never robbed a bank, Kathryn rose to the challenge and bought her husband a deadly new toy—a machine gun. After months and months of practice and innumerable rounds of ammunition, George amazingly became an expert with the lethal weapon.

Kathryn began dropping in at speakeasies and handing out .45-caliber cartridges as "souvenirs" from big, bad George's machine gun. Then Kelly's moll would imply that the notorious "Machine Gun" was up north pulling off one lucrative heist after another. Actually, her hero was at her mother's ranch fighting off the DTs.

George did go to Leavenworth, but not for robbing a bank. "The Legend" got arrested for pulling into an Indian reservation with a truckload of his booze, but then no one but Kathryn ever said George was smart.

After his brief stint in prison, Kathryn began promoting Machine Gun again and lined him up with some bank robbers who pulled off "big" jobs in Tupelo, Mississippi, and Wilmer, Texas. But bank robbing in the 1930s was simply not a rewarding profession, and the legend of Machine Gun began fading fast. Kathryn Kelly would make Shakespeare's shrewish Kate look like a devoted, doting wife, and George's Kate came up with her blockbuster plan—kidnapping. Dutiful George came out of a stupor long enough to agree.

Their first plan failed because Kathryn got drunk and bragged about the big heist to two undercover detectives. The next victim was millionaire oilman Charles F. Urschel of Oklahoma City. When the Kelly's broke into Urschel's home, the millionaire was playing cards with his wife and a friend, Walter Javitt. After Machine Gun snarled, "Which one of you is Urschel?" neither man answered, so the kidnappers took them both. Javitt was later released.

More comedy of errors followed before the Kellys finally got their loot of $200,000 in marked bills. Unlike many kidnap victims who are killed, Urschel was turned loose and given $10 for a cab.

The Kellys took off for gangster paradise in Chicago and spent their ill-gotten gains, leaving a trail of marked bills wherever they got drunk. The FBI quickly rounded up Kathryn's mother and step-father, the Shannons, on their seedy ranch at Paradise, Texas, where they made a living harboring criminals on the lam. George and Kathryn were apprehended in Memphis, Tennessee, giving up meekly without a single blast of the infamous machine gun.

Everybody got life imprisonment including the Shannons. Poor old "Pop-Gun" Kelly died in Leavenworth with these five words on his cell wall: "Nothing can be worth this."

Kathryn was released in 1958, but at least George spent his last 21 years away from his nagging wife.

This inhospitable cage of steel provided the last room and board of Bill Longley.

William Preston Longley (1851–1878)

Giddings

Bill Longley survived his first hanging. As the condemned Longley swung from his noose, the irate posse shot him to assure his demise. The first shot struck the gold belt around his body, and the second shot cut strands of the rope. The bullet also passed through Bill's jaw and broke one of his teeth, but those severed rope strands saved his life.

Longley was cut down by the 13-year old brother of the cattle rustler hanging on the noose next to Longley's. In revenge, Bill hanged one of the men who put the rope around his neck from the same tree. This time, the hanged man received five shots from Longley's gun—all hitting their mark. When Bill was arrested for the hanging, the jury deliberated one and one half hours and sentenced him to a year in a Galveston jail.

Bill Longley was an amazing marksman and could hit any target even from a galloping horse. As a teenager, Bill was involved in several senseless and deadly shooting scrapes around Evergreen, Texas. From there the fast gun ranged the Southwest, and death followed in his wake. Within 10 years the papers had recorded more than 30 Longley victims. Violently anti-Reconstruction, Longley's victims were mostly Federal soldiers, Negro police, and possemen.

Wild Bill did return home to Evergreen, but if there was ever a boy who should never have gone home again, it was Longley. Intent on killing Wilson Anderson, who Bill believed had murdered his cousin, the handsome young Longley was captured.

An iron cage with just a few slots for air stands by the museum in Lexington with the crude lettering that reads "a portion of the cell built for custodial security of Bill Longley while awaiting trial in Giddings." The cell did its work well, and Bill faced the gallows . . . again. One of Longley's last acts in prison was to write a letter bitterly protesting that Wes Hardin had gotten "only 25 years" for his misdeeds and he was going to hang.

An old-timer in Giddings told about how his father used to go to every hanging back in the days when public executions were social events. He remembered that Longley was the only one who had died bravely and with a smile on his face. The handsome murderer's last words were, "I see a lot of enemies out there and mighty few friends. I deserve this fate. It is a debt I owe for my wild reckless life. Goodbye, everybody." Longley was strung up for 11 minutes, and no lucky shots saved his life this time. He was 27 years old.

Bill may have been miffed over John Wesley Hardin's sentence, but Longley can rest assured in the fact that he rates a Texas Historical Marker, and Hardin has yet to earn Texas recognition.

A. J. Royal

Old Fort Cemetery
Fort Stockton

The epitaph reads:

A. J. Royal
Born Nov. 23, 1855
Assassinated Nov. 21, 1894
Sleep, Husband dear and take thy rest,
God called thee home, he thought it best,
It was hard indeed to part with thee,
But Christ's strong arm supported me.
Gone but not forgotten.

From that sentimental inscription, you would think A. J. Royal was a fine upstanding citizen and wonderful family man that was assassinated because he wanted to uphold law and order. The real truth is that a meaner, crueler, more despised man would be hard to find.

Andrew Jackson Royal had been involved in a number of serious offenses in Junction with several men buried as a result. His attitude did not change when he arrived in Fort Stockton, the last town he would ever terrorize.

In 1889 Royal had several assault and battery charges against him, and then he blasted a Mexican in the back with a shotgun saying the Mexican had threatened to kill him. After intimidating the witnesses, Royal was acquitted. Soon afterwards, rumors of Royal stealing horses and cattle were rife. When confronted, the thief dropped his claims to the stock.

Values were different back in the Old West. In 1892 Royal ran for sheriff and won with a good majority. The voters saw the error of their ways, however, when it became apparent that Royal was rotten clean through. His brutal attack on a citizen, the disappearance of a prisoner, and the death of Mexicans incensed the town.

On the frontier it was not unusual for the sheriff to operate the local saloon. However, when Royal opened the Grey Mule Saloon, he beat his competitor with a cane, and a feud erupted between the two saloonkeepers. When election time arrived, the judge of Fort Stockton sent for the Texas Rangers. Royal was favored by whites of bad reputation, and the crooked sheriff allowed a Mexican bandit to escape jail in order to gain Mexican support.

With six notches on his gun, Royal commanded such fear in the townspeople that the citizens decided Royal had to go. Royal lost the election, but that wasn't enough for the town. One November day, Royal was sitting at his desk with his pistol on and his gun close by. Two people were present and numbers of others in the hall. Suddenly, there was a blast from nowhere, and the town bully's head rested on his desk with blood coming from his mouth and streaming down his left arm.

The assassin was never apprehended. The story goes that a group of honest reputable citizens held a secret meeting to draw the black bean to rid Fort Stockton of its problem.

One of the best historical tours in West Texas is in Fort Stockton. While the ancient Comanche Springs no longer flow their 60 million gallons per day, the buildings from the old fort are in excellent repair, particularly the Annie Riggs Hotel. (See *A Guide to Historic Texas Inns and Hotels*, Lone Star Books, Houston, Texas.) Now one of the best pioneer museums in Texas, you can see A. J. Royal's desk. The tour ends at the Old Fort Cemetery. Soldiers who were buried here were moved long ago, but the records on the civilian tombstones indicate the harshness of life, for no one lived to be over 40. As for Royal's endearing epitaph, he was a good family man.

Judge Roy Bean

Whitehead Museum
1308 S. Main Street
Del Rio 78840
Hours: 8:30–4:30 Tues.–Sat.
512-774-3611
Admission free

 When it comes to legendary characters of the Old West, none can surpass the soiled and bewhiskered old, fat man that looked more like Santa Claus than a folk hero—Judge Roy Bean. (See *Traveling Texas Borders*, Lone Star Books, Houston, Texas.) On the lovely grounds of the Whitehead Museum in Del Rio is a plain concrete slab with nothing fancy written on it or above it that marks the grave of the "Law West of the Pecos."

The Judge was pressing sixty when he arrived in this untamed land west of the Pecos River. His neck had a permanent crook to it, from his own misfired hanging. The Judge said he was hanged because of a fight over a Mexican girl, and the senorita cut him down after he was left for dead. Just remember, the Judge was prone to altering the script as he told stories.

The character of Judge Roy Bean got its start from simple necessity. As the transcontinental tracks of the Sunset Route pushed across Texas' last frontier, the usual riff-raff followed the construction crews—bandits, cardsharps, ladies of the night, and gunmen. By 1882 the railroad was begging for help, so the Texas Rangers suggested a justice of the peace.

Roy Bean began his law career in a railroad camp called Vinegaroon after the scorpions that were the most numerous inhabitants of the area. As proprietor of a "store," Bean was a natural for the job. The next year he moved his "court" to Langtry.

Drunks often awoke to find themselves chained to the Judge's bed along with Bruno, his pet bear. One famous story has Bean declaring a man who murdered a Chinese man not guilty because he didn't "find any law in Texas against killing a Chinaman." After finding five dollars and a gun on a corpse, Bean fined the corpse five dollars for carrying a concealed weapon. When a man was accused of blowing daylight into a Mexican, the Judge pronounced, "It served the deceased right for getting in front of a gun."

For 20 years the Judge ruled the Pecos, and most of the time from his famed Jersey Lilly Saloon. It is true he named this oft-duplicated establishment for the beautiful actress Lillie Langtry. According to the story, the star's name was misspelled on the sign because the sign painter had indulged too liberally in the saloon's stock in trade. (There was also a railroad official with the name Langtry, but it is much more romantic to think it was named for Bean's idol.)

Judge Roy Bean created one of Texas' favorite legends with his Law West of the Pecos saloon.

The Judge saw the fabled Lillie on the stage in San Antonio, but never met her. After Bean's death, she did come to the town and offered to donate a water fountain. Supposedly, Langtry offered Lillie the Judge's pet bear, but Bruno broke and ran before the actress had to make the decision.

We all know of the Judge's "Jersey Lillie" but there was a Mrs. Roy Bean in the past. Her name was Virginia Chavez who left the Judge after they had adopted four children. Son Sam Bean lies in the grave next to his father.

Life in this dreary arid land was not all saloon keeping and dispensing justice. The Judge went into fight promotion with the world championship fight in 1896 between Maher and Fitzsimmons. The fight was judged illegal, and Rangers arrived to prevent the show. Mexico cooperated with the Rangers, but Bean just held the fight in the middle of the Rio Grande as lawmen and spectators from both sides watched Fitzsimmons score a knockout in less than three minutes.

The real Jersey Lilly stands in Langtry just as it did so long ago, now in a state park. A beautiful cactus garden has been added along with a new visitor center. His lawbook is here as well as the .41 caliber Smith and Wesson revolver he used as a gavel. A sign reads "No shooting, fighting, or loud cussing allowed and absolutely no spitting on the floor." The Texas historical marker reads, "On this exact site and this very building Judge Roy Bean dispensed hard liquor and harsh justice, all a part of his Law West of the Pecos." His justice was harsh, but Bean never hanged anyone; perhaps that crook in his neck was one hanging enough for him.

Candles of the faithful requesting health and happiness blaze in profusion at the grave of Don Pedrito.

Don Pedrito Jaramillo (1830–1907)

FM Road 1418
Falfurrias

In 1881 a Mexican man in his fifties arrived at Los Olmos Ranch near present-day Falfurrias and announced himself as a *curandero* or healer. He was certainly needed, for there was but one doctor between Corpus Christi and Laredo, and the Mexican population preferred a curandero to a doctor.

This unusual curandero was not the run-of-the-mill healer who also inflicted curses, removed curses, and prescribed herbs; this curandero used faith in the all-powerful God as his weapon. Today, in a small unpretentious shrine just outside of Falfurrias is a grave adorned with photographs, drivers licenses, and a pyrotechnic display of candles. Don Pedrito has been dead since 1907, but his influence is as strong as ever among the inhabitants.

When the Saint of Falurrias arrived at Los Olmos, he had spent his life as a poor laborer in Mexico working for half a bushel of corn and five dollars a month. This good man was charitable and sincere and believed he had a God-given mission to help the poor. Don Pedrito became the local priest, attorney, sheriff, and psychologist.

Don Pedrito became a curandero when he suffered from an affliction of the nose. During one night of agony, he went to a pool of water, lay down, and buried his painful face in mud. In three days the future healer was well and returned home. As he slept, a voice awakened him and told him he had received the gift of healing from the Lord God. After his holy visitation, the curandero's first cure was achieved when he prescribed a tepid bath for an ailing neighbor.

For 25 years, no other man worked so hard to relieve the suffering of his people as did Pedro Jaramillo. The local doctor, J. S. Strickland, remarked, "How do I know that Don Pedrito's prayers don't do more good than my pills?" Even the saintly parish priest, Father Bord, explained that where there were so few doctors, God saw fit to bestow on this humble man the power of help.

When the famous curandero went on a mission of mercy, he left at home groceries to feed the faithful who came to his house and waited for his return. Don Pedrito told his patients repeatedly, "I have no healing power, it is the power of God released through your faith which heals you." To help faith along, the healer offered such counsel as "Take a glass of water for nine nights, go out into the yard, raise your eyes to the heavens and say, 'In the name of God,' then take a taste and throw the rest out." This simple prescription resulted in a cure of epilepsy.

For violent headaches, all a sick man had to do was get up at the same hour for three mornings and drink a glass of water. Another remedy that was successful was for a woman to dip her head into a bucket of water before bedtime and the next morning put a can of tomatoes into each shoe and wear them all day *sin verguenza* (without shame).

Tomatoes were used in numerous cases, and one story goes that Don Pedrito was trying to help a shopkeeper who had overstocked with tomatoes. Regardless, the violently insane Colonel Regalo was brought to Don Pedrito, and the curandero merely prescribed a can of tomatoes every morning for nine mornings. At the end of his treatment, Colonel Regalo was a well man.

At times Don Pedrito refused to prescribe for his patients, telling them they either had too little faith or their affliction gave them too much pleasure. He refused to counsel clients in business or romantic affairs, nor did he tell fortunes. The curandero preferred mud, water, and spittle, as did his Savior, Jesus Christ.

Don Pedrito has not been formally recognized by the Catholic Church, but his followers arrive at his shrine in droves for the elusive gifts of health and happiness with the dead saint's help.

In the gift shop next door, you can buy statues of the Saint of Falfurrias, candles, books, herbs, pictures of the curandero, dashboard medallions, rosaries, and cold drinks.

Headless Horseman

Ben Bolt

This is a story that should begin with, "In the days of the Old West when frontier justice took bizarre forms . . ." for the tale of the Headless Horseman of Texas is unique in the annals of criminal punishment.

Down around Ben Bolt is a clump of scrubby trees surrounding some rotten wooden crosses, remnants of an old forgotten graveyard. The inhabitants are unknown except that one grave is that of El Muerto, the headless one.

The grave site is hard to find, because you have to know the specific clump of trees, and around Ben Bolt there just aren't a lot of people to ask. But, if you persevere, climb a few barbed wire fences, and plow through a few pastures, you will find the spot where El Muerto finally made his last ride.

During the days when Texas was a republic, law and order were sparse commodities, and cattle rustling big business. If the thieves were caught, how justice was dispensed depended on how everyone felt about the thief at the time.

One particular thief called Vidal stole some of Creed Taylor's horses. Taylor, in hot pursuit, ran into Big Foot Wallace who joined in the chase. Vidal was shot by his pursuers, and Taylor and Big Foot decided to teach all would-be thieves a lesson. They decapitated Vidal, tied the body to the strongest, wildest mustang they could find, and propped the corpse upright in the saddle. Then, they tied the head on the saddle horn and turned the mustang loose.

This strange apparition panicked everyone from Corpus Christi to Eagle Pass, as the eerie headless rider rode through the brush country of South Texas. Reports of the rider who refused to die created quite a legend in this raw wilderness.

Finally, the ghostly rider was run down at a waterhole, and the rustler's body was riddled with bullet holes. El Muerto did not stop the rustling and stealing, but he did originate a great Texas ghost story.

Bonnie Parker (1910–1934)

Crown Hill Memorial Park Dallas

Clyde Barrow (1909–1934)

West Dallas Cemetery Dallas

"As the flowers are all made sweeter
By the sunshine and the dew,
So this old world is made brighter
By the lives of folks like you."

These child-like lines are just a few of the many, many verses written by one of the most notorious criminals in the annals of U.S. crime. The composer of such innocence died with more than 50 bullet holes in her body and her right hand shot away. Bonnie Parker was 24 years old.

The saga of Bonnie Parker and Clyde Barrow lasted a brief two years. After they met in 1930, Clyde was sent to prison for auto theft and burglary. To get out of hard labor, Clyde had a fellow prisoner cut off two of his (Clyde's) toes. He was released in 1932, and by May 23, 1934 he and Bonnie had kidnapped seven victims and killed nine law officers and three civilians.

The greatest manhunt of the 1930s was led by Ted Hinton and lasted 17 months. There was no rapid communication in those days, and not everybody wanted to see the pair caught. Even the newspapers tended to romanticize Bonnie and Clyde's crimes.

The climax came at Gibsland, Louisiana, in 1934. Hinton deduced that the pair would come looking for their old cohort, Henry Methvin, who lived near Gibsland. Hinton pretended to have a flat on the road to the Methvin house where he waited two nights and one full day for a tan V-8 Ford and its two doomed passengers. About 9:15 A.M., just as Hinton was ready to give up, the stolen Ford came around the bend.

Bonnie and Clyde never knew what hit them. Bonnie still had a sandwich and a Louisiana roadmap in her hand. Clyde's shoes were off and his guns never fired. In a stunning example of overkill, the car was riddled with 167 bullets. In addition to a shotgun, 9 pistols, 4 Browning Automatic rifles, 1,000 rounds of ammunition, clothing,

One of Texas' favorite grave rubbings is Bonnie Parker's epitaph.

food, and camping equipment, Clyde had also carried his saxophone.

Hinton described the surrounding populace as becoming "crazy as loons." People were on their hands and knees gathering up shell casings and digging out bullets embedded in trees. The procession into Arcadia, Louisiana, of 200 cars was led by the wrecker dragging the mutilated car and bodies. When it stopped in front of the schoolhouse, the kids flew out and tore Bonnie's red dress and smeared their hands in her blood. The car was ripped apart for souvenirs, and by nightfall, Arcadia had 9,000 sightseers.

Bonnie's grave marker is now a favorite item for people who collect grave rubbings. Her funeral was attended by 40,000 spectators. Clyde is across town in an unkept corner next to his brother Buck, who had also died in a gun battle as part of Clyde's gang the year before. Clyde only attracted 30,000 to his funeral.

Hinton summed up the manhunt with "We didn't catch 'em. They was never *captured*. They was killed. Once they knew, beyond the shadow of a doubt, that capture could only mean death in the electric chair, they resisted capture, and sometimes they resisted by killing their would-be captors. They could continue this way only so long, until they would die. They stuck together, and they loved each other. That just about tells it."

The death car was a new "Desert Sand" Ford Jesse Warren of Topeka, Kansas had bought for $785.92. Bonnie and Clyde had driven it 7,500 miles in 23 days. Ruth Warren had to go to Arcadia and hire a lawyer to get her car back two months later.

Shipped to Topeka, the car was leased to John R. Castle, who exhibited it, and then to Charles Stanley, who bought it. Between 1934 and 1940, lots of Bonnie and Clyde cars were seen. In 1952 Ted Toddy bought the real car for $14,500 and ended up storing it in a warehouse. When the movie "Bonnie and Clyde" broke boxoffice records, Toddy got the car out of storage and grossed over $1 million exhibiting it. Wouldn't Bonnie and Clyde have been envious!

Eccentrics

Sometimes it is difficult to separate just plain crazy from odd human quirks. But Texas is proud of the unusual personalities and their interesting peccadilloes that add to the Texas mystique.

Bailey's Prairie

Highway 35
Between West Columbia and Angleton

Between West Columbia and Angleton somewhere on the prairie stands an eccentric extraordinaire, Brit Bailey. Since about 1832, Brit has been "standing" on his prairie, because of having said in his will, "All my life I have traveled west, and I never looked up to any man, so I do not want it said, 'here lies old Brit Bailey'... have my remains interred erect with my face fronting the West."

Also, according to the story, Brit wanted his rifle in his hand and his faithful jug "Old Bubba" at his feet. When Brit died of the fever, Mrs. Bailey went along with the rifle as the coffin was lowered feet first into a standing position, but at the last minute changed her mind about including "Old Bubba."

James Britton Bailey spent the first 42 years of his life as a hunter and Indian fighter. He was never seen unarmed and carried a rifle, a pouch with 150 bullets, and two pistols. Brit thought death would only transport him to new hunting grounds and fields of battle, and he wanted to be prepared.

Brit Bailey arrived in Texas even before Moses Austin, and he became one of Texas' first squatters. When Stephen F. Austin arrived with his 300 colonists, Austin was determined to rid his landgrant of Brit and Nancy Bailey and their six children. Bailey defied the empressario, and Austin finally allowed Bailey to stay. Brit even became a lieutenant in Austin's militia. In 1832, Bailey, armed to the teeth as usual, was right in the midst of the Battle of Velasco, and when he returned to his prairie home, he became somewhat of a hero.

Brit died that same year and never made it to the Revolution.

The exact spot where Brit's remains stand is lost, but Brit still makes his presence known. For a few years after his death, his ghost wandered around his house frightening its tenants. Then, in the 1850s people began seeing a bright light moving across the prairie but floating out of reach when chased. The ghost light was seen even during the 1960s. Some wits claim it's old Brit looking for "Old Bubba." Who knows, maybe all those ghost light seekers have enjoyed their own "Old Bubba" too well.

Anyway, when you are down on Bailey's Prairie, if you don't see Brit looking for his jug, stop and read the historical markers shaped like gravestones, telling you all about one of Texas' most unique individuals.

Out on a lonely hill stands the Johnson Mausoleum, erected by the founder of the now abandoned town of Thurber.

William W. Johnson Mausoleum

Thurber

On the list of famous Texas ghost towns, Thurber has got to be up there in the top ten. (See "Texas Underground.") The town's remnants sit on thousands of tons of bituminous coal that no one wants. The man who brought Thurber to its zenith by discovering this vast coal deposit never left. William W. Johnson and his family are still there in a "house" of sandstone sealed for eternity.

On a hill overlooking absolutely nothing stands a small fortress with no way in or out. It contains four caskets, and this crypt is the only reminder of the Johnson family.

In 1885 the Johnson's three-year old daughter Marian died. Anna, her mother, was absolutely devastated and could not bear to see her baby buried. She built her a little "house." Nine years later, another tragedy struck the Johnsons as their only son, Harvey, age seven, died. This time a new "house" was built, and it was not long before the mother joined her two children. In 1922 the fourth casket was added to the "house" of native stone on the Johnson ranch. In a final touch of irony, the town died the same year its founder did.

A visit to the Johnson house is not advised. It is on private property behind locked gates in a rough pasture infested with rattlesnakes. Besides, the Johnsons would probably prefer their isolation, or they would have built their "house" in a public cemetery.

Howard Hughes

Houston

Howard Hughes' biographers have not been kind to this dead eccentric. For years the public believed that Hughes had the Midas touch, and every venture he made turned to gold. But, Hughes was a man that created legends, even though few were true. What can you expect

of a man who spent the last 18 years of his life in a sealed bedroom addicted to narcotics.

Howard Hughes, Jr. was born on Christmas Eve, 1905. His father was just beginning the Hughes millions with the invention of a rock bit that was a boon to the oil industry. Howard Jr.'s mother doted on him, but he still grew up rather shy with no close friends. Even though Howard never finished college, his powerful ability for total recall convinced people he was a genius. But, somehow, Howard Hughes never learned to convert his knowledge into practical application.

After his parents' deaths, the young millionaire became interested in the movie industry, and at 21 directed his first film, *Hell's Angels*. It was a World War I silent movie epic that called for numerous flying scenes. Hughes bought up old planes all over Europe and accummulated the largest private airforce in the world. Hughes even flew and crashed one of the planes himself, but he was not seriously injured. Three other pilots died filming the movie, and *Hell's Angels* was finally finished at an exhorbitant cost. Ironically, before it could be released, the film was obsolete, for *The Jazz Singer* had tolled the death knell for silent films.

As his original heroine spoke with a Norwegian accent, Hughes was persuaded to try an unknown actress named Jean Harlow. With sound, *Hell's Angels* was a smash, and it set the theme for all of Hughes' productions—rich in entertainment, low on philosophy and message, and packed with sex and action. *Hell's Angels* launched the Hughes legend.

The next big Hughes production was *Scarface*, starring George Raft. Then came *The Outlaw* and the publicity for a new brassiere Hughes had invented for his leading lady, Jane Russell. "The Outlaw" was not a success and never made money in spite of all the emphasis on Miss Russell's anatomy.

Hughes' next interest was the world of flight, and the intense pilot became absorbed in flying around the world. Finally, in 1938 Hughes did set a world's record for around-the-world flight. He was lionized by the entire country.

Hughes Aircraft secured a government contract to build a flying boat, the Hercules or HK-1. Most of the time the awkward-looking plane was referred to as the *Spruce Goose*, a nickname that made Hughes furious. Constructed of plywood, the *Spruce Goose* was and still is the largest plane ever built. But, the war was over before the plane was tested. In 1947 the lumbering old gal was able to get off the ground for a few minutes, but it was woefully underpowered. Rather than demolish it, Hughes leased the big mistake back from the Government for $1 million a year to preserve it.

Hughes also contracted for a new plane, the XF-11. While he was testing it, the props reversed and he crashed. With multiple injuries and fractures, Hughes was told he would not live. Incredibly enough, Hughes not only survived the crash, but he had no permanent disabilities. Hughes said it was because he drank huge quantities of orange juice. The XF-11 ended up as scrap.

Back in the movie business, Hughes' next major film was *Jet Pilot*. There were thousands and thousands of feet of aerial photography for he could not bear to cut any of the footage. It took so long to edit, the "jet pilot" was flying obsolete planes. The film cost millions and was a total waste. With Hughes as owner, RKO lost money and their rank as one of the top five film companies in America.

By now Hughes was becoming more aberrant and eratic than ever. He imagined people were listening to his conversations. He would hold talks in bathrooms with the water running so no one could hear him, or he would rent auditoriums and sit in the center in order to have a private talk.

Hughes also developed a strange phobia about dirt. His aides had to wear gloves whenever they handled anything. They also had to buy three newspapers, and the eccentric would take the one in the middle. To escape dust, Hughes ordered windows and doors sealed with masking tape. The millionaire began to go without shaving, and his clothes were often filthy.

By the mid 1950s, a few of his major holdings were Hughes Aircraft Company, Hughes Tool Company, Hughes Productions, and Trans-World Airlines. Hughes married Jean Peters, a Hollywood star in a deserted mining town in Nevada, and both used assumed names. Jean and Howard spent most of their married life in separate houses, but they seemed fond of each other, and the marriage lasted several years.

In the end, Hughes' phobias became too much for him. In the sealed bedrooms of his various hotels, he became addicted to narcotics to such a degree that his autopsy showed needles broken off in his arms. His reputation as a recluse kept the world from knowing of his addiction and madness until his death. Howard Hughes was a classic example of the man who desired to be master of everything, yet could not master himself.

The Last Roundup

The post-Civil War era in Texas saw the beginning of the huge cattle drives to the Kansas railheads. Texas' sole source of wealth was a few million tough, stubborn, and lean old Longhorns. The only way to get them to the beef-hungry East was walk them to the railroads. The great cattle ranches emerged during this period as did the romance and legends of the famous cattle trails.

Oliver Loving

Weatherford

The real pioneer of the herds bawling their way "up the trail" was Oliver Loving. With John Durkee, Loving drove a herd to Chicago in 1858, the first occasion on record of Texas cattle going directly to market.

During the Civil War, Loving furnished beef to the Confederacy and in 1866 joined with his friend Charles Good-

night to sell cattle in New Mexico. The two cattle kings established the Goodnight-Loving Trail from Fort Belnap, Texas, to Fort Sumner, New Mexico. They also organized the first great cattle drive from Weatherford to Kansas.

On one of the drives, Trailmaster Charles Goodnight nailed a stout cupboard, called a chuck box, right onto the back of a wagon, as an efficient method of feeding his trail hands, and invented the famed chuck wagon.

In 1867 tragedy befell Loving. The Dean of the Trail Drivers was en route to Fort Sumner with Goodnight. Riding lookout with one-armed Bill Wilson, the two men were attacked by Indians, and Loving was seriously wounded. Loving, believing himself to be dying, sent Wilson to warn Goodnight who was following with the herd. Before Wilson reached Goodnight, Loving was rescued by Mexicans and taken to Fort Sumner.

Goodnight arrived, overjoyed to find his friend alive and his wound healing. But, in those days when infection was a mystery, gangrene developed, and in three weeks Loving was dead. The cattle baron told Goodnight, "Take me back to Texas. Don't leave me in foreign soil."

The trails these cattle kings blazed were followed by thousands, and in 1887 the last county organized in Texas was named for Oliver Loving. Loving County had 3 people in 1890 and 227 in 1950 (see *Traveling Texas Borders*, Lone Star Books, Houston, Texas), and is still the least populated county in the state.

Goodnight honored his friend's last request, and Loving lies under a plain concrete marker beneath beautiful oak trees not too far from the trails he made so famous. Here in the heart of Texas rests the man who did not want to be left in foreign soil.

Abel "Shanghai" Pierce

Hawley Cemetery
Blessing

Many years ago an old black man sat and rocked away his remaining years on the porch of the Blessing Hotel. He delighted and thrilled the youngsters with stories of his boss, the famous cattle baron, Shanghai Pierce. The youngsters are old men now, and the storyteller is dead, but you can still see Shanghai in the nearby Hawley Cemetery.

"There stands Old Pierce," Shanghai would say as he rode by, and Old Pierce stands today with Shanghai beneath him. This full-sized statue of one of Texas' most famous cattlemen surveys his former domain from a 40-foot pedestal of solid bronze through bullet-riddled eyes. Some vandal or foe (or even Old Pierce himself) shot out the statue's eyes.

Abel Head Pierce was born in 1834 in far away Rhode Island. At 19 he stowed away on a schooner bound for Indianola, Texas. His first job in Texas was as a rail splitter for $14 a month. Not a very auspicious beginning for a future cattle baron.

After Pierce began to acquire his own cattle, he ran them under the AP brand, but the Civil War ruined him. He later established Rancho Grande on the Trespalacios River, but once again tragedy struck. His wife and infant son died, and Pierce left for Kansas.

Kansas didn't last, and the cattleman was back in Texas with 250,000 acres. He formed a cattle company that sent thousands of head of beef up the trails.

There are two stories of how Pierce acquired his famous sobriquet, "Shanghai." One says it was because he stowed away to come to Texas. Another tale goes that John B. Stetson wore a hat with a large brim and high crown made of untanned rabbit fur. Stetson called the hat "The Great Provider" because of its protection from the elements.

When the fun-loving Pierce came to Denton and tried on the hat with a crown that stood up like the comb of a proud cock, he shook his spurs and crowed, "By damn, this hat with these spurs make me look like a Shanghai rooster."

Other stories abound about Shanghai. He could raise as much hell as any cowboy and had several run-ins with Wyatt Earp for conduct unbecoming a cattle king. According to his devoted black hand, "Mr. Shang was a good man, but a hard man." His faithful servant carried Shanghai's money, and wherever Mr. Shang stayed, he stayed.

When the $10,000 statue arrived from Italy, Shanghai stood back and walked round and round his likeness. He

Through gunshot eyes, "Shanghai" Pierce stares at his former kingdom. (Photograph courtesy of John S. Runnells.)

then asked his black treasurer, "What do you think?" The man replied, "Mr. Shang, it's a fair likeness." Shanghai never did like the eyes, and with his fondness for drink, it is quite possible he shot out the eyes himself.

But, Shanghai did the cattle industry a tremendous service. He concluded that ticks caused cattle fever, and he toured Europe searching for a breed immune to ticks. He correctly picked the Brahmans as the most likely breed to resist the dreaded ticks.

In 1900 Shanghai lost more than $1 million in the Galveston storm and bad investments. On December 26, a cerebral hemorrhage caused the demise of one of the most celebrated trail drivers to ever cross the Red River. His estate later imported Brahman cattle which furnished Texas with the basic stock. No one had to build a monument to Shanghai's colorful memory; he had already done it himself.

John S. Chisum

Washington Street
Paris

The novice history buff often confuses the legendary Chisholm of "Trail" fame with John Simpson Chisum so vividly portrayed by John Wayne in the epic movie *Chisum*. There were Chisum Trails, but they were from Fort Sumner to Las Animas, Colorado, and Fort Sumner to Tascosa, Texas. Neither trail achieved the romance and adventure of Jesse Chisholm's trail, but the great Duke saw to it that Chisum would be remembered as well.

The Chisum family migrated from Tennessee to the Red River country in 1837. As a young man, Chisum entered the cattle business and soon had the largest "outfit" in that part of Texas. During the Civil War, Chisum sold beef to the Confederacy at $40 a head, but astutely turned his money back into cattle instead of being wiped out with useless Confederate money.

At the end of the war, Chisum moved to New Mexico near Roswell, and Charles Goodnight handled his cattle. The Chisum brand was a "rail" from shoulder to thigh, and his earmark slit the ear so deeply the lower part dangled limply. This "jinglebob" mark was so well known, the cattleman was called "Jinglebob John" and "Boss of the Jinglebob."

John Chisum was probably the biggest cattle baron in the 1800s with over 60,000 head.

In 1854, at age 30, John opened his ranch in the northwestern part of Denton County. He was a good fiddler, and his home became a social center. During one horrendous week of rain, a party was marooned at the Chisum ranch, and the longest dance in Texas reeled away the whole week.

By 1864 the Chisum herds covered many counties over a vast free territory. (Chisum never purchased any of the land in Concho county at all.) Chisum suffered financially during the Lincoln County War, and his herds began melting away. A throat infection caused his return to Paris, Texas, where he died in 1884. A huge ornate piece of weathered marble, marks his grave in Paris.

The Final Curtain Call

When the stage lights dimmed for the last performance of some of Texas' great stars, they came back to the home they knew before they were rich and famous.

Jim Reeves Memorial

Highway 79 East
Carthage

If I, a lowly singer, dry one tear
Or soothe one humble human heart in pain,
Then my homely verse to God is dear
And not one stanza has been sung in vain.

 These words are carved on the granite monument at Jim Reeves' grave. Atop a pedestal is a life-sized statue of the singer, and a guitar-shaped walk leads to the memorial. Inscribed on a disc in the center of the guitar is:

JIM REEVES
GENTLEMAN
TIME: AUG. 20, 1923   PRODUCER: GOD
JULY 31, 1964

"Gentleman Jim" Reeves was far from being a lowly singer. Not only was he one of the first American singers to bridge the gap between country and pop music, but Jim also recorded four gold records. Even after his death, Reeves'

records continue to sell in enormous quantities, and his version of "It's Nothing to Me" became a Top-20 hit in 1977.

Jim was born a few miles east of Carthage at Galloway. His father died when he was very young, and his mother worked in the fields. Jim traced his interest in music to hearing the great Jimmy Rodgers' recordings. But, Jim was also interested in being the high school baseball team's leading pitcher. He entered the University of Texas, and his baseball expertise gained him a contract with the St. Louis Cardinals. An unlucky slip on a wet pitch gave Jim an ankle injury that ended his sports career, but made the halls of country music a great deal richer.

Jim and his wife, Mary, flipped a coin to decide whether to go to Dallas or Shreveport. The luck of the toss was with them, and Jim landed a job as announcer of KWKH, the

Gentleman Jim Reeves never sang a stanza in vain.

station that owned the Louisiana Hayride in Shreveport. (See *Traveling Texas Borders*, Lone Star Books, Houston, Texas.)

One night in 1952 Hank Williams failed to show for a performance, and Jim was asked to fill in. It was a moviescript success story. In the audience was Fabor Robison, owner of the Abbott Record Company, and Jim was signed straight away. With "Mexican Joe" in 1953, Jim reached No. 1 on the charts, achieved his first gold record, and became a featured star on the Louisiana Hayride.

The second gold record came in 1956 with "Bimbo," and a string of hits followed. Reeves then joined the Grand Ole Opry in Nashville and began touring Europe. The release of "Four Walls" in 1957 was a major turning point for the star. "Four Walls" was a smash in both country and pop fields and turned gold. But, Reeves' all-time greatest hit was in 1959 with "He'll Have To Go." His dark, intimate, velvet tones that glided over a muted background were something different again, and with this gold disc came international stardom. With the sixties came "I Love You Because," "You're the Only Good Thing," "Am I Losing You?" "Welcome to My World," and "I Won't Forget You."

Reeves was always considered to be one of the friendliest and most courteous of all the celebrities in show business. Because of his well-mannered personality, Reeves earned the title of "Gentleman Jim," which followed him to his death.

On a fateful day in July, Jim and his manager Dean Manuel flew a single engine plane from Arkansas to Nashville. Only a few miles from landing, they ran into heavy rains, and the plane disappeared from the radar screen. Two days later the wreckage and bodies were discovered amid thick foliage.

After his death, Jim's body was flown back to Carthage where hundreds filed past the coffin. Inquiries came from all over the world requesting information concerning his place of burial. He now rests in a lovely park studded with large oak and pine trees, which Jim loved so well. In 1967 he received the highest award given to a singer; he was voted into the Country Music Hall of Fame. None of Jim Reeves' stanzas have been sung in vain.

"Blind" Lemon Jefferson

Wortham

The Wortham Cemetery is nothing spectacular, and if you hunt for celebrities or unusual interments, you will never find them there. However, in the smaller Wortham Negro Cemetery nearby, you will find one of the greatest blues musicians that ever lived.

One of seven children, Lemon Jefferson was born blind on a farm outside of Wortham in 1897. He worked as an itinerant singing beggar at farm parties, picnics, and on the streets of the town. By 1914, Jefferson's "field-holler-work shout" form of singing took him to the streets and brothels of East Dallas and Galveston. A few years later, "Blind" Lemon Jefferson hoboed extensively as a singer on the streets throughout the South, still performing for picnics, suppers, and parties, or wherever he could get work. He never stayed in one city very long.

By the late twenties, the great blues singer was recording on the Paramount label in Chicago and the OKed label. Jefferson spent his entire life, however, as a street singer. His heart attack and death from exposure was on the streets where he had spent most of his life.

"The blues" are synonymous with sorrow. Jefferson left behind a formidable list of "blues" songs, and all are sad: "Bad Luck Blues," "Chinch Bug Blues," "Rabbit Foot Blues," along with the hobo songs, "Prison Cell Blues," "Tin Cup Blues," and "One Dime Blues."

The list of future musicians influenced by Blind Lemon reads like a Who's Who in the Music World. To name a few: Louis Armstrong, B. B. King, Leadbelly, Jelly Roll Morton, Jimmie Rodgers, Bessie Smith, "T-Bone" Walker, Tommy Dorsey, Bix Beiderbecke, and Harry James. Even a rock group popular in the 1960s was the Jefferson Airplane.

The small Texas marker over Blind Lemon Jefferson reads, "One of America's outstanding original musicians." His song "See That My Grave is Kept Clean," has been taken literally, and Blind Lemon Jefferson's only monument is his music.

Tex Ritter

Oak Bluff Memorial Park
Port Neches

In 1952 Dimitri Tiomkin was scoring a movie already finished, and he needed the singer for the theme song. Tiomkin's one and only choice to sing the Academy Award winning score was Tex Ritter. Twenty years later, *High Noon* was still Tex's most requested number whenever he performed.

Woodward Maurice Ritter was born in Panola County, but the family moved to Nederland, and Tex always considered this Dutch community his hometown. When Tex enrolled at the University of Texas, he fully intended to become a lawyer, but his love of cowboy music led him to study under folklorists J. Frank Dobie and John A. Lomax. After transferring to Northwestern, Tex Ritter began singing western and mountain songs publicly, and in 1929 became a featured singer for Station KPRC in Houston. His law career ended before it ever began.

Stardom was on the horizon when Tex landed several roles in Broadway plays including *Green Grow the Lilacs*, a predecessor to *Oklahoma!* Franchot Tone sang the song in the play, but Tex recorded it. In one album Tex narates the story of how American troops sang this old song in their camps along the Rio Grande during the Mexican War. When Mexican soldiers heard the lyrics in the late evenings across the river, they heard the words as "Gringo." So, from this song evolved the Mexican term for Americans.

By 1936 Tex was in Hollywood following Gene Autry as a singing star and cranking out Grade B "oaters." Out of 85 features, 78 movies were westerns, and the format seldom varied from film to film.

In these low budget films, the sets were always identical from movie to movie, the bartender or side-kick provided the comic relief, and absolutely nobody took their hat off. Tex did come out with one winner, however; he married Fay Southworth, his leading lady in most of his westerns. John Ritter, one of their two sons, inherited his father's love of the stage and stars in the ABC–TV sitcom *Three's Company*.

The "oaters" declined in popularity as the adult or psychological westerns became the vogue, but Tex was still one of country music's biggest sellers. When the unforgettable *High Noon* was released in 1953, the entire country sang along with Tex Ritter.

After Tex moved to Nashville, he became active in the Country Music Foundation and president of the Grand Ole Opry. In 1964 Tex Ritter was elected as the fifth inductee in the Country Music Hall of Fame, the first living performer so honored. Unfortunately, Tex acted on a lifetime desire and ran unsuccessfully for the U.S. Senate. The debts he incurred were to haunt him until his death by a heart attack in 1974.

This great singer did not have a great voice, but his unusual accent, odd slurs and phrasing, plus an enduring strong sense of honesty made his sometimes plaintive, sometimes gruff, voice one of the most appealing in country music's history.

Tex's long list of hits include his rendition of "Boll Weevil" sung as it was taught to him by a black man, Robert Williams, with a deep East Texas Panola County accent. In the 1940s, Tex Ritter was number 1, 2, 3, and 5 on the charts. Those were the days you could have a hit on both sides, and "Jealous Heart" and "You Two-timed Me Once Too Often" were on the same disc. Other firsts on the charts were "Let Me Go, Lover" and "You Will Have to Pay," but the one that outsold the most before "High Noon" was "Have I Told You Lately That I Love You?"

The first record Tex made was "Rye Whiskey" in 1933 in New York, and in 1943 it became a hit again. The song was originally titled "Jack O'Diamonds," and Tex used it in his first movie.

In a little Dutch windmill in Nederland on Boston Avenue are a few mementos of one of the greatest country-western singers of all time. A plaque outside proclaims the W. M. "Tex" Ritter Park.

Dan Davis Blocker

Woodmen Cemetery
Dekalb

In an age where nothing seems very permanent, you could at least always count on the folks at the Ponderosa to entertain you every Sunday evening. For a miraculous 13 seasons or 440 episodes, the Cartwrights rode the range of television land in the smash *Bonanza* series. Pa, Little Joe, Adam, Jim, and Hop Sing delighted

Known by millions as Hoss Cartwright, Dan Blocker smiles his shy grin in his hometown of O'Donnell.

millions of viewers, but the most beloved Ponderosa resident of them all was "Hoss."

In the fantasyland of TV, Hoss was a big, bumbling, not-too-bright, but devoted, honest, and diligent son. Hoss never got the girl, was often the brunt of Little Joe's jokes, and never missed one of Hop Sing's meals. From 1959 to 1973, this creation of David Dortort for NBC made television history as the longest running of any show since the television set was invented.

In real life, Dan Blocker was an astute businessman, a college graduate with a masters degree, and in 1965 was voted Texan of the Year.

Dan was always big, however, and he was born in DeKalb at a record-breaking 14 pounds. At 12, Dan was 6 feet tall, weighed 200 pounds, and was still growing. When he arrived at Sul Ross State Teachers College, Blocker was a giant at 6 feet, 4 inches, and 275 pounds. This coach's dream led Sul Ross through an undefeated football season to the conference championship.

Naturally, the football star was made many tempting offers in professional football and boxing, but Dan refused and got his B.A. in speech and drama. After serving in Korea, the big man returned to Sul Ross for his masters and married his childhood sweetheart, Dolphia Lee Parker. When Dan was five, the Blockers moved to O'Donnell which Dan always thought of as home.

After teaching school a few years, Dan moved his family to Los Angeles where he began work on his Ph.D. at UCLA. After landing the part of Hoss, Dan never returned to school. When he died in 1972 following complications from an operation, millions of television viewers mourned.

Even though Dan is buried in Dekalb, a museum in the little town of O'Donnell has many photographs and clippings of its famous resident. The Blockers and their four children spent many days in this tiny West Texas town. O'Donnell also erected a bust of Hoss with his familiar shy-sweet smile and characteristic tilt of his head bearing the inscription:

"Thanks to film, Hoss Cartwright will live. But, all too seldom does the world get to keep a Dan Blocker."

The Last Inning

The Hornsby graveyard is filled with historical markers, but Rogers got crossed baseball bats.

Two of the greatest baseball players in the history of the game were Texans. Rogers Hornsby's family was here long before Texas was a state and in Austin before it was a capital. Tris Speaker was the first nominee to be voted into the Texas Sports Hall of Fame, and both athletes set records yet unbroken.

Rogers "Rajah" Hornsby

Hornsby's Bend Cemetery
Austin

When you go to the Hornsby Cemetery, you keep bumping into historical markers, for Hornsby's Bend was the first settlement in Travis County. Reuben Hornsby was part of the Austin Colony, and established his headright of 4605.5 acres in 1832. From then on, the Hornsby family was destined to play an important role in Texas history.

One of the most incredible stories of pioneer ESP occurred at Hornsby's Bend that same year. A survey party of five men was attacked by Indians at what is now Manor and East Fifty-first Street in Austin. Two men were killed, and a third, Josiah Wilbarger with arrows in both legs and a rifle ball in his neck, was left for dead.

Amazingly, Wilbarger was still alive. He came to his senses to find he had been scalped and stripped naked except for one sock. Josiah crawled to water and managed to soak his head with the sock. As the poor man lay in agony, he had a vision of his sister, Margaret Clifton in Missouri, telling him not to despair. That same night, Sara Hornsby, Reuben's wife, dreamed Wilbarger was not dead and saw the exact spot he was lying. She demanded her husband take a rescue party and save the scalped victim. After his rescue, Wilbarger discovered his sister had died the day *before* he was scalped by the Indians.

The Hornsby name continued to shine through Texas history, and then one of Reuben's descendents created a Hornsby legend of a different sort. On September 10, 1915, the name Hornsby showed up for the first time in a St. Louis box score. No one in the sports world got very excited over a 19-year-old Texas kid who played shortstop for the Cardinals. Yet, this unknown baseball player was destined for the very peak of sports records. Before leaving St. Louis, "Rajah" led the National League 7 times in batting (3 times with averages over .400), and the Cardinals won their first pennant and the city's first world championship in 38 years.

The world's greatest righthanded hitter was born in Winters, Texas, in 1896. Older brother "Pep" was a right-handed spitball pitcher and probably inspired "Rajah" to carry a baseball and glove wherever he went. Pep took Rogers to spring training with the Dallas team, but the skinny kid couldn't make the grade. Rogers signed with Denison in a class-D league.

Rogers was not a spectacular star at first. In fact, he only batted .232, and no one saw any real potential in his performance. When the Cardinals' second team played an exhibition game in Denison, its manager, Connery, was impressed with young Hornsby's pep and life on the field as well as his strong arm and hands. For the magnificent sum of $500, Rogers went to the Cardinals, but was told to "put on some muscle."

After consuming vast quantities of milk and steak, the rookie arrived in 1916 at spring camp 30 pounds heavier. In no time, Rogers became one of the game's most feared hitters. By 1919, "Rajah" was playing second base where he found his calling. By 1920 his batting average was .370, and the Hall of Fame was in sight. In 1922 he posted a .401 average, and later hit back-to-back .400s with a .424 in the 1924 season and a .403 in 1925.

"Rajah" became the Cardinals' manager that year, and in 1926 when the team broke spring training, "Rajah" told the players they would win the pennant. If they didn't believe it, they weren't wanted. Sure enough, the Cardinals held their one-run lead (thanks to Grover Cleveland Alexander), and won the seventh game of the Series.

"Rajah" was not known for his sweet nature and was traded to the Giants. Then, he was traded to the Boston Braves in 1928 where he again won the league batting average with a .387. Then, the record-breaker went on to the Chicago Cubs, where he was voted Most Valuable Player in 1929. Returning to the Cardinals, "Rajah" ended his 22-year major league career in 1936 with a lifetime batting average of .358, the highest in National League history.

"Rajah" continued in baseball as coach and manager for various clubs, and died in Chicago while teaching in a city youth program. Hornsby never attended movies or read during his playing career for fear of injuring his amazing eyesight. A habitual horse player, "Rajah" even gambled away an automobile given to him after winning the 1926 World Series.

Rogers Hornsby is buried among his famous Texas pioneer ancestors at the family plot, Hornsby's Bend. As per Rogers' request, he rests at the foot of his mother's grave.

Tristram "Tris" Speaker

Hubbard

The first member of the Texas Sports Hall of Fame was one of the greatest outfielders in the history of baseball. Called "Spoke" and "The Gray Eagle" (the latter because of his prematurely gray hair), Tris Speaker's records are a sports statistician's dream: most putouts, 6,706; most assists, 449; chances accepted, 7,195; most doubles in major league history, 793; and he stole 433 bases.

Speaker's style of fielding was so unique no one, before or since, has played center field so close to the infield. Tris had an uncanny ability to gauge the speed and distance a ball would travel. He was always there—under it and catching it when it fell.

Called a "fifth infielder," Speaker threw out 30 or more men in 4 seasons; twice he threw out 35. The records show that two times in April 1918, Tris had unassisted double plays at second base.

All of those records are about an outfielder, but Tris started in baseball as a pitcher—and a poor one. He was signed by Cleburne, not for his pitching, but because he could hit and field the ball. Houston purchased him and put him in interfield, and he played this position the rest of his career.

After Tris's great year of 1912 with a .383 for the Boston Red Sox and a Most Valuable Player award, the Red Sox played the New York Giants in the World Series. With his team behind 2 to 1 in the tenth inning, Speaker singled in the tying run. In 1920 Tris was back in the World Series, this time with the Cleveland Indians. He batted .388, socked in 50 doubles and 11 triples among 214 hits and drove in 107 runs. With that kind of record, no wonder Cleveland won the Series.

After this victory, Speaker brought the team to his home town, Hubbard, for a visit. They played a game so the home folks could see big leaguers in action. Tris loved his hometown and returned there often. On one of those visits, the great Tris Speaker suffered a fatal heart attack. Hubbard and the team wanted to erect a monument to this all-time baseball hero, but his wife insisted on a plain granite marker. Speaker's monument stands in baseball's record books.

Boot Hills

"Boot Hill." Dodge City, Kansas, named it, and the West adopted it, for no term better described the cemeteries of lawless towns where so many graves were for those "who died with their boots on." In this raw land of the frontier, about the easiest thing in life was leaving it. Even the law-abiding and God-fearing lie next to those who reached a violent end. Texas was one of the most savage parts of the frontier, and yet only two Boot Hills are marked in the state.

Boot Hill of Tilden

Tilden

Down in Tilden a rickety old sign and single wooden boot proclaim the town's Boot Hill. Originally called Dog Town because the local ranchers used packs of dogs to round up cattle, Tilden's name was supposedly changed to honor a defeated presidential candidate. Tilden was a stage stop between San Antonio and Laredo and had a rather lurid past.

This pathetic little cemetery began with the grave of a suicide, and its occupants testify to the tough frontier life. Dick Gosset was killed in a gunfight while John Smithwick was merely murdered. Samuel Wm. McCreery was also murdered at his sheep ranch, and Jim ? was assassinated from the door of an old rock store. The same gun battle that got Jim ?, got another unknown, a mere bystander. Another unnamed went to his reward from a prank Clabe Young played (details are not included about the prank). Other graves include those of an anonymous drowning victim and a man thought to be a member of the Dalton gang, who murdered James Minter.

Poor Glenn Greer was thrown from his horse, and Lige Harrison, Jr. was killed at age 17 in a hunting accident. The only ones buried in Tilden's Boot Hill who died nonviolently are four cholera victims. A rich full life was not standard operating procedure in Dog Town.

Boot Hill of Tascosa

Tascosa

On a lonely, little hill overlooking Cal Farley's famous Boy's Ranch stands an old cemetery— all that is left of one of the most rootin' tootin' wildest towns in the West. Down the streets of Ol' Tascosy strolled the famous and the infamous, but all that is left behind are the legends.

Because the Canadian River offered an easy crossing at this point, Old Tascosa grew to be a thriving den of thieves, gunfighters, comancheros, Indians, and lawmen. No wonder it was called "the Cowboy Capital of the Plains."

Charles Goodnight arrived with the first cattle in this free-grass empire in 1876, and the land boom was on. With the rip-roaring saloons, crooked card games, and "loose" women, Tascosa became the epitome of a Hollywood western town.

The town's first sheriff, Cope Willingham, shot the cowboy who filled Boot Hill's first grave. Other occupants include a saloon keeper who lost a fight over his wife, a tough trail boss who was hit with two barrels of buckshot, and a Dutchman who was gunned down from the distance of one foot.

In the late 1870s an Irishman named Mickey McCormick arrived to operate a saloon. One of the belles of Tascosa was "Frenchy," who earned her livelihood dealing monte. Frenchy took up with Mickey and married him, but she continued dealing for such famous guests as Billy the Kid,

Dave Rudabaugh, Charles A. Siringo, Pat Garrett, and Bat Masterson.

When Old Tascosa died and Mickey followed in 1908, Frenchy remained all alone in the ghost town. Finally, the old, old lady was moved to Channing, where she died in 1941, but she was buried beside Mickey not far from Tascosa.

As with all of the wild and wooly western towns, barbed wire and no railroad killed Old Tascosa more effectively than all the gunfights fought there. When barbed wire was introduced on the nearby Frying Pan Ranch in 1882, and the XIT fenced itself in, the cattle drives were over. With its lifeblood drained dry and bypassed by the railroad, the "Cowboy Capital of the Plains" crumbled into dust. The courthouse still stands on Cal Farley's Boys Ranch as a museum, but there is nothing left of Ol' Tascosy for a self-respecting ghost to haunt.

Boot Hills are a source of endless fascination with tourists, because most of the deaths are a testimony from a bygone era that is still tinged with action and adventure. Looking at the graves, all sorts of stories could be written about their occupants and the violent lives they lived.

The First, Last, or Only in Texas

Some of Texans' favorite adjectives are "first, last, and only." Lone Star citizens are also partial to "largest" and "richest," but will settle for the first three.

Elizabeth Crockett's Grave

Only Grave That Is a State Park
Acton

Lots of famous people are buried in Texas, but outside of the State Cemetery in Austin, only one grave has become a state park all to itself. With an area of .006 acres, it is, naturally, the smallest state park in Texas. Here lies the wife of a man who was in Texas only two months, and she did not arrive here until 18 years after his death. Elizabeth Crockett never gained the fame her husband Davy achieved at the Alamo, but she is honored nonetheless.

Both Davy and Elizabeth were widowers with five children between them when they married. They became the parents of three more. Tennessee was a good place to live,

Elizabeth Crockett stands majestically in the smallest state park in Texas.

and Davy was elected a U.S. Congressman. Unfortunately, Davy could not abide Andrew Jackson's politics and stalked out of Congress with the words "I wear no man's collar."

As did so many others in those days, Davy headed for a new life in Texas. William B. Travis had come to Texas after a sensational trial over his wife's lover's murder, Jim Bowie's Mexican wife and children had died; Mirabeau Lamar's wife was deceased, and his brother had committed suicide, and even Sam Houston's wife had left him for mysterious reasons before he came to Texas. Davy arrived in San Antonio in 1836 to find its citizens had proclaimed Texas a republic. Leaping right in to the spirit of the times, Crockett promptly joined the Texas forces, and as every schoolboy knows, was killed two months later at the Alamo.

Crockett loved tales about the endurance and stamina of pioneer women. In his *Almanac*, Elizabeth was a regular female Paul Bunyan. She had a bearskin petticoat and one "died red with tiger's blood." Elizabeth "could tell a bear from a panther in the dark by the feel of his bite."

In 1854 Texas granted Elizabeth some 1,280 acres in what is now Hood County, 7 miles from Acton. When the widow and her son Robert arrived, Acton was a prosperous community. She lived an exemplary life, not at all like a lady with a bearskin petticoat. She died in 1860 at age 72.

In 1911, mainly due to the efforts of Senator Ward, the state appropriated funds to erect a granite memorial. Carved in Italy, Elizabeth Crockett's statue looks westward, just as Elizabeth did in Tennessee while waiting for a husband who never returned.

First Visitor from Outer Space

Aurora

You won't find Aurora on the official Texas highway map, but it is north of Fort Worth, and at one time was a thriving cotton town. By the 1890s overplanting, land erosion, and boll weevils had toppled King Cotton from his Aurora throne, and the town was dying.

A local cotton buyer, S. E. Heyden who was also a newswriter, had lost his wife and two sons to "spotted fever," with two more sons blinded and crippled by the disease. Aurora was packing it in and heading out, as they blamed the water supply for the plague.

In April of 1897 newspapers began printing reports of "mysterious flying objects" seen by citizens of surrounding towns. Dallas citizens even organized lawn parties to watch for these eerie objects. Hayden saw a chance to put Aurora back on the map, and the Dallas and Fort Worth newspapers carried an April 18, 1897, report:

"The airship previously sighted over Aurora . . . collided with J. S. Proctor's windmill and went to pieces with a tremendous explosion . . ."

Hayden described in great detail "a little man" and T. J. Weems, U.S. Signal Service officer, was of the opinion the pilot was a native from Mars. Papers found on the little pilot were written in some unknown hieroglyphics and were undecipherable. A Christian funeral was held for this nineteenth-century "E.T." and his records buried with him.

Rumor and tradition have kept this spaceman story alive since 1897. There was a T. J. Weems, but he was the Aurora blacksmith, and even though the historical marker tells the legend, Aurora's spaceman is accepted as Hayden's hoax. On the other hand, suppose Hayden wasn't lying. . . .

Frost Thorn (1793–1854)

Nacogdoches

When it comes to making money, Texas is mighty proud to have so many millionaires, but there had to be a first, and that title goes to Frost Thorn. Frost was from Glen Cove, New York. In 1825 he and Haden Edwards obtained empresario contracts from Mexico to bring 800 families to East Texas. Thorn refrained from trying to remove all the old settlers as Edwards had tried to do, and no mention is made of Thorn in the days of the Fredonia Rebellion. (See *Traveling Texas Borders*, Lone Star Books, Houston, Texas.) In fact, Thorn seems to have led an unexciting, exemplary life.

The first millionaire married Susan Edwards, one of the five single white women in Nacogdoches. His chief interest was in the acquisition of land and he had contracts with Ben Milam and Green DeWitt. With hundreds of thousands of acres, Thorn built up a trade route between Texas and the United States. He also owned a store, a bank, a salt mine, lumber mills, and farms. He donated land for churches, aided Austin's colonists, and was elected to the state legislature of Coahuila and Texas. You would think there would be some excitement in the fact that Thorn was the richest man in Texas, but it seems that all he did was make money.

A weatherbeaten gravestone is the only reminder of Frost Thorn, Texas' first millionaire.

General Walter Williams

When Walter Williams died in 1959, he was 117 years old. That alone would rate an extraordinary burial ceremony, but Williams' death caused the entire nation to honor his memory. With the passing of Walter Williams, the last survivor of the bloodiest war in the history of the United States was gone. This former Confederate soldier had outlived all the other 4 million men who had fought in the Civil War.

No one knew Walter Williams was a Confederate veteran until he applied for his Confederate pension in 1932. Williams stated he had served with Company C, 5th Regiment, Hood's Brigade, in May 1864 until the end of the war. The veteran did not achieve notoriety until his one hundredth birthday, but from then on, the old soldier became quite a celebrity.

A lesser man would probably have been bedridden, but Uncle Walt flew in a plane for the first time to make TV appearances, and he really enjoyed his old age. At 107, Williams could no longer scream the Rebel Yell, and he had to retire from being the oldest fox hunter in the world.

In 1956 when Williams was 114, the last Yankee survivor died, leaving only Walter. President Eisenhower gave this enduring old man the honorary rank of General. At 116, the Texas Heritage Foundation awarded Williams their Distinguished Service Medal and Citation, as he "finally won the war for the South," and it was signed by Governor Price Daniels. In December of 1959, Walter Williams died at age 117.

No sooner was the General's death known, than the usual swirl of controversy raged over his Civil War record. Opan Beckett of Miamitown, Ohio, had grown up near the Williams' farm and advised the Ohio papers that General Williams was "the biggest joke on the American people I ever heard." She did not mind Uncle Walt getting his pension, but the military funeral was too much. Records did prove that the brigade Williams claimed to have served in never existed at the time of his enlistment, but Governor Daniels stood behind Williams' claim, and so did the nation.

Wearing the Confederate uniform of a general, the body lay in state for 48 hours with an 8-man honor guard. The funeral procession through downtown Houston was a pageant of pomp and circumstance. Sons of the Confederacy came from Ohio as did the Sons of Veterans of Union Forces from Mount Vernon, Ohio, where the composer of "Dixie" was born. To the strains of "Onward Christian Soldiers," "Dixie," and "Yellow Rose of Texas," General Williams was laid to rest. In an ironic twist of fate, the flag Walter Williams had fought against flew at half-mast at his death.

Unsung Heroes

Haunting the graveyards of Texas are innumerable unsung heroes. Somehow their deeds never made the bigtime, and records of their accomplishments are difficult to locate. Fame and glory went to the lawmen, outlaws, presidents, governors, generals, tycoons, and other superstars.

Tucked away in Fort Worth's Pioneer Cemetery is a plain concrete obelisk inscribed "Unknown Soldier of the Indian Wars." No eternal flame, no honor guard, no elaborate monument decorates the grave, and even the particular Indian War that cost him his life is omitted. No story is told, no dates are given. You are left to speculate who chose the monument, the dead soldier to be placed here, and how the soldier lost his life.

Fortunately, details about some of Texas' unsung heroes can be found, and their forgotten stories told.

Reverend J. T. Upchurch

In a sad little cemetery lost among the buildings of UT at Arlington are gravestones of girls with only their first names listed. Perhaps they did not want their last names known, for these girls probably considered themselves guilty of unforgivable sins. Here was the site of the Berachah Home for Wayward Girls and Unwed Mothers founded in 1903 by the Reverend J. T. Upchurch.

"Berachah" means "blessing" in Hebrew, and the Berachah Rescue Society was organized in 1894 by Upchurch (not to be confused with the Berachah Church founded in 1935).

The Berachah Industrial Home was opened nine years after Upchurch's home for girls. Included was a print shop for the publication of a "Purity Journal."

The home closed in 1935, but Upchurch's daughter, Allie Mae, operated an orphanage on the site until 1942. Upchurch does not rest here, but more than 80 graves, large and small, are filled with girls and the innocent results of their sins.

In an era when birth control existed only in abstinence, the Reverend Mr. Upchurch must have found little financial support for his home. History does not mention the girls' benevolent benefactor, but despite the number of graves in the Berachah Cemetery, there probably would have been many more without the Reverend J. T. Upchurch's kindness and aid.

Captain Joe Byrd Cemetery

Texas Department of Corrections
Huntsville

> You can walk forever down this long gray hall,
> And when you reach the end,
> You have gone nowhere at all.
>
> Denver Dean
> Eastham Unit

One of the saddest and perhaps most macabre graveyards in Texas is the well-tended Captain Joe Byrd Cemetery at the State Prison in Huntsville. This felon's field could easily be mistaken for a military burial ground, because all of the headstones are neatly lined row on row and all have numbers. But the numbers are convicts' prison numbers, and in some graves, their execution number.

During the days of the Texas Republic, the penal code dictated the death sentence for arson, burglary, rape, murder, and robbery. The theft of $20 or more was punishable with 39 lashes and "T" branded on the right hand. When the Huntsville prison opened in 1849, about three convicts per month arrived. One of the most infamous prisoners was John Wesley Hardin who managed to get a law degree while confined in its walls.

Another inmate was the Kiowa chief, Satana. Satana, Satank, and Big Tree were captured after the Salt Creek Massacre in 1871. Satank escaped after chewing the flesh from his arm, but was later killed. Satana and Big Tree were the first Indians ever tried in a white man's court. Sentenced to death, both sentences were later commuted to life imprisonment, and then both were paroled. Satana broke his parole and returned to Huntsville. In 1874 the great Kiowa warrior jumped to his death, and is buried in the prison cemetery.

For many years convicts suffered the added indignity of burial in a potter's field. Called Peckerwood Hill by the convicts (a "peckerwood" was a southern term for poor white trash), the cemetery was a morass of tangled weeds, brambles and briars. When an unclaimed body arrived in a pine box for interment, a clearing just sufficient for a grave was hacked out of the wilderness.

Finally, a compassionate man made it his service in life to dignify death, even for the rejects of society. Captain Joe Byrd obtained permission to clean up the cemetery using prison labor. More than 500 gravestones were uncovered, mostly blank from the destruction by the elements. Some graves were determined only by sunken outlines, but 923 graves were found, and 1870 was the earliest decipherable date on the markers.

More than 200 graves are those of executed men, and of the first 100 criminals to die in the electric chair, all but a dozen lay in Peckerwood Hill. Along with these lie those slain while trying to escape and those who died during a devastating flue epidemic. The most imposing tombstone belongs to Lee Smith, who though good with horses was mean to his fellow inmates. Smith was killed while trying to steal another prisoner's money, but the prison cowboys chipped in and bought him a big stone.

Plain crosses made from prison-quarried stone mark these lowly graves today, thanks to a caring and compassionate Captain Joe Byrd. Occasionally bodies are claimed, and in 1963 Satana was exhumed and buried at Fort Sill, Oklahoma, by his grandson, James Auchiah.

Today, few burials occur at this depressing cemetery. If bodies are unclaimed after a certain interval, many are sent

One of the saddest and most macabre cemeteries is at Huntsville State Prison. (Photograph courtesy of Texas Department of Corrections.)

on to medical schools. Those that do lie in Huntsville no longer remain in "pits of shame," but in a quiet peaceful resting place under beautiful trees because of a guard captain with a gentle heart who served the prison system 47 years.

There were years when the warden of the prison was also a pastor and could not take a human life. Captain Joe Byrd not only gave the criminals a decent burial, his duties required that he also be their executioner.

Henry Zollner

Rockwall

Banners will never wave, eternal flames never blaze, nor 21-gun salutes ever be fired over Henry Zollner's monument in the Rockwall Cemetery, but here lies a true unsung Texas hero.

Henry's father, Matt, and his uncle, Charlie, came to Rockwall County from Germany in 1876 by way of Australia. The Zollner brothers settled in tiny Fate, and to get started on their farm, the Zollners took in transient labor.

The term "hobo" was not originally used to describe a vagrant. After the Civil War, bands of migratory farm laborers followed the crops. As there was no farm machinery, most operations involved hand labor with a hoe. A wandering workman was a "hoe boy."

"Hobo Ranch" was not a true description of the Zollner farm; more applicable was "Zollner Haven," for the farm hands were not bums. True, the workers were transient and a man could always find room and board and work in season, but many of the farm's residents found much more.

Henry asked few questions and made only two demands: His workers must behave and bathe once a week and boil their clothes. Because of this policy, Zollner's farm provided a rest stop between vocations, a place to get a new start, and a spot to disappear. Among the lost souls who took refuge here were doctors who had lost their patients, lawyers who had lost their clients, men who wanted to die, a future judge, the son of a state senator, and a man who built a Houston skyscraper. Men from all walks of life found a place to rest and regain their lost self confidence at Zollner's bunkhouse and table.

The great farm had numerous buildings and a dining room that fed 200. Young men came, but most of the diners were old—those whom others would not hire. Zollner never refused a man succor because of his age and actually preferred the elderly. They had what youth often lacks—dependability. They could work as much or as little as they wished and turn in their own time, as the farm was run on the honor system.

On Thanksgiving, Christmas, and New Year's, the cooks turned out a feast of turkey and the trimmings. Also at Christmas, Henry remembered his workers with tobacco, socks, handkerchiefs, fruit, and candy, for the Zollner family ate with friends not hobos.

Some residents never left Zollner's farm. At 96, J. E. Bennett was called "The Kid" and had lived at Hobo Ranch 45 years. At 80, R. S. Cates had been with Zollner 52 years. When the oldsters qualified for pensions, most stayed on at Hobo Ranch rather than live with relatives that did not want them. Down in Hackberry Creek in a pretty spot amid the trees, many "hobos" found a permanent rest at the home they loved.

One old chap left behind $1,500 in his money belt. When Zollner notified the next of kin, they came and saw the home their disappeared relative had loved. The $1,500 was donated to Zollner for a Rockwell Cemetery lot for their family member and other "hobos" who followed.

Even those workers who moved on treasured their days at Hobo Ranch. Men befriended years ago dropped in for warm visits, while others came to spend their vacations with the Zollners who had helped them in their hour of need. Fights were almost unheard of, and the only time one man snitched on another was when he didn't bathe or boil his clothes. "Henry, he ain't a boilin," they would say.

Several times when the farm was losing money, Henry asked himself if he should rent his farm, sell out, retire, or make an easier living—but the answer was always, "Those men who have been with us all those years are as much a part of the place as I. I have an obligation to them." Henry Zollner was indeed his brother's keeper.

Hobo Ranch is deserted now. Minimum wage, mechanization, and welfare were as fatal to Hobo Ranch as Henry's death. Ben, Henry's son, is a Rockwall lawyer and occasionally allows indigent families to live in one of the buildings, but Hobo Ranch is now as extinct as the "hoe boys" that gave the ranch its name.

Index